Learning
Windows Vista

Ramesh Bangia
B.Sc., Dip. Comp. Sc.
Formerly: Managing Editor, Software Today
Formerly: Incharge Computer Centre, Hindustan Copper Ltd., New Delhi

KHANNA BOOK PUBLISHING CO. PVT. LTD.

Learning Windows Vista — Ramesh Bangia

Published by SHEETAL KHANNA
Khanna Book Publishing Co. Pvt. Ltd.
1694 Nai Sarak
Delhi - 110 006
Tel. 23256658, 23283211
e-mail: **contact@khannaedu.com**

First Edition 2007

Typeset at

MAYANK CONSULTANTS 65/80 New Rohtak Road, New Delhi 110 005
Tel.: 2871 5968, 2872 7854

Printed: Ziya Offset Works,

Preface

Learning of a software is both easy and difficult. It depends upto what level you are planning to learn. If you are learning only for the working use, then it is very easy. But, when you try to go deep into it, then you realise how difficult it is to master it.

Windows Vista is such a vast subject that it will take a lot of time to understand it fully. This book has been written in mind to make you aware of the options available in the software and how they can be used. It is like telling the child about the steps and stairs. You are the one who is to climb the stair. This book will just guide you how to use the stairs.

I am indeed debited to my publishers Khanna Book Publishing Co. Pvt. Ltd., specially Shri Sheetal Khanna for their suggestions and encouragement given in producing this book.

I would like to thank my family specially my wife Sadhna, kids Mayank and Samarth, for without their criticism this book would not have seen the day.

Suggestions for improvement of the book are indeed welcome.

Ramesh Bangia

CONTENTS

5. Maintain and Protect Your System with Windows Vista 129

1 Introduction to Windows Vista

Introduction

Windows Vista is the new version of ever popular operating system called Windows. It is an enhancement of the different released till now, i.e., Windows 95, Windows 98, Windows NT, Windows 2000, Windows ME and Windows XP.

Windows Vista comes in five different versions: Home Basic, Home Premium, Business, Enterprise, and Ultimate.

Exploring the Desktop of Windows Vista

As was in the earlier versions of Windows, Windows Vista too has a familiar desktop from where you can launch your programs using their shortcuts. A Windows Vista desktop is shown below, with all the relative icons. You may or may not have the same desktop on computer. But, it will be quite similar.

On the desktop, there are few icons, most of them are by choice, i.e., you can have them or not, the choice is yours only. But, the ones that you should have are: **Computer**, **Recycle Bin**, etc.

However, the most unfamiliar object on the desktop is the Start button, which used to be there since Windows 95, well, it has been replaced by a real button and does not have a name since by now everybody knows what that button means.

Another different feature is the presence of Gadgets on the right hand side of the desktop. There are few available and you can choose which one to have on the screen.

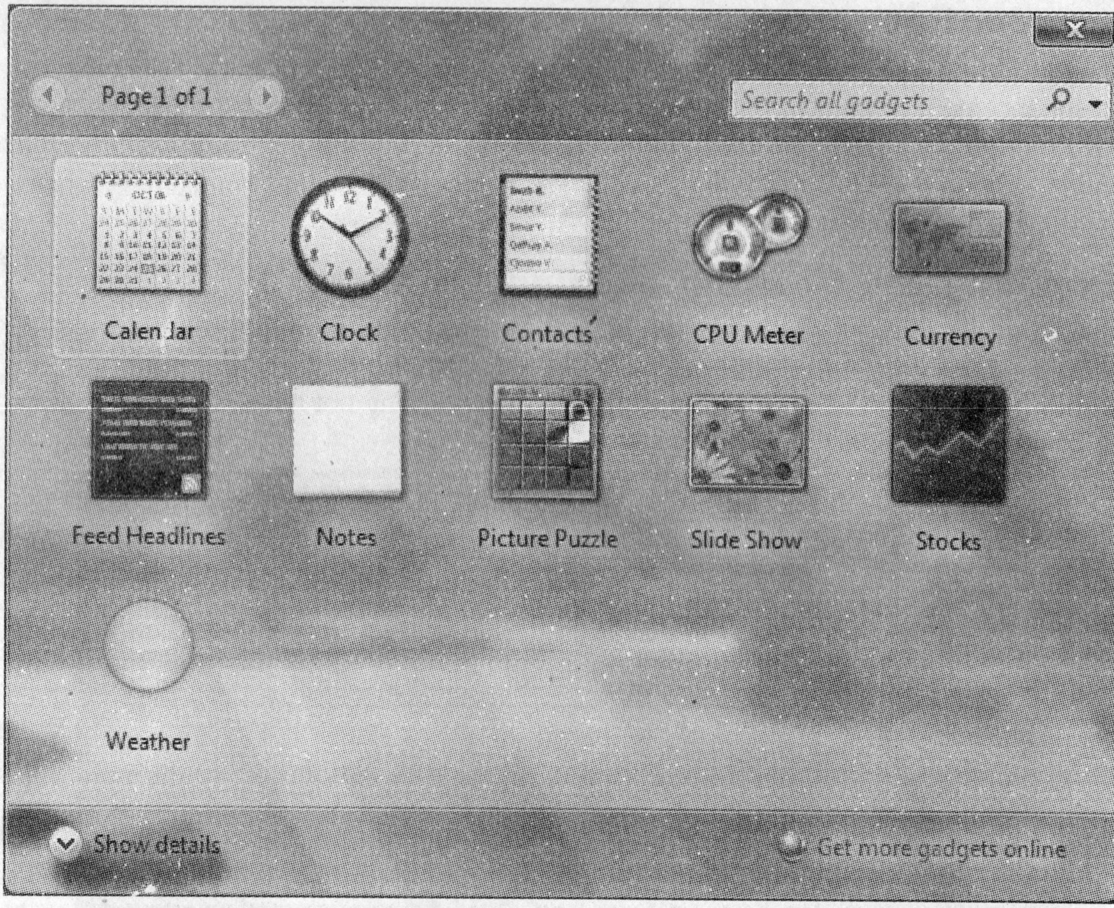

On pressing the Start button, as usual you would see the various programs which can be used by just clicking at them. It is in 2 cols. The first column gives the recently used programs at the bottom and favourite programs at the top.

The favourite ones are:

Internet : It opens up Internet Explorer version 7.0 for you to access Internet.

e-mail : If opens up Outlook Express for you to send and receive e-mail.

Next we have a list of the various programs which have been recently used. So you may have something different from this.

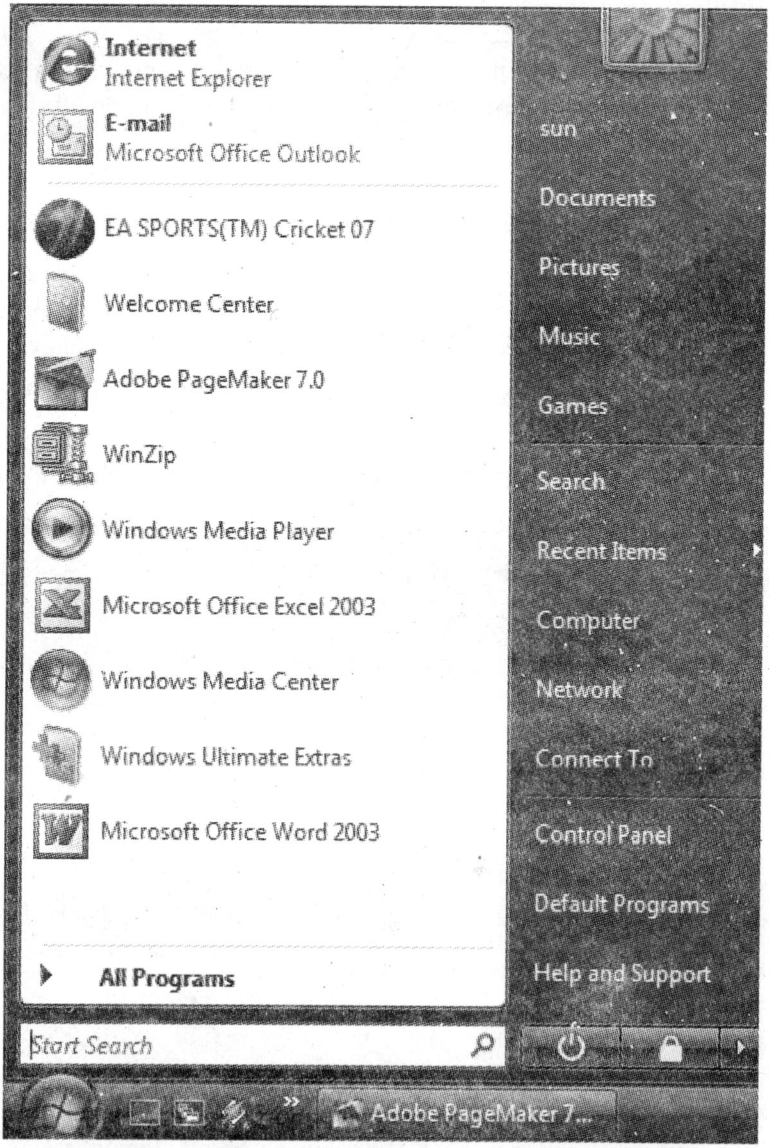

Exploring the Taskbar

It the bottom key line on the desktop. Starting with the right most corner, we see the following:

Date and Time

It shows you the date and time of the system.

Sound

It shows you the volume level which has been set.

Network

If your system is connected to a network, it shows.

WinZip Quick Pack

You can launch WinZip quickly from here.

Windows Defender

You will read more about it when we study Control Panel.

Windows Security Alerts

This alerts you when your system is at a security risk of being attacked by a virus.

Quick Launch Toolbar

Various icons here are the ones used for launching different programs. You have an option to put these icons here for the programs which you often use.

Running Tasks

When you have a program running in youı system, its name will be reflected here on this taskbar to show that this program is open.

Computer

It helps you browse the contents of your computer, open folders, open documents and run your favourite applications. As shown here, it is divided into 2 sections, Favorite Links and Details. You click at any icon on the right hand side of the dialog box and then choose the option on the left hand side.

Details will give you the detail of the item selected. You can access other places by clicking at any one of them.

On the right hand side, you have the options of the followings:

Name: It gives you the option of sorting the icons by Name or by from A to H and I to Z.

Type: You can choose the type from CD Drive, Local Disk and System Folder and then Stack by Type.

Total Size: You can set the drives according to their size.

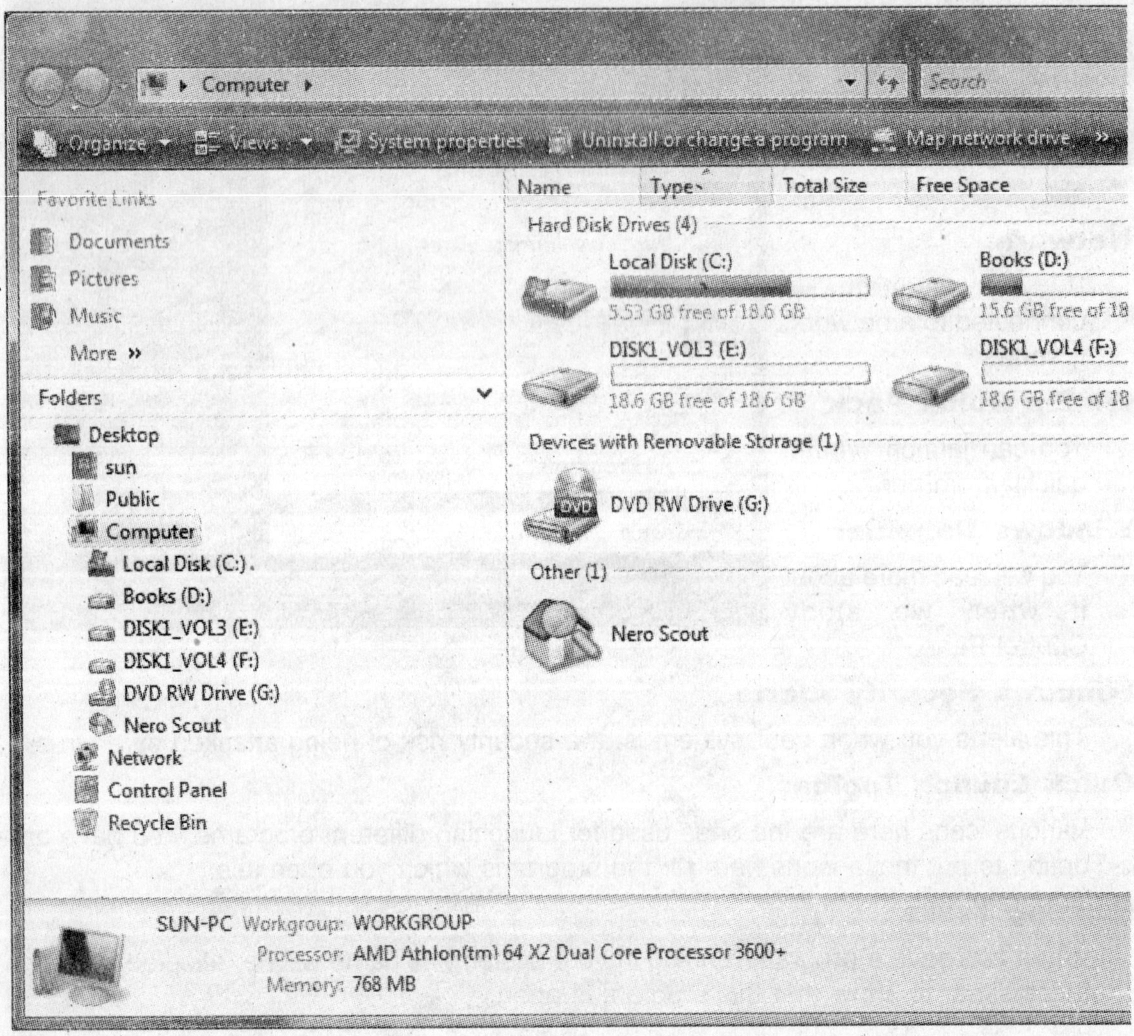

Free Space: You can set the drive to show how much space is available in them and list them according to the size, as shown below.

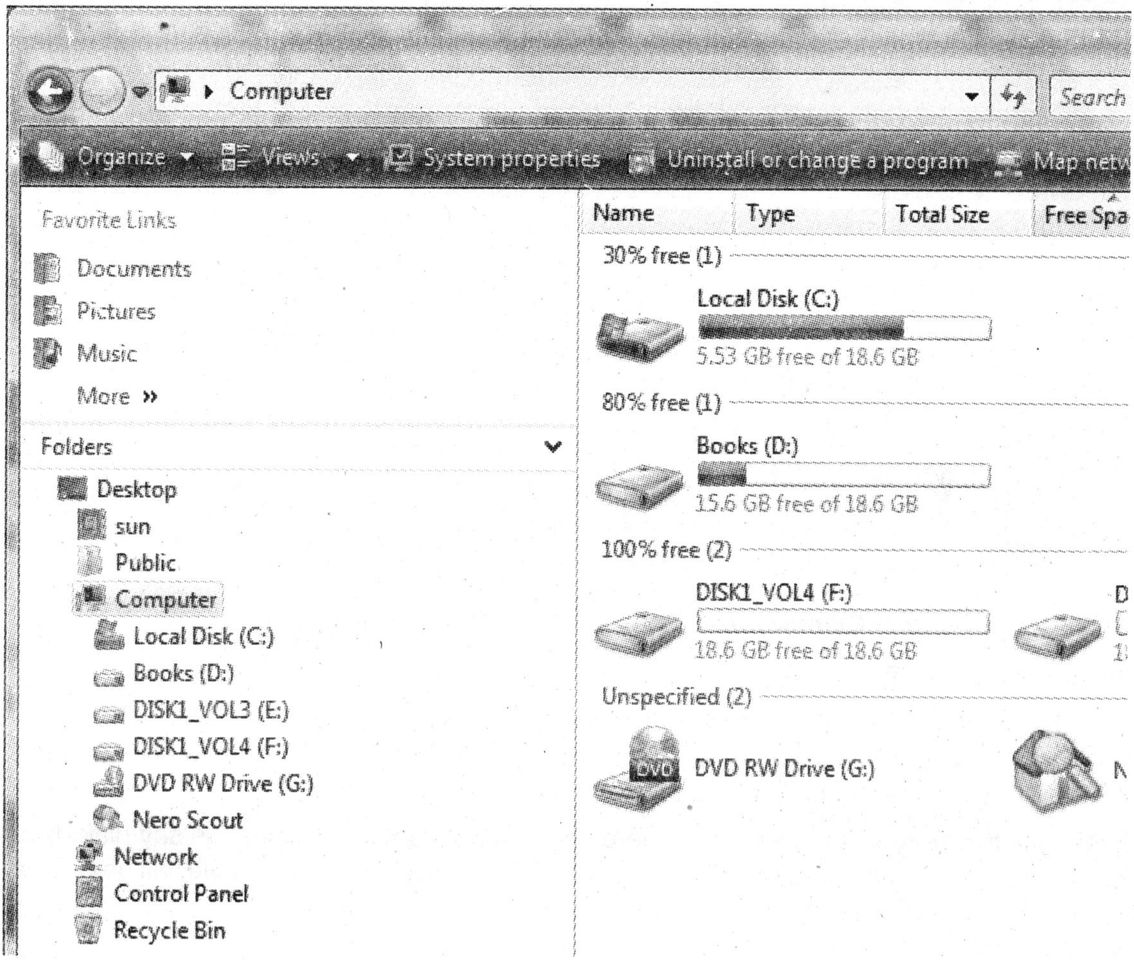

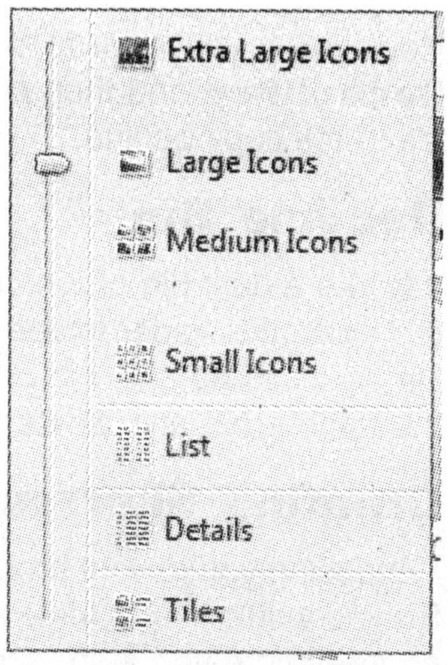

On the top there are buttons like this:

Organize: This allows you to organize the folders and files according to your liking. Like creating a New Folder, Cutting, copying, pasting of folders/files. Other options are shown here.

Views: It gives the option of viewing the folders/files in different views.

System properties: Shows information about your computer, such as the processor speed and the amount of installed memory.

Uninstall or change a program: Allows you to uninstall or change any program in the fixed drive.

Map network drive: It allows you to map a network drive.

Details of the folders available in the hard disk drive C: are shown here.

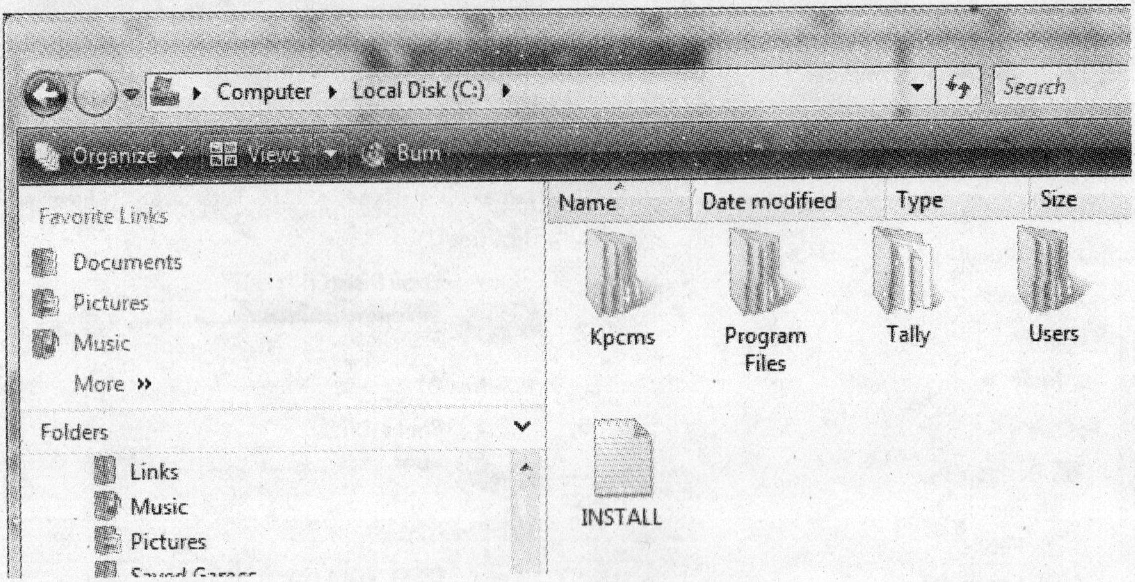

Now let us see how **Computer** is used for working with files.

Copying of Files

Supposing you have to copy a file from one drive to another. Open the folder of hard disk and the particular file where it exists. Click the file to make it selected. Now click at Copy in the Organize menu.

Now click the other folder/hard disk where you want to copy the file. Let us say disk drive F:. Now again go to the Organize menu and click at Paste, this time. The file will be pasted in the disk drive F:, as shown next. Similary you can copy and paste folders from one place to another.

However, if you want to copy without leaving the copy of the file in the source, press **Control Key** and then click the mouse to drag the file. This will copy the file and not leave the copy behind.

Recycle Bin

It is like a dust bin of the computer. All the deleted files are transferred here. You can in fact open this folder to see the files present in it. If you want at any stage to retrace any file, you can do it, if it is present in the **Recycle Bin**. However, if you choose to empty the recycle bin and delete the files altogether, then you cannot restore any of the file.

Creating Shortcuts

Supposing you have a program loaded into the computer and you are quite often using it. So you would like to have a shortcut for it. For example, I use **PageMaker**, quite often, so I have created a shortcut for this and it is available on the desktop.

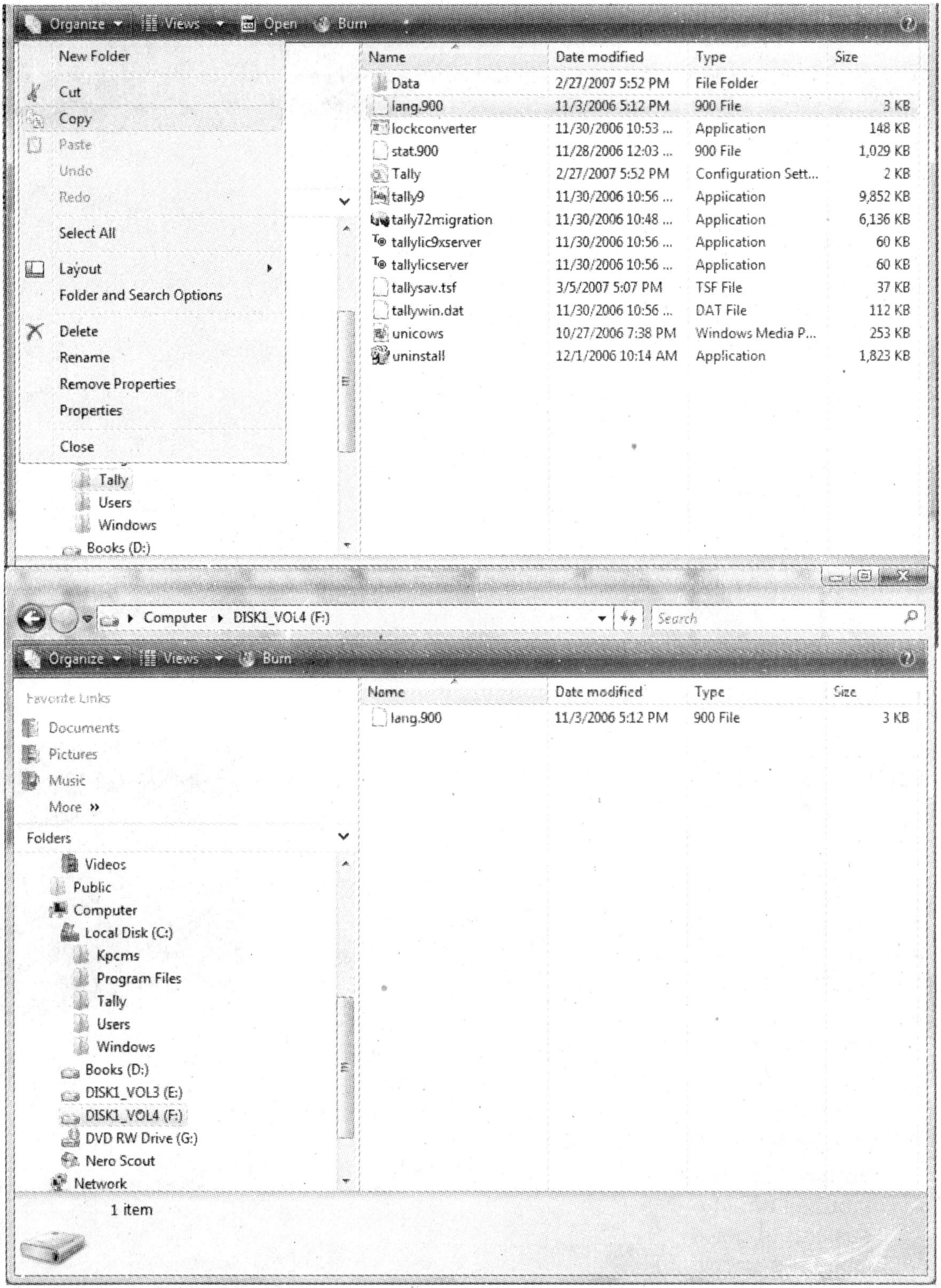
Organize
Views
Open
Burn
New Folder
Cut
Copy
Paste
Undo
Redo
Select All
Layout
Folder and Search Options
Delete
Rename
Remove Properties
Properties
Close
Tally
Users
Windows
Books (D:)
Name
Date modified
Type
Size
Data 2/27/2007 5:52 PM File Folder
lang.900 11/3/2006 5:12 PM 900 File 3 KB
lockconverter 11/30/2006 10:53 ... Application 148 KB
stat.900 11/28/2006 12:03 ... 900 File 1,029 KB
Tally 2/27/2007 5:52 PM Configuration Sett... 2 KB
tally9 11/30/2006 10:56 ... Application 9,852 KB
tally72migration 11/30/2006 10:48 ... Application 6,136 KB
tallylic9xserver 11/30/2006 10:56 ... Application 60 KB
tallylicserver 11/30/2006 10:56 ... Application 60 KB
tallysav.tsf 3/5/2007 5:07 PM TSF File 37 KB
tallywin.dat 11/30/2006 10:56 ... DAT File 112 KB
unicows 10/27/2006 7:38 PM Windows Media P... 253 KB
uninstall 12/1/2006 10:14 AM Application 1,823 KB
Computer ▸ DISK1_VOL4 (F:)
Search
Organize
Views
Burn
Favorite Links
Documents
Pictures
Music
More »
Folders
Videos
Public
Computer
Local Disk (C:)
Kpcms
Program Files
Tally
Users
Windows
Books (D:)
DISK1_VOL3 (E:)
DISK1_VOL4 (F:)
DVD RW Drive (G:)
Nero Scout
Network
Name
Date modified
Type
Size
lang.900 11/3/2006 5:12 PM 900 File 3 KB
1 item

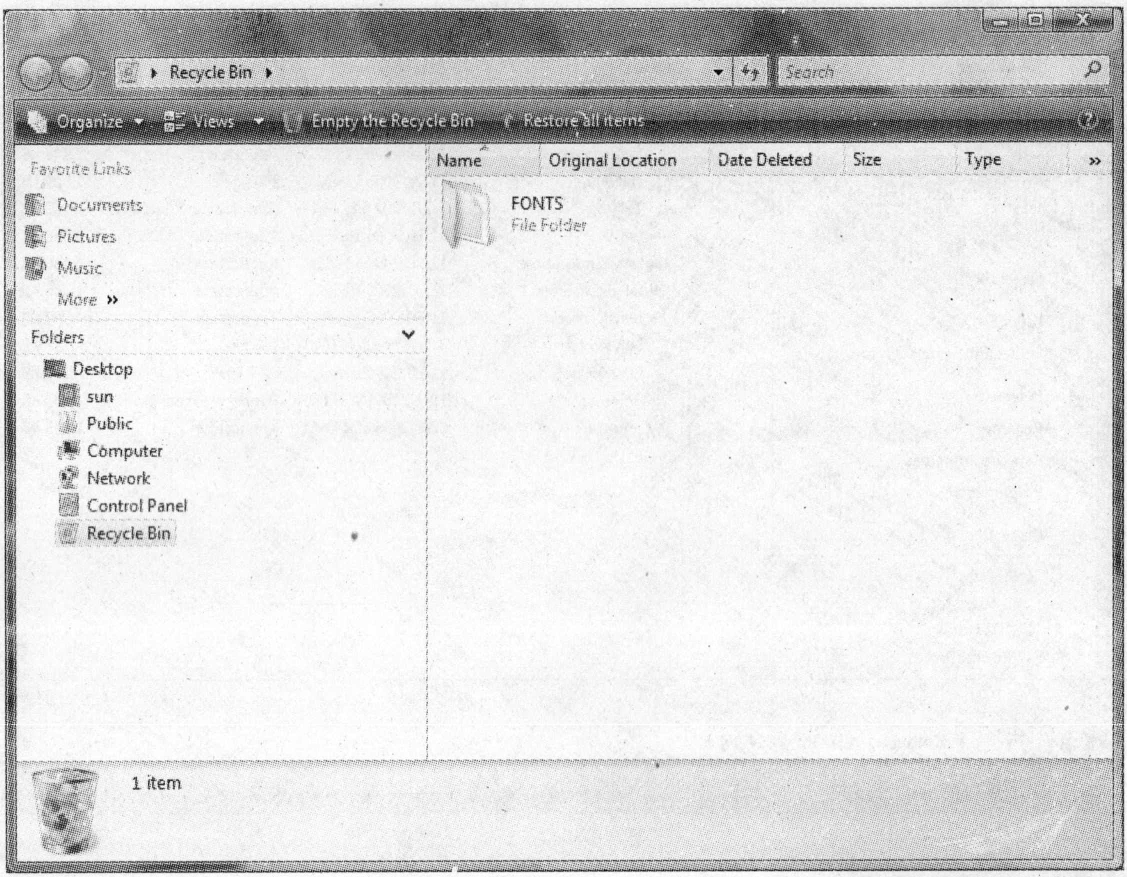

Supposing you are using a program called **Paint** quite often during your use of the computer. You would like to create a shortcut for it. Lets see how it is created. For this you follow the steps here.

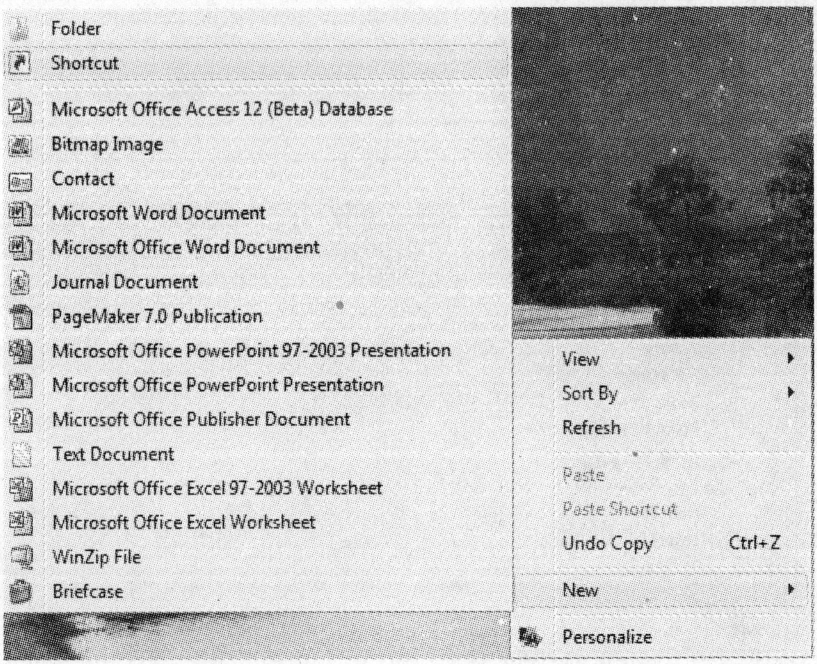

1. Minimize all your opened programs.
2. Click at the right button of the mouse on the desktop to get a menu, as shown here.

3. Click at **New** to get the new menu, as shown. Click at **Shortcut** to create one.
4. This will give rise to a dialog box, as shown. Side by side, you will notice that it has created a new folder with **New Shortcut** as the name.
5. Click at the browse button to locate the file associated with the new shortcut. In our case it will be **Paint** or **Paintbrush**. In this case, as the picture shows that the file is available in the Windows folder under the name **mspaint.exe**.

   Once selected it will be filled up in the File name column. Click

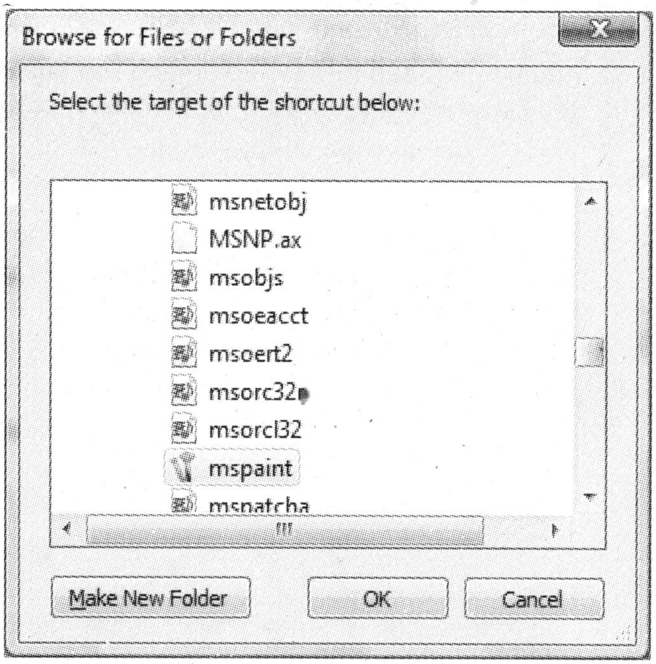

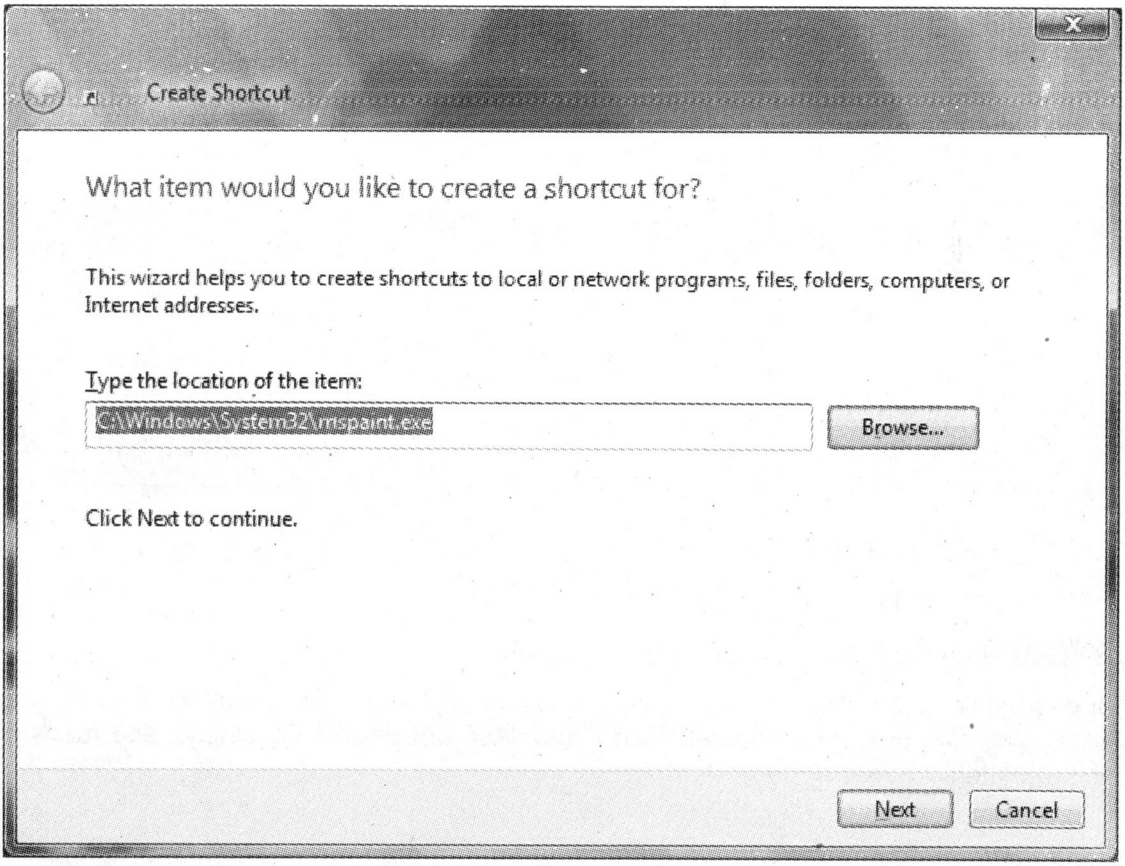

it to open it. This will lead us back to the main dialog box of **Create Shortcut**.

6. You will now see that the command line has been filled up with the exact location of the file which is to be Run for launching of this shortcut from the desktop.
7. Click at **Next** to get the next dialog box. This will ask you fill up the name you want to give to the shortcut. Here we have given it as **PAINT**.
8. Clicking at **Finish** will end the procedure to create the shortcut. Once done, it will create a new shortcut named **PAINT**on the desktop. You can now use it to launch Paint.

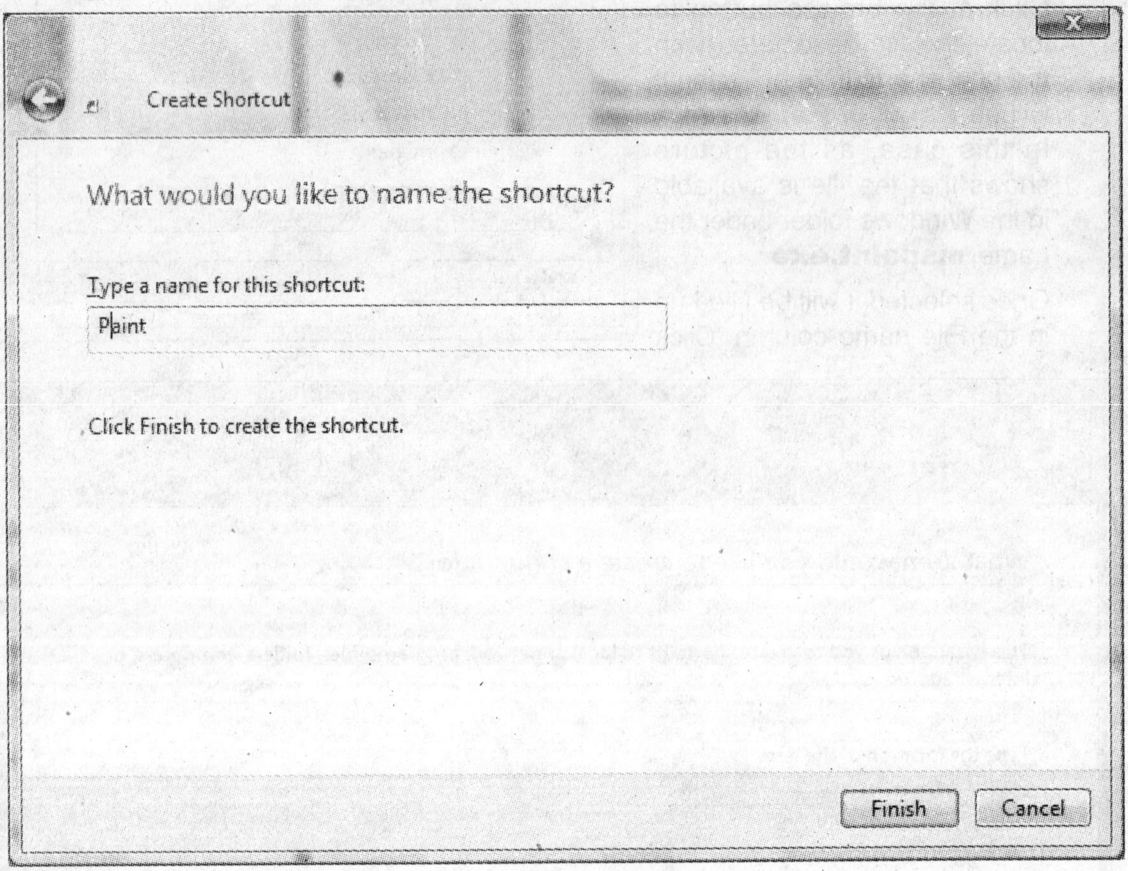

9. This can be seen on the next page.

Let us now see what is new in Windows Vista.

What's new in Windows Vista

Explore new features for searching, staying connected, networking, syncing devices, and managing files on your computer. Find things fast, get down to business, and focus on what matters to you.

Searching and organizing

In every folder in Windows, the Search box appears in the upper right corner. When you type in the Search box, Windows filters the view based on what you're typing. Windows looks for words in the file name, tags that you've applied to the file, or other file properties. To find a file in a folder, type any part of a file name in the Search box to find what you're looking for. You can also use Search folders when you don't know where a file is located or when you want to do an advanced search using more than just a single file name or property.

Security

Features such as Windows Firewall and Windows Defender can help keep your computer more secure. Windows Security Center has links for checking your computer's firewall, antivirus software, and update status. BitLocker Drive Encryption allows you to encrypt the entire system partition, which can improve security by preventing hackers from

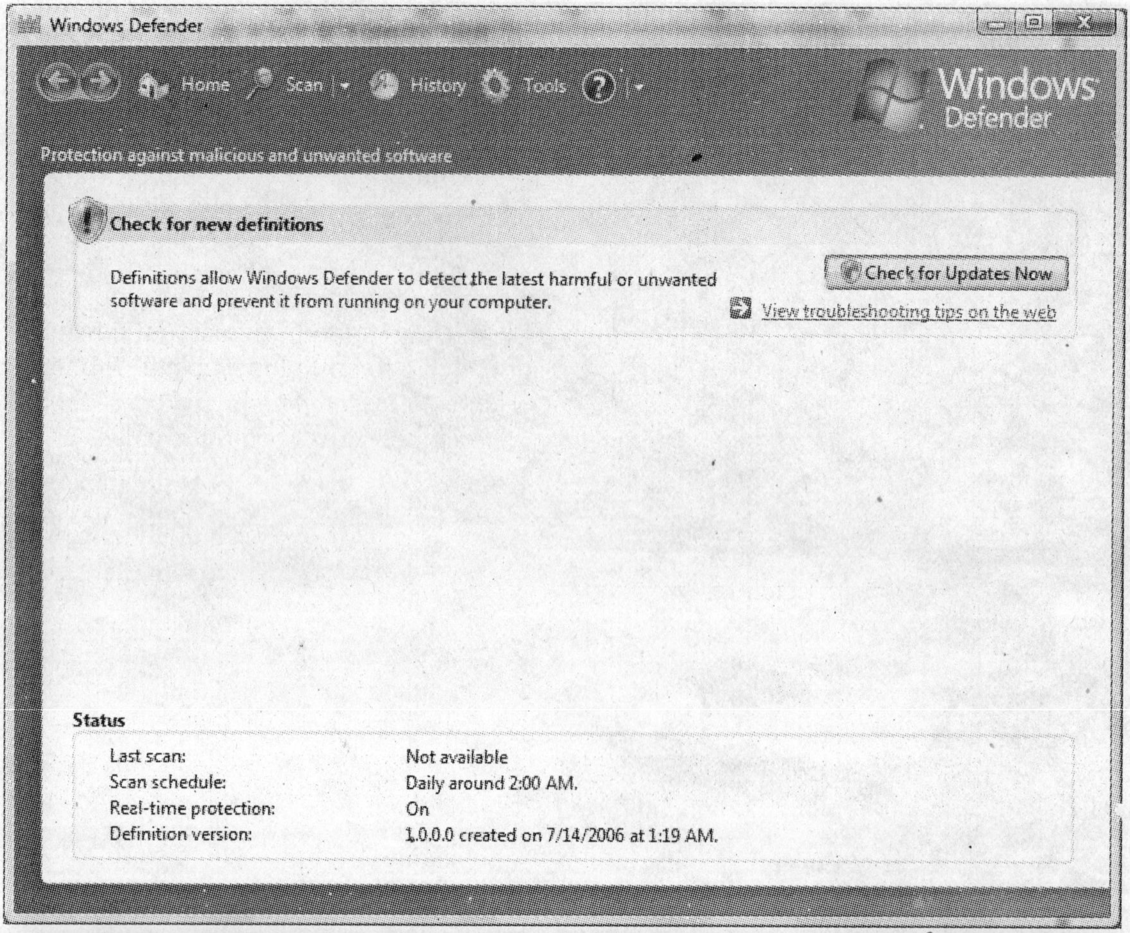
Windows Defender
Home
Scan
History
Tools
Windows Defender
Protection against malicious and unwanted software
Check for new definitions
Definitions allow Windows Defender to detect the latest harmful or unwanted software and prevent it from running on your computer.
Check for Updates Now
View troubleshooting tips on the web
Status
Last scan: Not available
Scan schedule: Daily around 2:00 AM.
Real-time protection: On
Definition version: 1.0.0.0 created on 7/14/2006 at 1:19 AM.

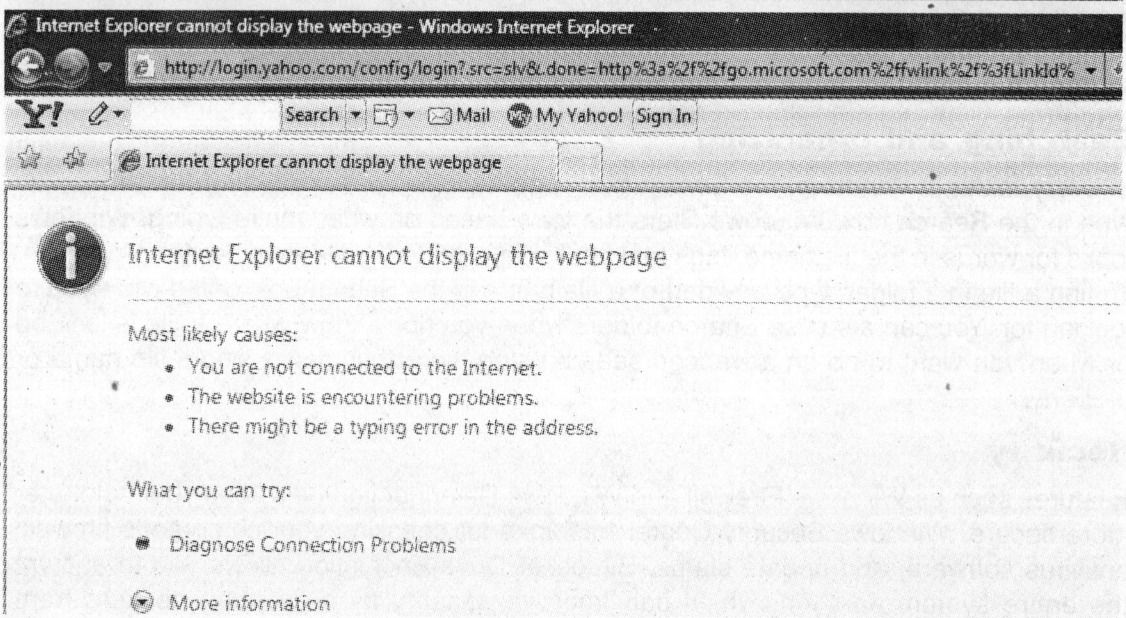
Internet Explorer cannot display the webpage - Windows Internet Explorer
http://login.yahoo.com/config/login?.src=slv&.done=http%3a%2f%2fgo.microsoft.com%2ffwlink%2f%3fLinkId%
Search
Mail
My Yahoo!
Sign In
Internet Explorer cannot display the webpage
Internet Explorer cannot display the webpage
Most likely causes:
You are not connected to the Internet.
The website is encountering problems.
There might be a typing error in the address.
What you can try:
Diagnose Connection Problems
More information

accessing important system files. User Account Control (UAC) can help prevent unauthorized changes to your computer by requiring permission before performing actions that could potentially affect your computer's operation or that change settings that affect other users.

Internet Explorer

Web feeds, tabbed browsing, and always-available search are just a few of the new features available in Internet Explorer.

Web feeds provide frequently updated content published by a website that you can subscribe to for automatic delivery to your web browser. With a feed, you can get content such as breaking news or updates to a blog without having to go to the website. Tabbed browsing allows you to open multiple websites in a single browser window. You can open webpages or links on new tabs and then switch among them by clicking the tabs.

Sync and sharing

Sync with other devices such as portable music players and Windows Mobile devices. With Sync Center, you can keep devices in sync, manage how your devices sync, start a manual sync, see the status of current sync activities, and check for conflicts.

You can also share files and folders with people on your network, even if they use a computer that's not running Windows. When you share files and folders, other people can open and view the files and folders just as if they were stored on their own computer. And they can make changes, if you allow that.

Ease of Access Center

The new Ease of Access Center replaces Accessibility Options in earlier versions of Windows. The Ease of Access Center comes with several improvements and new features, including centralized access to accessibility settings and a new questionnaire that you can use to get suggestions for accessibility features that you might find useful.

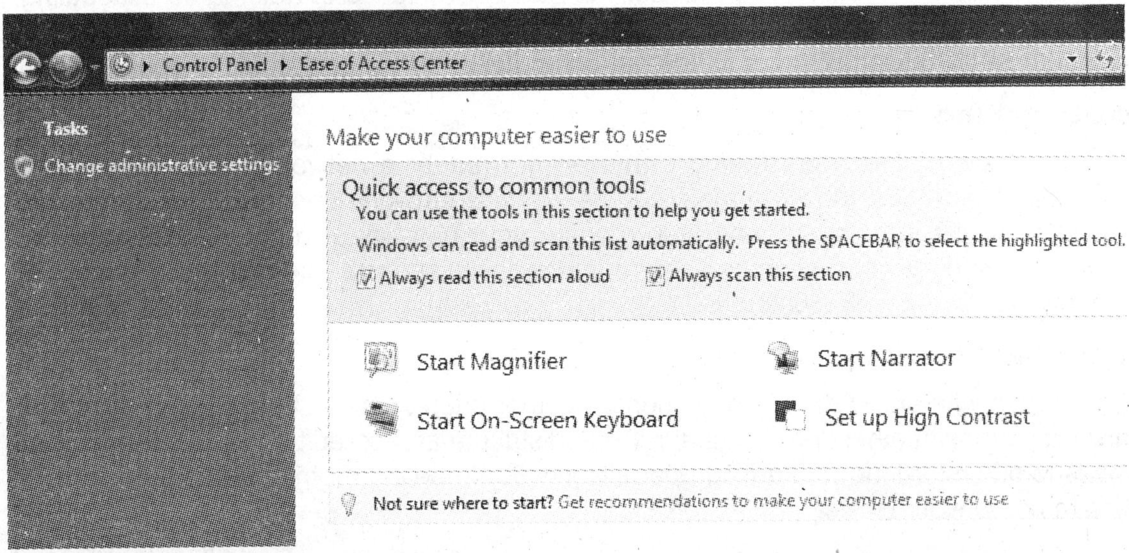

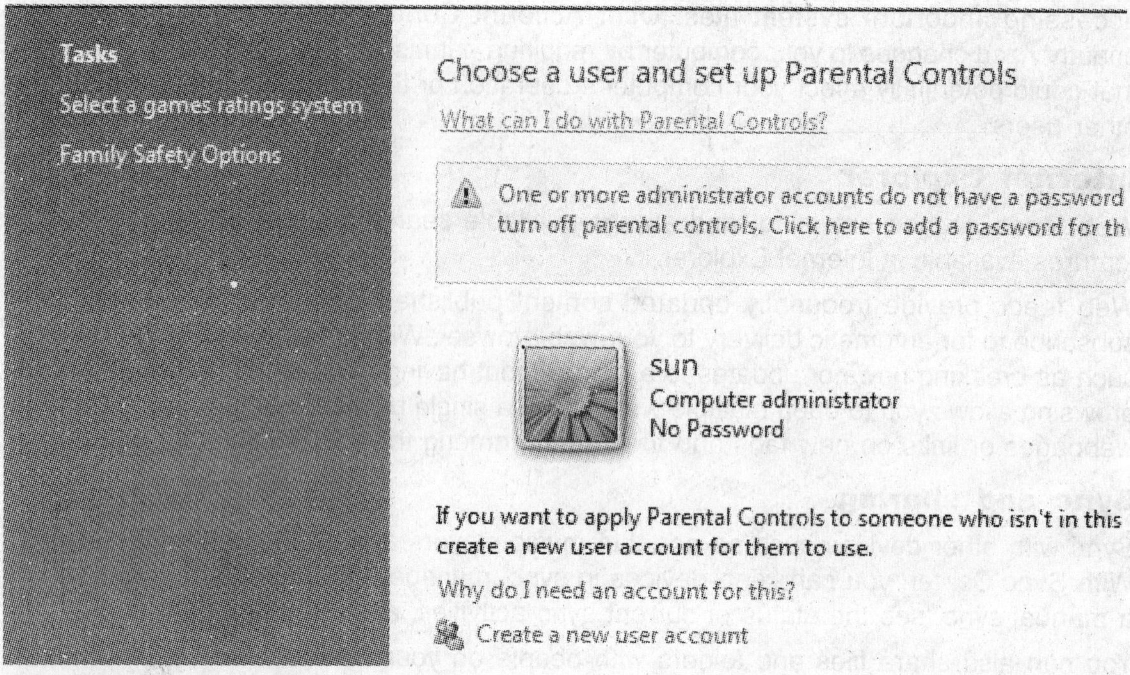

Parental Controls

Parental Controls makes it easy for parents to designate which games their children are allowed to play. Parents can allow or restrict specific game titles, limit their children's play to games that are rated at or below a certain age level, or block games with certain types of content that they don't want their children to see or hear.

Back Up and Restore Center

The Back Up and Restore Center makes it easier to back up your settings, files, and programs when and where you choose, with the convenience of automated scheduling. You can back up to a CD or DVD, an external hard disk, another hard disk on your computer, a USB flash drive, or to another computer or server connected to your network.

Networking

Use the Network File and Sharing Center to get real-time network status and links to customized activities. Set up a more secure wireless network, connect more securely to public networks in hotspots, and help monitor your network security. Access files and shared network devices, such as printers, more easily and use interactive diagnostics to identify and fix network problems.

Windows Meeting Space

Collaborate with and distribute documents to other people online. Share your desktop or any program with other session participants, distribute and co-edit documents, and pass notes to others. Windows Meeting Space works in a meeting room, a favorite hotspot, or where no network exists.

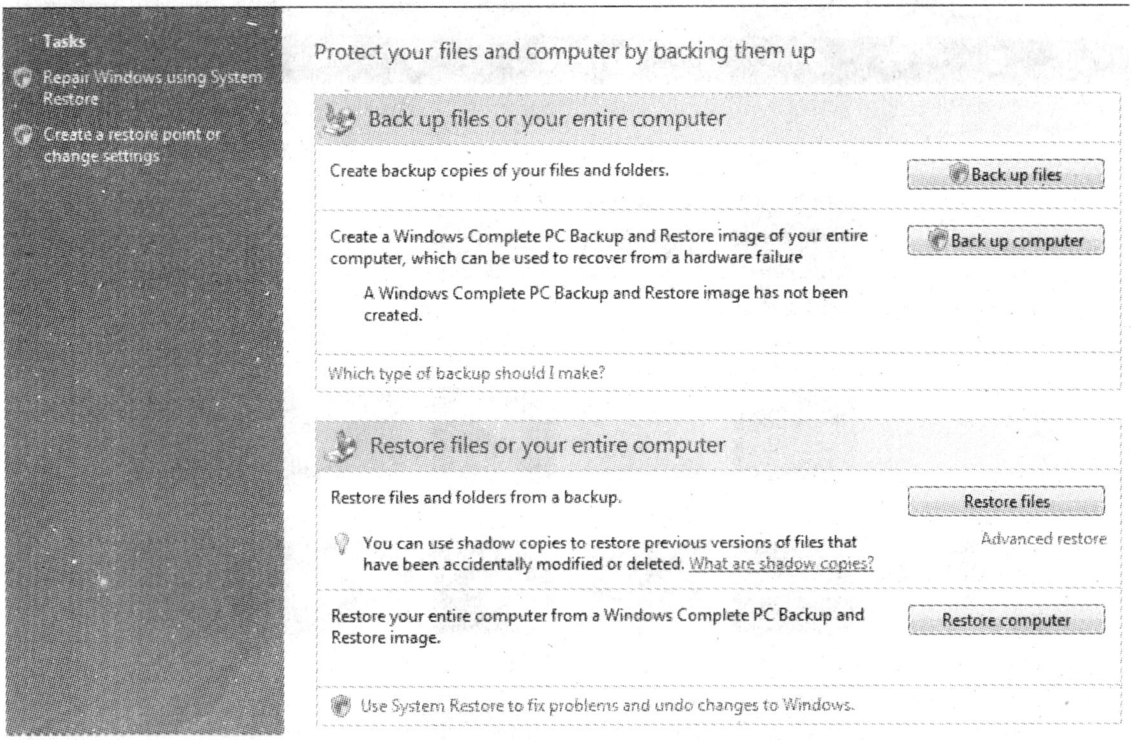

Windows Media Center

Enjoy all your favorite digital entertainment—including live and recorded TV, movies, music, and pictures—in one place with the Windows Media Center menu system and remote control. Windows Media Center in Windows Vista includes enhancements for expanded support of digital and high-definition cable TV, an improved menu system, and the ability to create a consumer-electronics-quality living-room experience, as well as new options for multi-room access to your entertainment through Media Center Extenders, including Microsoft Xbox 360.

Pictures

The Pictures folder and Windows Photo Gallery make it easy to view, organize, edit, share, and print digital pictures. When you plug your digital camera into your computer you can automatically transfer your photos to the Pictures folder. From there, you can use Windows Photo Gallery to crop photos, remove red eye, and make color and exposure corrections.

Mobile PC features

Use the Mobility Center to adjust settings you regularly change when you move from place to place (such as volume and screen brightness) and to check your connectivity status. Use a secondary, or auxiliary, display to check for your next meeting, read e mail, listen to music, or scan news without opening your mobile PC. You can also have an auxiliary display on a device, such as a cell phone or TV.

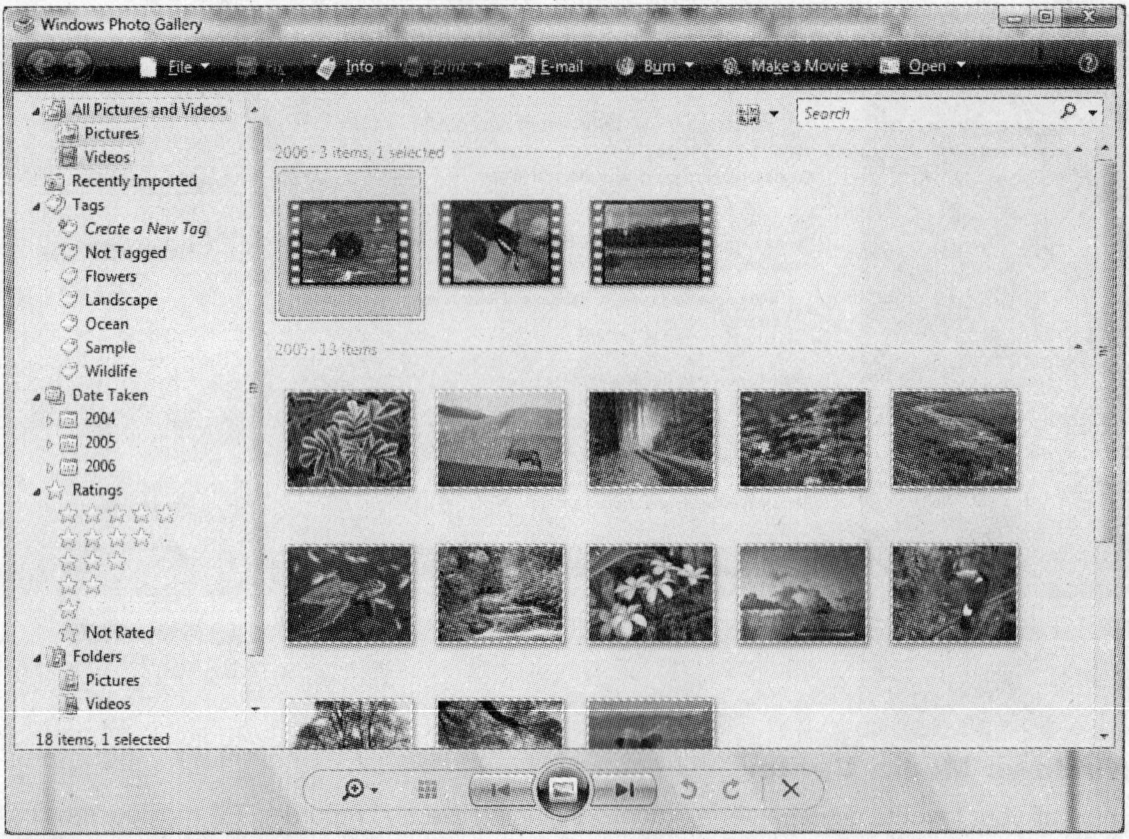

Tablet PC features

Improve handwriting recognition by personalizing the handwriting recognizer. Use flicks to navigate and perform shortcuts with your pen. See pen actions more clearly with optimized cursors. Use the Input Panel to handwrite, or use the soft keyboard anywhere on your screen. Use the touch screen to perform actions with your finger (the touch screen is only available if you have a touch-enabled Tablet PC).

2 Accessories of Windows Vista

Introduction

As in earlier versions of Windows, Windows Vista too has its own set of accessories for making the working under Windows Vista easier. Most of the earlier one have been retained but some new ones have also been added.

Calculator

You can use Calculator to perform addition, subtraction, multiplication, and division. Calculator also offers the advanced capabilities of scientific and statistical calculators.

You can perform calculations by clicking the calculator buttons, or you can type calculations by using your keyboard. You can also use the numeric keypad to type numbers and operators by pressing NUM LOCK.

Most of the button look just like the ones on the plastic calculator that's probably in your desk drawer at this very moment, but several require special explations:

Slash / means divided by in computer language.

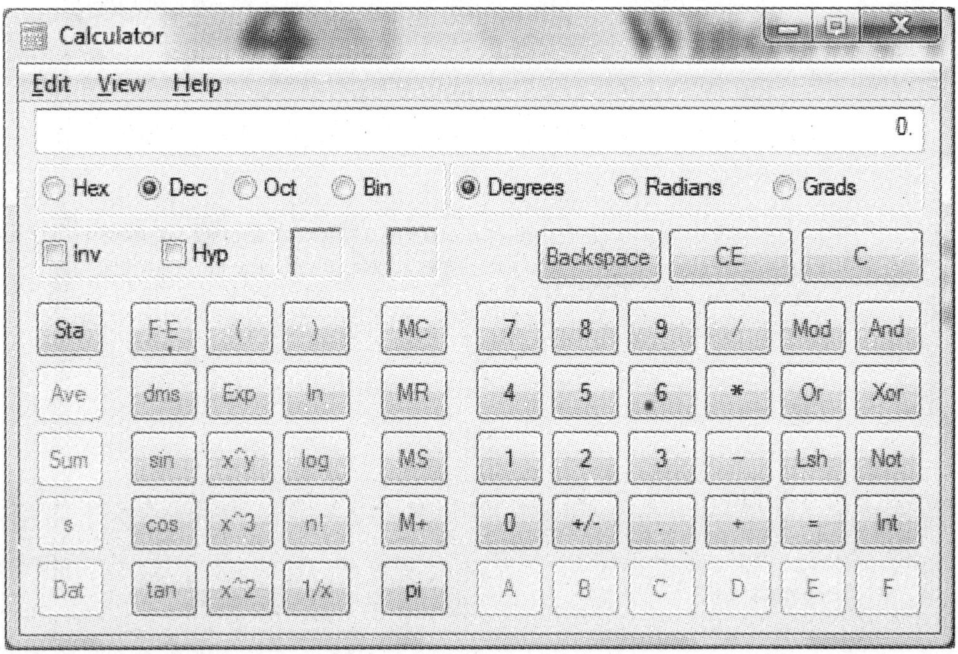

Asterisk	* is used for multiplication.
Sqrt	click this button to find the square root
%	click this to find the percentage

Command Prompt

This is for running the old DOS based commands

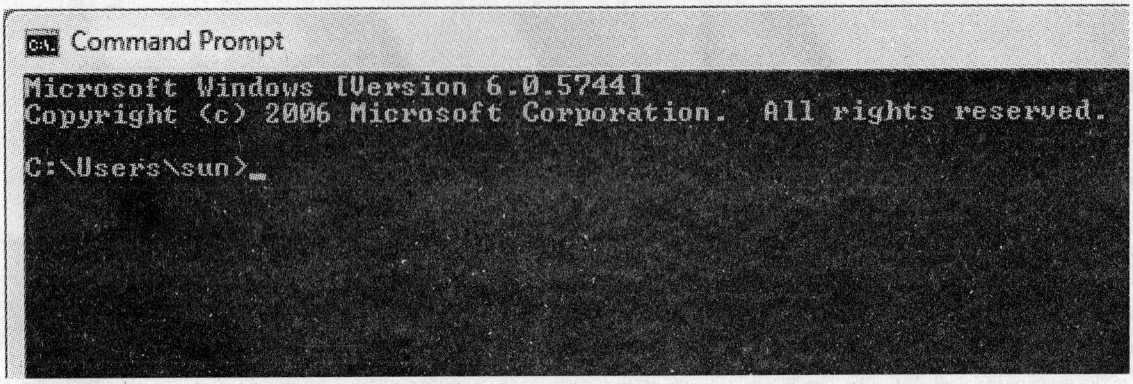

Connect to a Network Projector

This little wizard is designed to detect, and connect your PC to a network projector—a video projector that can project the image from any computer on the network. You, the pitchmaster, can stand in the conference room on the eight floor, where the projector is, showing your awestruck co-workers a PowerPoint presentation that's actually sitting on your PC in Accounting down on the fourth.

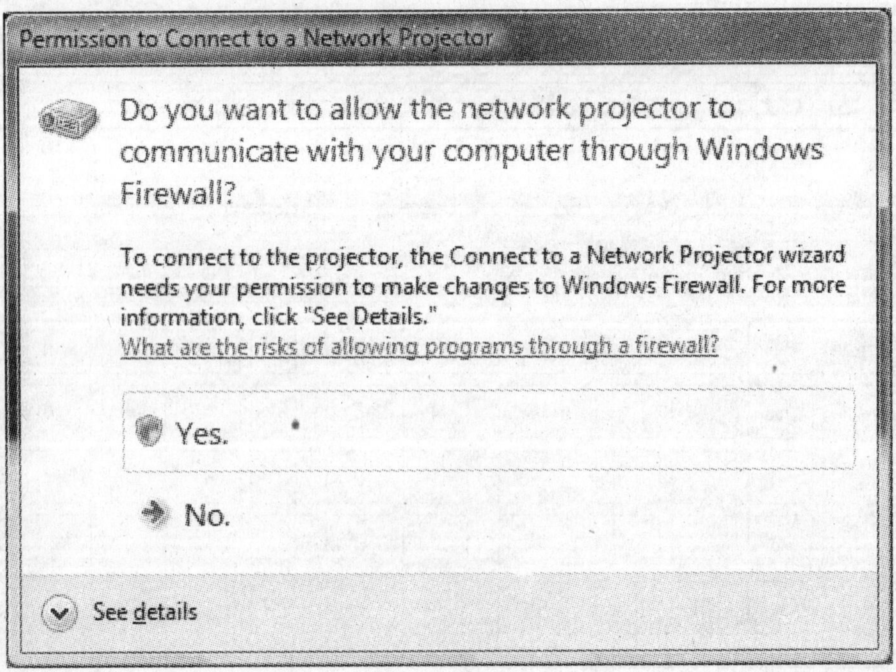

Notepad

It is a text editor, which means that it lets you open, create, edit files that contain plain, unformatted text, like the Read Me text files that usually accompany new programs. You can also use Netepad to write about short notes or edit text that you intend to paste into your email program after editing it.

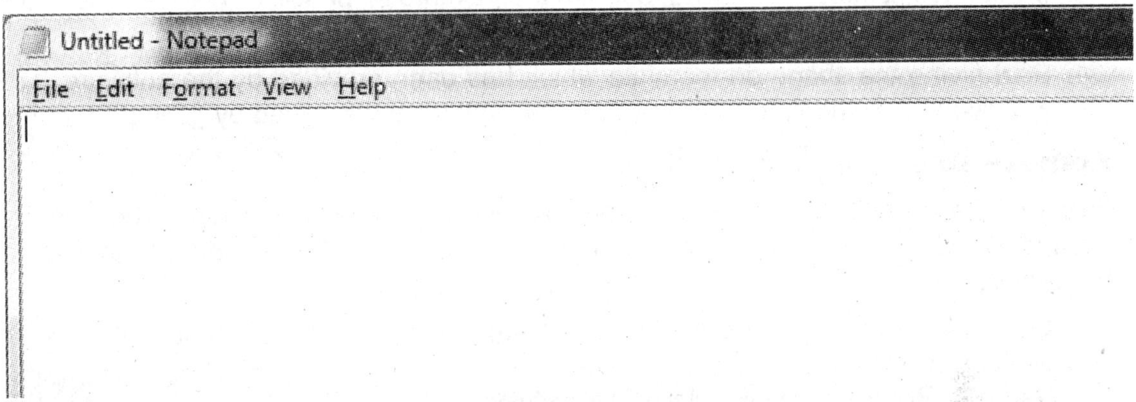

Paint

You can use Paint to create simple artwork or edit graphc files from other sources. Common tasks for this program include making quick sketches, fixing dust specks on scanned photos, and entertaining kids for hours.

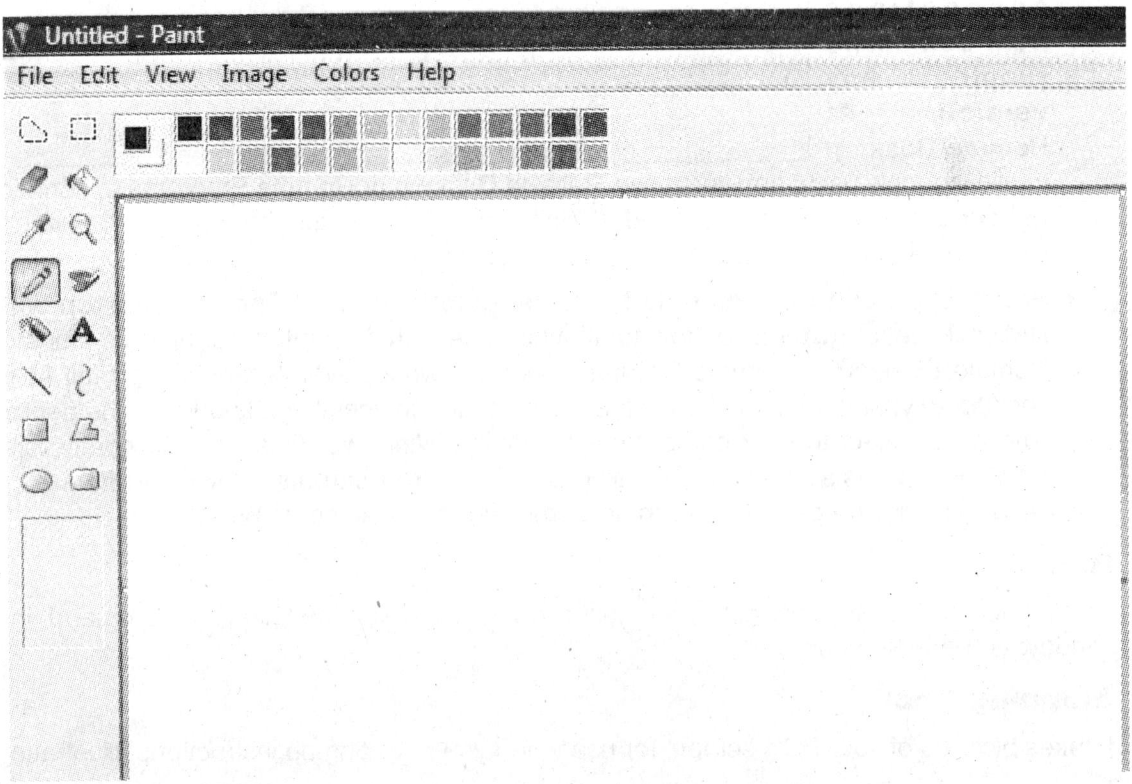

For creating a small painting on the screen do the following:

1. Choose Image>Attributes to specify the dimensions of the graphic you want to create. Click Ok.
2. Click a tool on the left hand side.
3. If you have selected a painting tool, like the paintbrush, pencil, or line tool, click color from the palette at the bottom of the window.
4. Start giving the shape on the slate which has been provided by the software. This will give rise to the figure which you draw, which can be saved by giving it a name.

Remote Desktop Connection

This allows you to site at home PC and run your office PC by remote control. The following information will help you decide which setting to choose on the Remote tab in System Properties:

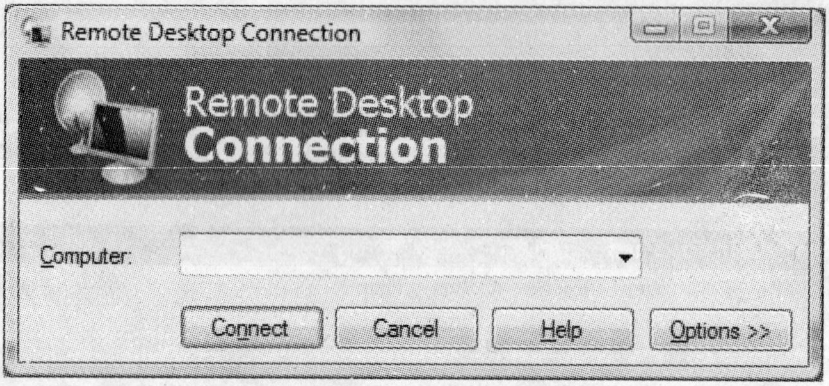

- Select **Don't allow connections to this computer** to prevent anyone from connecting to your computer using Remote Desktop or Remote Programs.
- Select **Allow connections from computers running any version of Remote Desktop** to allow people using any version of Remote Desktop or Remote Programs to connect to your computer. This is a good choice if you don't know the version of Remote Desktop Connection that other people are using.
- Select **Allow connections only from computers running Remote Desktop with Network Level Authentication** to allow people with computers running versions of Remote Desktop or Remote Programs with Network Level Authentication (NLA) to connect to your computer. This is the most secure choice, if you know that the people who will connect to your computer are running Windows Vista on their computers. (In Windows Vista, Remote Desktop uses NLA. You can also download NLA as a service pack on computers running some earlier versions of Windows.)

Run

When you want to open somthing with just a few keystrokes, the little Run command-line window is there for you.

Snipping Tool

It takes pictures of your PC's screen, for use when you're writing up instructions, illustrating

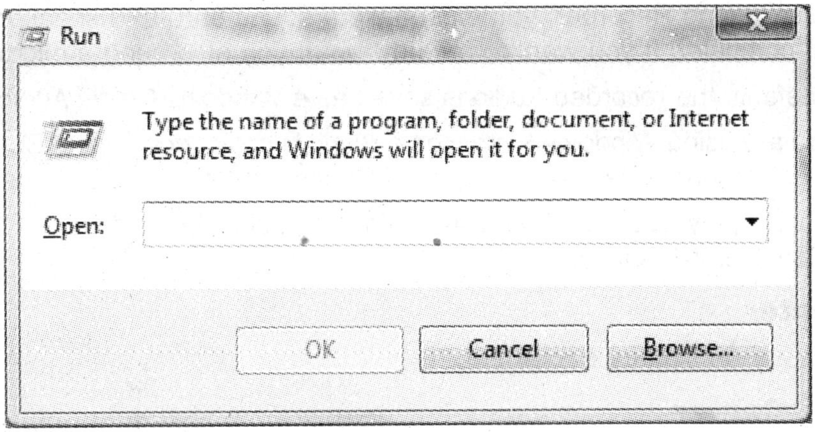

a computer book, or collecting proof of some secret screen you found buried in a game. You can take pictures of the entire screen or capture only the contents of a rectangular selection. When you are finished, Snipping tools displays your snapshot in a new windows, which you can print, close without saving, edit, or save, ready for emailing or inserting into a manuscript or page-layout program.

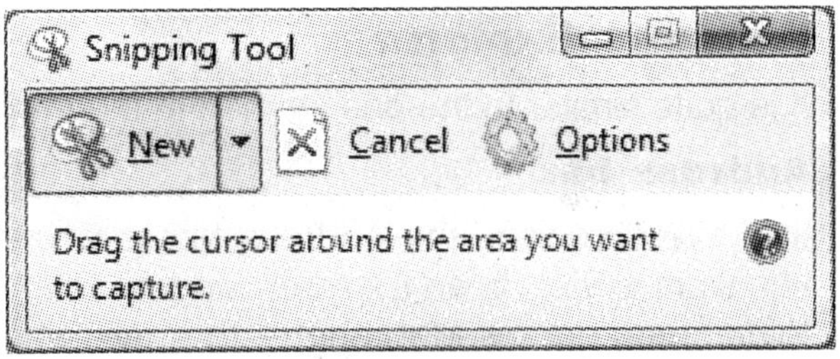

Sound Recorder

Using Sound Recorder, you can record sound as a digital media file on your computer from a variety of devices, such as a microphone that is plugged in to your sound card. The types of audio input sources you can record from depend on the audio devices you have, as well as on the input sources that are available on the sound card that is installed on your computer.

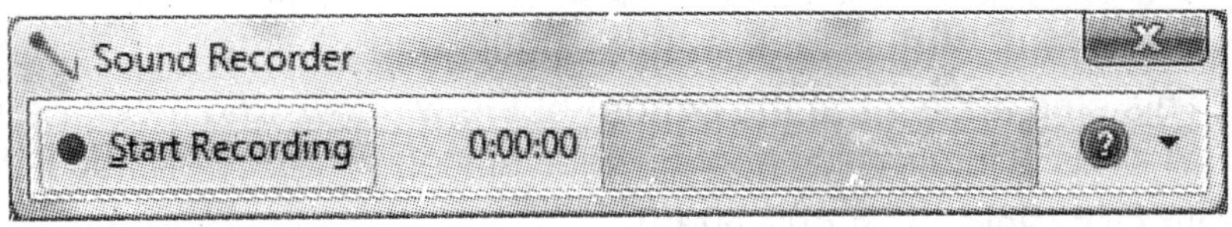

1. Make sure you have an audio input device, such as a microphone, connected to your computer.
2. Click Start, click All Programs, click Accessories, and then click Sound Recorder.
3. Click Start Recording.
4. To stop recording audio, click Stop Recording.
5. Do one of the following:
   - If you want to continue recording audio, click Resume, and then continue to record sound.
   - If you want to save the recorded sound as an audio file, click the File name box, type a file name for the recorded sound, and then click Save.

- To use Sound Recorder, you must have a sound card and speakers installed on your computer. If you want to record sound, you also need a microphone.
- By default, the recorded audio is saved as a Windows Media Audio (WMA) file.

  If you are using Windows Vista Home Basic N or Windows Vista Business N, your Sound Recorder files are saved as .wav files rather than .wma files.
- You can play your recording in a digital media player program that supports playback of WMA files.

Sync Center

See the chapter on Control Panel

Welcome Center

Discussed in Contol Panel

Windows Explorer

It is quite similar to the one we had in the earlier versions of Windows. It has the following:

Address bar

In a Web browser, the Address bar is where you type the addresses of the Web sites you want to visit. In an Explorer window, the Address bar shows the path you have taken—folders you burrowed through—to arrive where you are now.

Search Pane

The Search pane appears across the top of the windows, just below the address bar. Of course, the Search box already appears in every Explorer window, next to the Address bar—so why do you need a Search pane as well?

Details Pane

This strip appears at the bottom of the window, and it can be extremely useful. It reveals all kinds of information about whatever icon you have clicked in the main part of the window: its size, date, type and so on.

Preview Pane

The Preview oane appears at the right side of the window. That's right: Microsoft has now invented information strips that wrap all four sides of a window.

Navigation Pane

The Navigation pane has two halves: Favorite Links and Folders.

Favorite Links List

The main purpose of this area is to list places to which you want quick access. One click on a folder name opens the corresponding window. This list also offers icons for Recently Changed and Searches. These links refer to saved searches.

Folders List

The bottom of the Navigation pane, if you have chose to view it, is a hierarchical folder

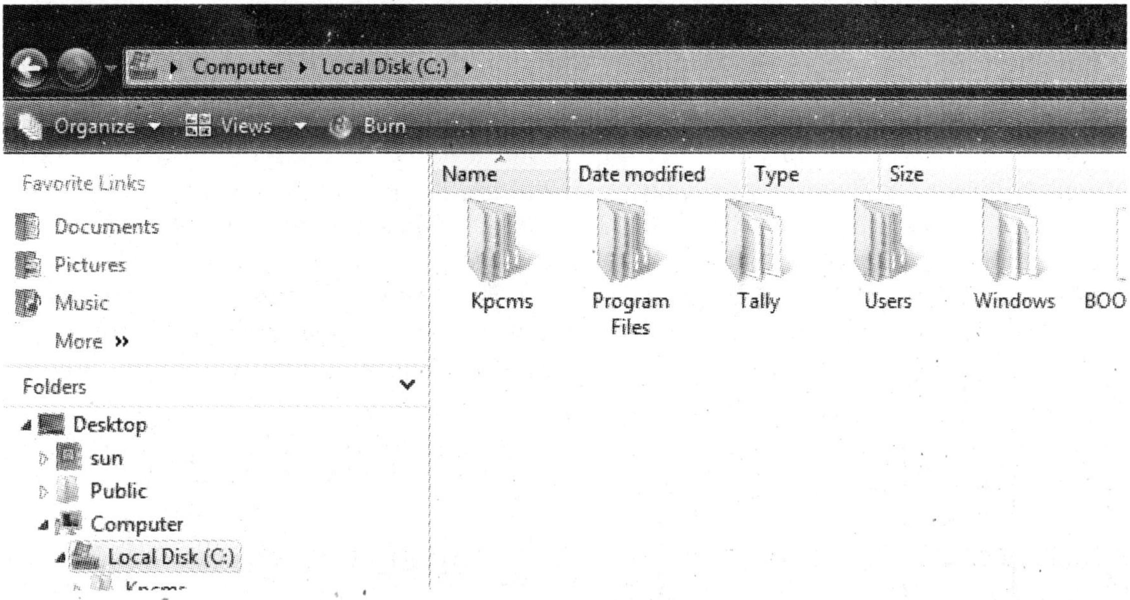

"tree" that shows the hierarchy of your entire computer. In essence, this view shows every folder on the machine at once. It lets you burrow very deeply into your hard drive's nest of folders without ever losing you bearings.

Windows Sidebar

It has been covered in chapter on Control Panel.

WordPad

WordPad is a very basic word processor. It however, fails in front of big word processing software like Word. WordPad is limited to opening and creating plain text files, Rich Text Format documents and Microsoft Write documents.

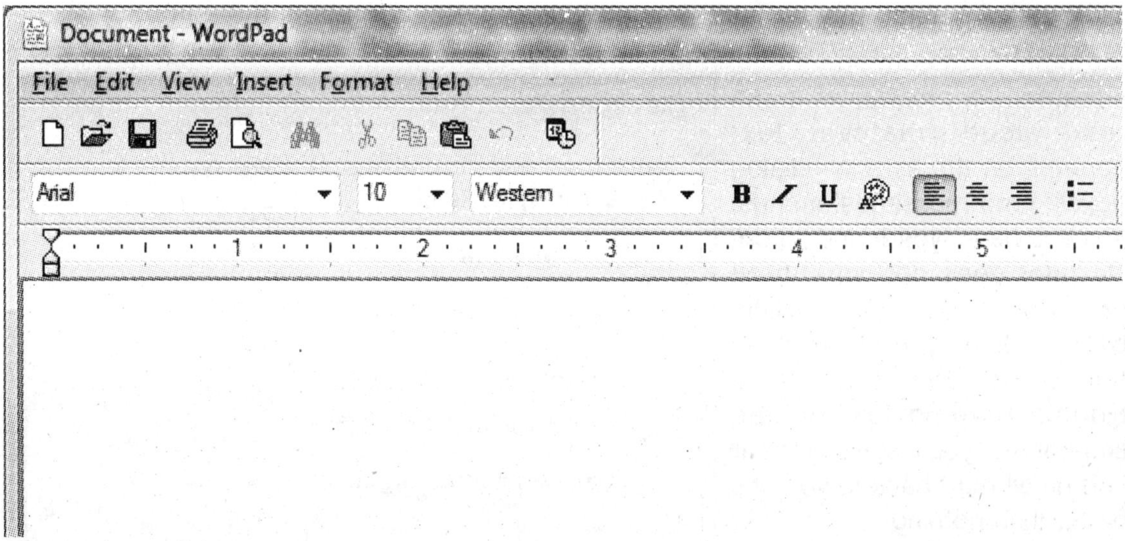

Ease of Access

It has the following programs: Magnifier, Narrator, On-Screen Keyboard and Windows Speech Recognition.

Magnifier

Magnifier is like a software magnifying glass that fills the top portion of your screen. The actual size version appears in the bottom half. The magnified area scrolls as you mover your cursor, tab through a dialog box, or type, enlarging whatever part of the screen contains the action. Using the Magnifier Settings dialog box shown here, you can specify how much magnification you want, which area on the screen gets magnified, and so on.

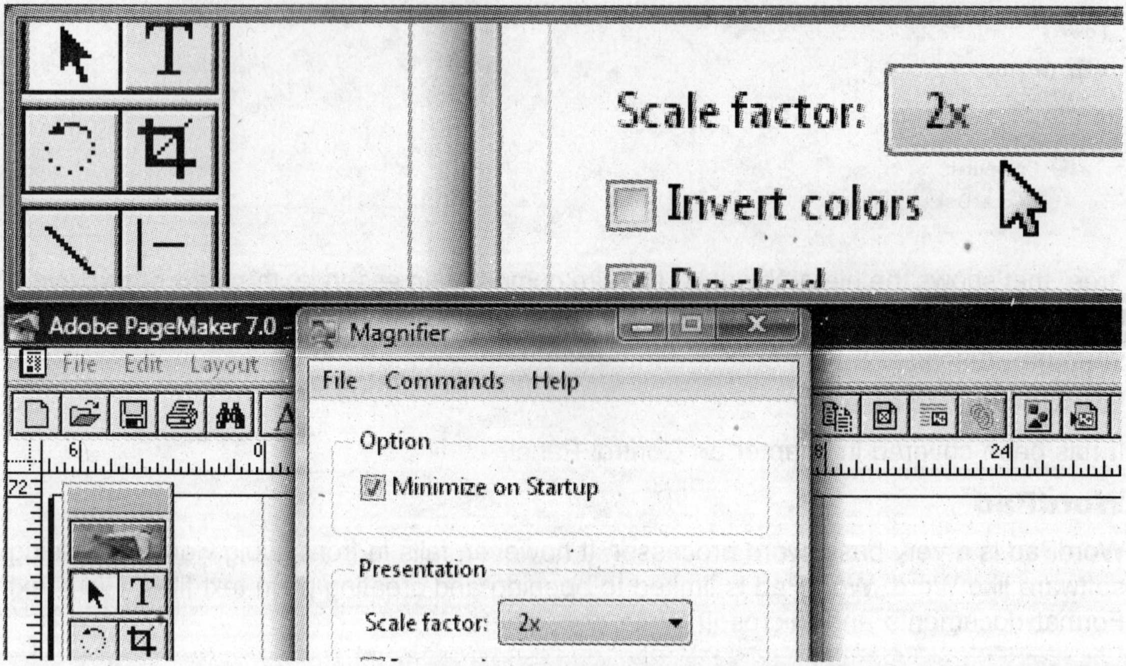

Narrator

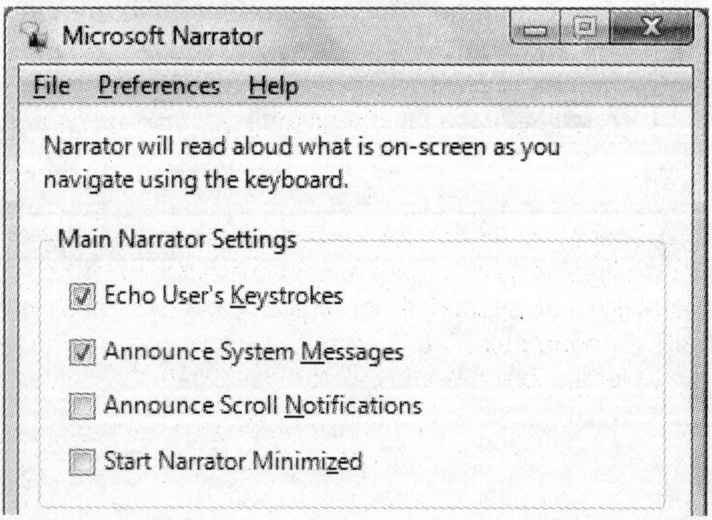

Narrator is a program that can read aloud whatever text appears on the screen—dialog boxes, error messages, menus, text you have typed, and so on. Narrator does not work in all programs, and it sounds a little bit like a Norwegian who has had few drinks. Still, if you have trouble reading text on the screen, or if you just like to hear you email read back to you, it's better than nothing.

On-Screen Keyboard

If you are having trouble typing keep the On-Screen Keyboard program in mind. It lets you type just by cliking the mouse-–an option you may find useful.

Windows Speech Recognition

A program that allows you to control your computer by speaking commands into a microphone. In Vista, it is far more powerful than what it was in earlier versions. It has various steps which have to be followed. First few steps are shown here.

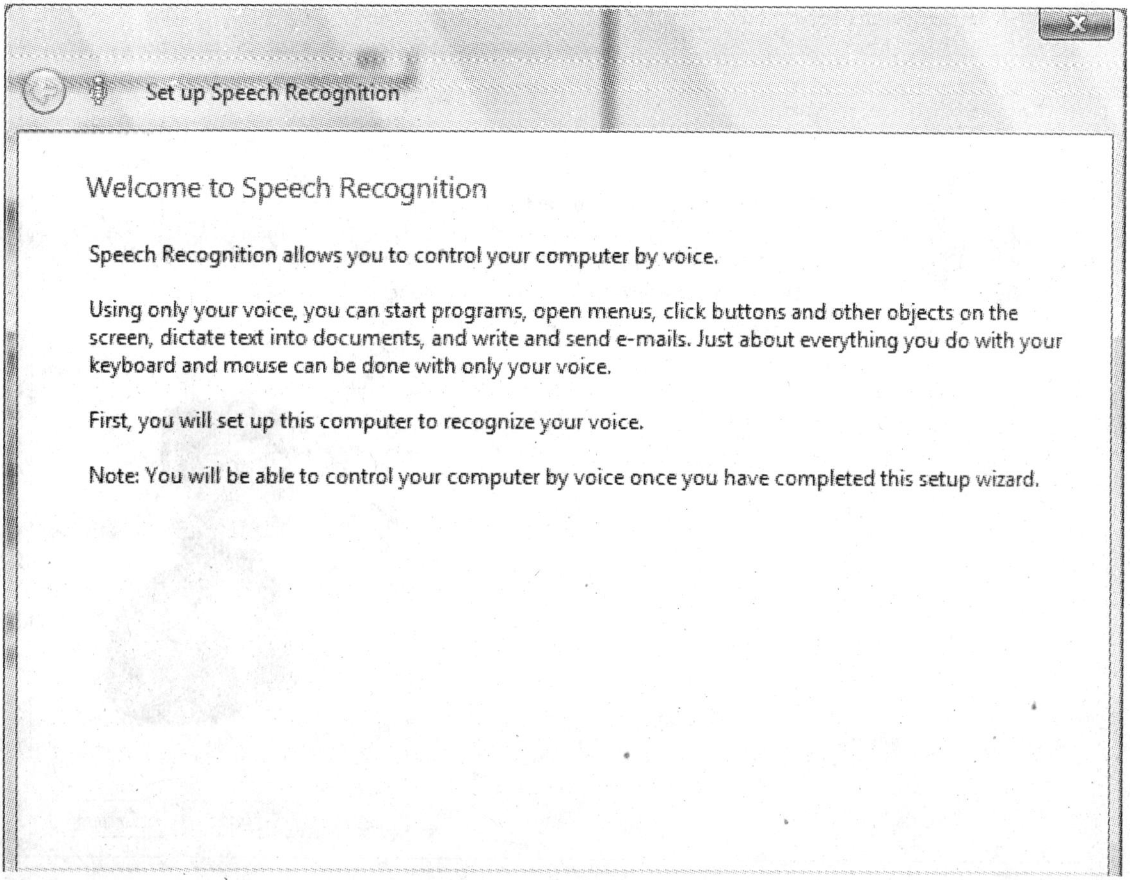

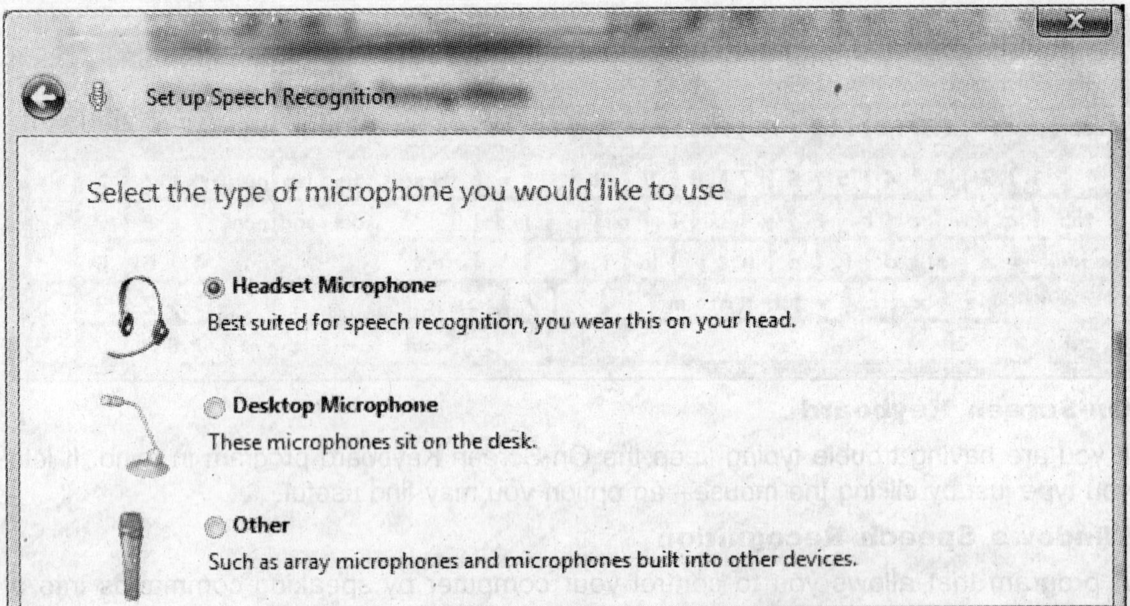
Set up Speech Recognition
Select the type of microphone you would like to use
Headset Microphone
Best suited for speech recognition, you wear this on your head.
Desktop Microphone
These microphones sit on the desk.
Other
Such as array microphones and microphones built into other devices.

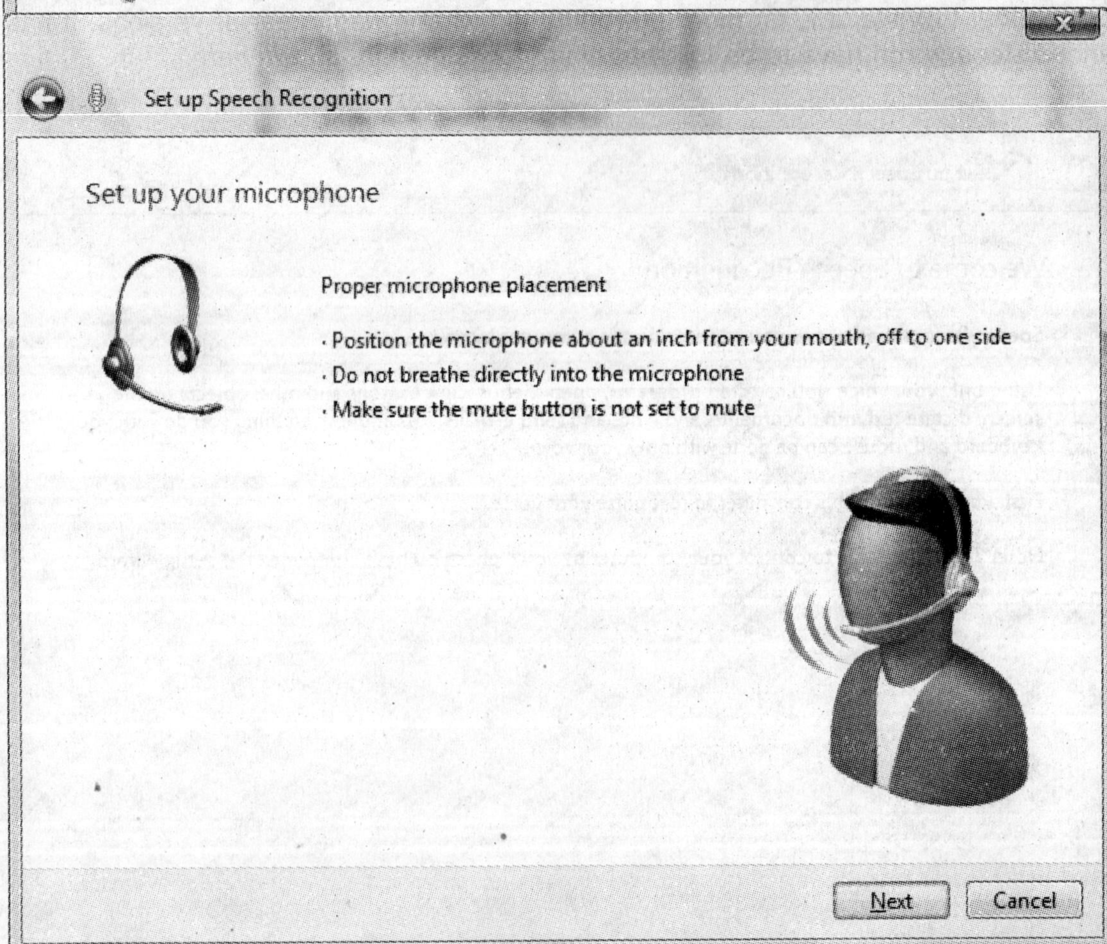
Set up Speech Recognition
Set up your microphone
Proper microphone placement
· Position the microphone about an inch from your mouth, off to one side
· Do not breathe directly into the microphone
· Make sure the mute button is not set to mute
Next
Cancel

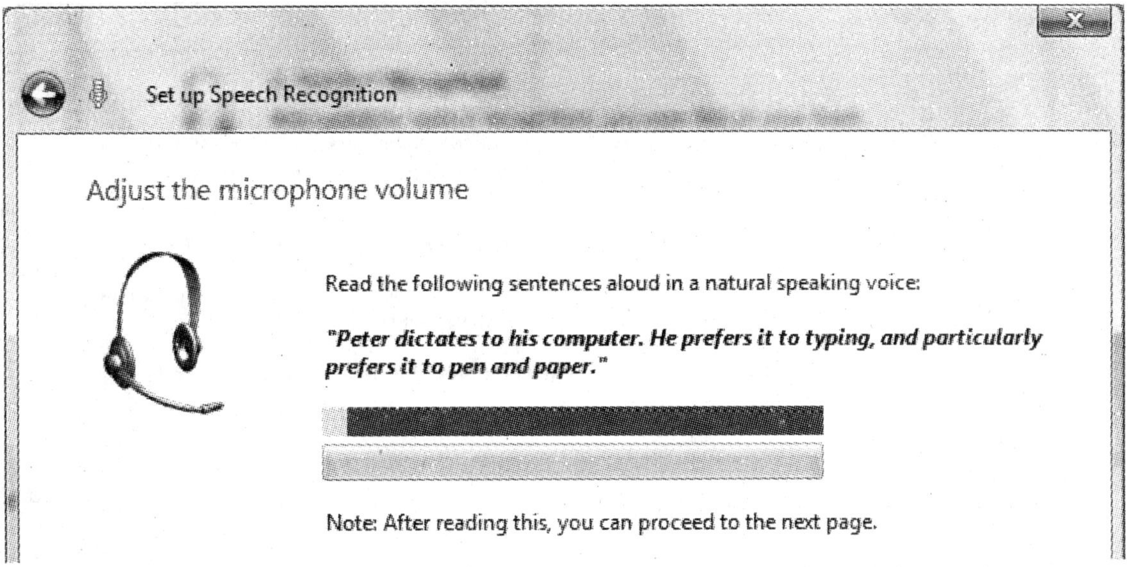

System Tools

Next set of tools help you in maintaining and troubleshooting the computer. They are: Backup Status and Configuration, Character Map, Computer, Control Panel, Disk Cleanup, Disk Defragmenter, Internet Explorer, System Information, System Restore, Task Scheduler, Windows Easy Transfer.

Backup Status and Configuration

Backups help ensure that your files aren't permanently lost or damaged. With automatic backups, you don't have to remember to back up your files. You can change your automatic backup settings (such as how often you back up, the type of storage you use, or the types of files you back up) whenever you want to.

To set up automatic backups

1. Click to open Back Up and Restore Center.
2. Click Back up files, and then follow the steps in the wizard. If you are prompted for an administrator password or confirmation, type the password or provide confirmation.

To change automatic backups

1. Click to open Back Up and Restore Center.
2. Click Change settings.
3. Click Change backup settings, and then follow the steps in the wizard. If you are prompted for an administrator password or confirmation, type the password or provide confirmation.

Character Map

A special character is a character that cannot be found on your keyboard. You can insert

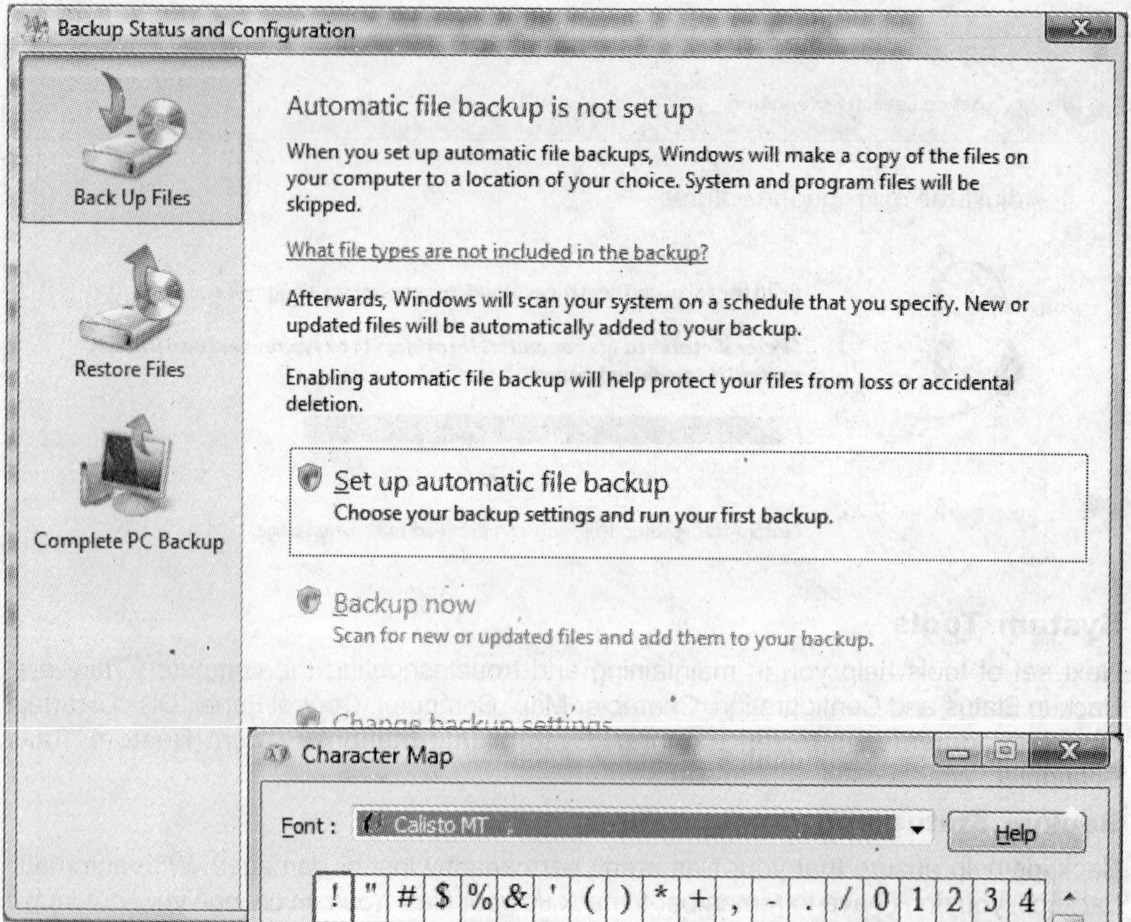

special characters by using Character Map or by pressing a combination of keys on your keyboard.

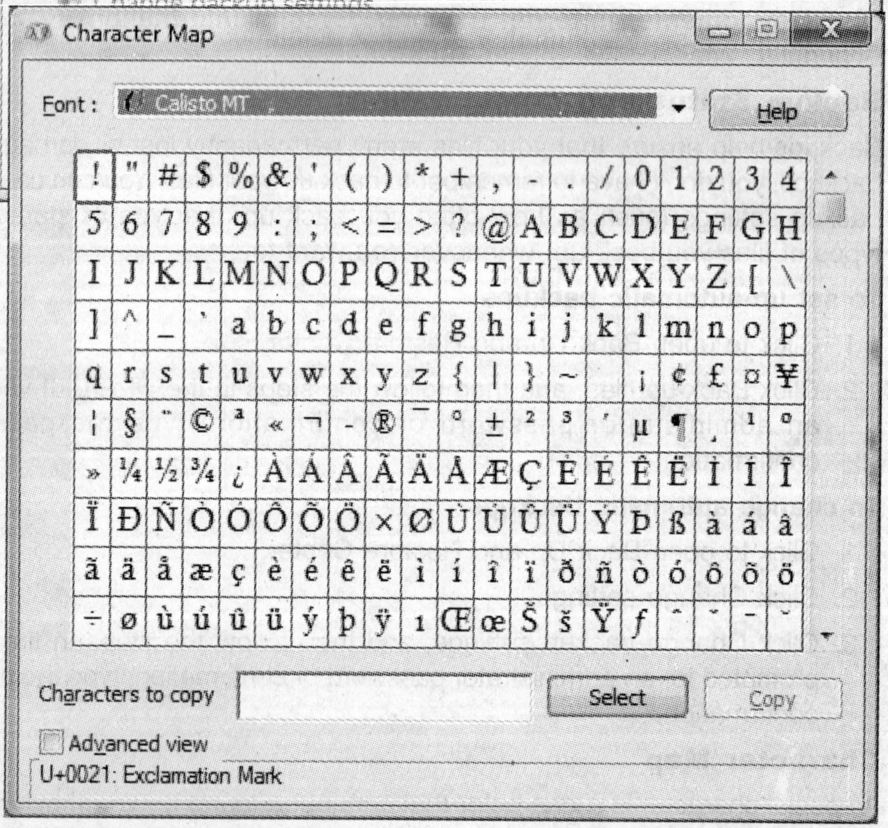

Character Map enables you to view the characters that are available in a selected font. Using Character Map, you can copy individual characters or a group of characters to the Clipboard and paste them into any program that can display them.

How to insert a special character into a document?

1. In Character Map, click the Font list, and then click the font you want to use.
2. Click the special character you want to insert into the document.
3. Click Select, and then click Copy.
4. Open your document and click the location in the document where you want the special character to appear.
5. Click the Edit menu, and then click Paste.

Computer

It has been described in an earlier chapter

Control Panel

See the chapter on the Control Panel

Disk Cleanup

As you use your computer, Windows litters your hard disk with temporary files, programs, utilities, and Web sites scatter disposable files everywhere. If you could see your hard drive surface, it would eventually look like the floor of a minivan whose owners eat a lot of fast food.

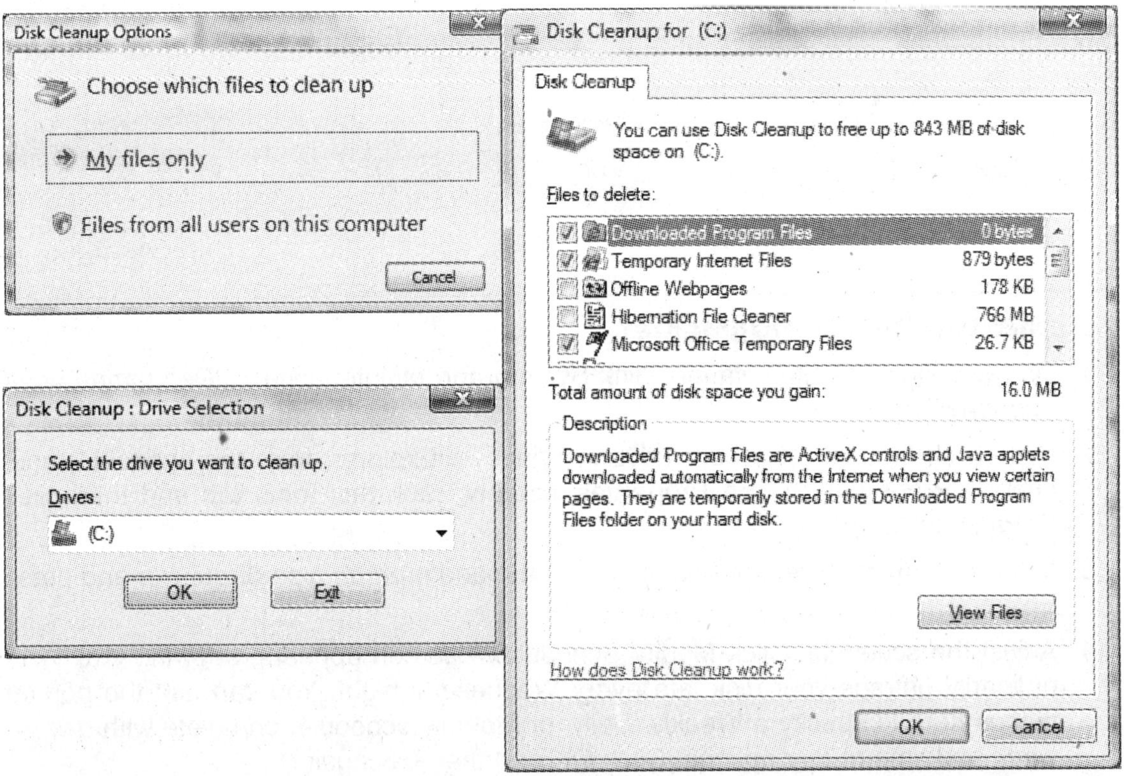

Disk Defragmenter

Disk defragmentation describes the process of consolidating fragmented files on your computer's hard disk.

Fragmentation happens to a hard disk over time as you save, change, or delete files. The changes that you save to a file are often stored at a location on the hard disk that's different from the original file. Additional changes are saved to even more locations. Over time, both the file and the hard disk itself become fragmented, and your computer slows down as it has to look in many different places to open a file.

Disk Defragmenter is a tool that rearranges the data on your hard disk and reunites fragmented files so your computer can run more efficiently. In this version of Windows, Disk Defragmenter runs on a schedule so you don't have to remember to run it, although you can still run it manually or change the schedule it uses.

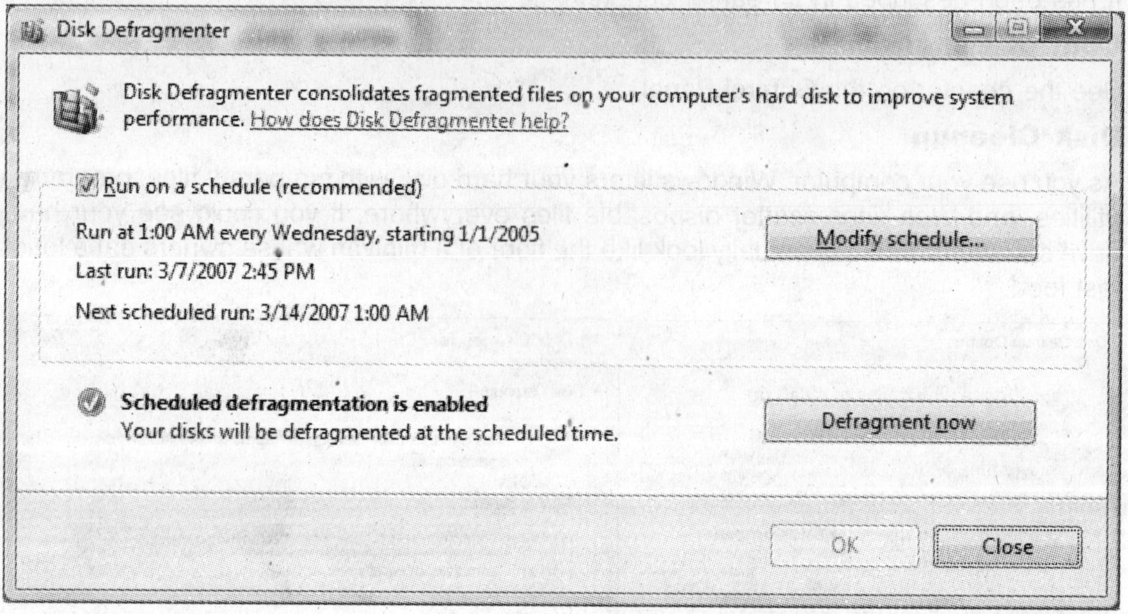

To start the Disk Defragmenter

1. Choose Start > Control Panel. Click System and Maintenance > "Defragment your hard drive".
2. Right-click the icon of a hard drive in Windows Explorer: from the shortcut menu, choose Properties. In the Properties window, click the Tools tab and then click Defragment Now.
3. In the Start menu's search box, or at a command prompt, type dfrgui.exe and press Enter.
4. Adjust the schedule. Click Modify Schedule. A screen appears, showing that Vista ordinarily defrags your disk late every Wednesday night. You can use the pop-up menus here to specify a Weekly, Daily, or Monthly schedule, complete with day-of-week and time-of-day options. Click OK and then OK again.

Internet Explorer

Here are some of the ways that Internet Explorer makes browsing the web easier, safer, and more enjoyable.

Increased security and privacy

New security and privacy features allow you to browse the web more safely.

- Phishing Filter can help protect you from phishing attacks, online fraud, and spoofed websites.
- Protected mode can help protect your computer from websites that try to install malicious software or to save files on your computer without your consent.
- Higher security levels can help protect you from hackers and web attacks.
- The Security Status bar displays the identity of secure websites to help you make informed decisions when using online banking or merchants.
- Internet Explorer's lets you start Internet Explorer without toolbars, ActiveX controls, or other add-ons that might slow your computer or prevent you from getting online.

New features

- Tabbed browsing is a new feature in Internet Explorer that allows you to open multiple websites in a single browser window. If you have a lot of tabs open, use Quick Tabs to easily switch between open tabs.
- The new Instant Search box lets you search the web from the Address bar. You can also search using different search providers to get better results.
- Internet Explorer now lets you delete your temporary files, cookies, webpage history, saved passwords, and form information from one place. Delete selected categories, or everything at once.
- Click the Favorites Center button to open the Favorites Center to manage favorites, feeds, and history in one place.
- Printing now scales webpages to fit the paper you're using. Print Preview gives more control when printing, with manual scaling and an accurate view of what you're about to print.
- The Zoom feature lets you enlarge or reduce text, images, and some controls.

System Information

System Information (also known as msinfo32.exe) shows details about your computer's hardware configuration, computer components, and software, including drivers.

System Information lists categories in the left pane and details about each category in the right pane. The categories include:

- System Summary. Shows general information about your computer and the operating system, such as the computer name and manufacturer, the type of basic input/output system (BIOS) your computer uses, and the amount of memory that is installed.

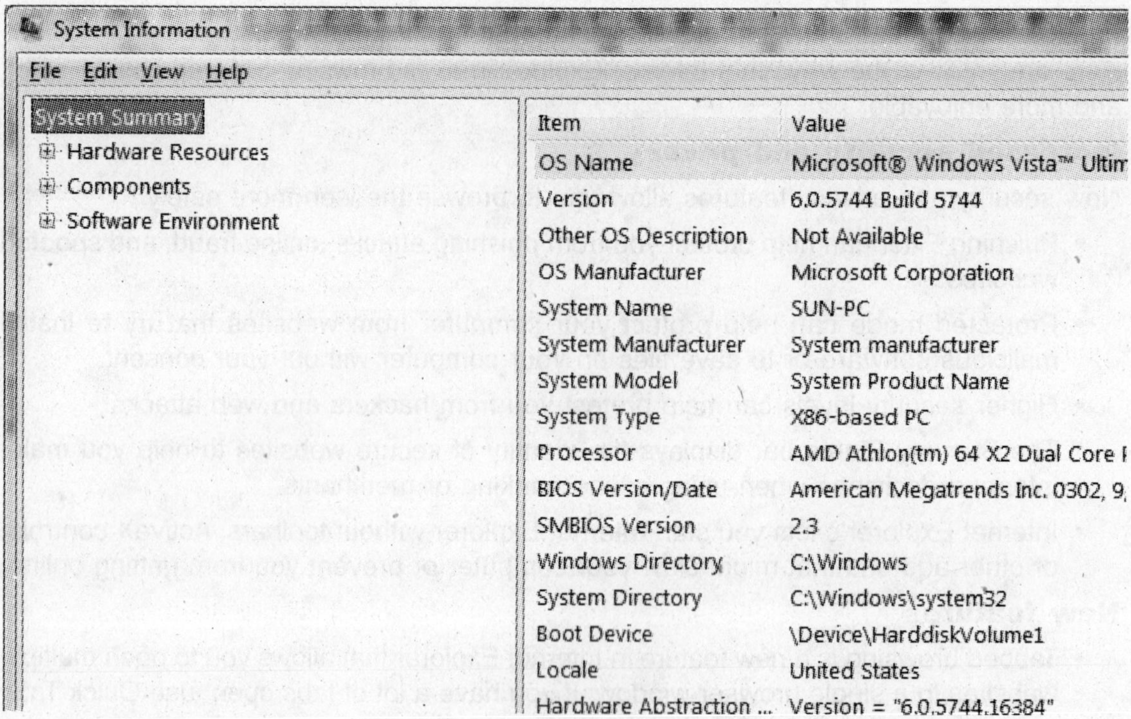

- Hardware Resources. Displays advanced details about your computer's hardware for IT professionals.
- Components. Displays information about disk drives, sound devices, modems, and other components installed on your computer.
- Software Environment. Shows information about drivers, network connections, and other program-related details.

To find a specific detail in System Information, type the information you're looking for in the Find what box at the bottom of the window. For example, to find your computer's Internet protocol (IP) address, type ip address in the Find what box, and then click Find.

System Restore

System Restore helps you restore your computer's system files to an earlier point in time. It's a way to undo system changes to your computer without affecting your personal files, such as e mail, documents, or photos.

Sometimes, the installation of a program or a drivercan cause an unexpected change to your computer or cause Windows to behave unpredictably. Usually, uninstalling the program or driver corrects the problem. If uninstalling does not fix the problem, you can try restoring your computer's system to an earlier date when everything worked correctly.

System Restore uses a feature called System Protection to regularly create and save restore points on your computer. These restore points contain information about registry settings and other system information that Windows uses. You can also create restore points manually.

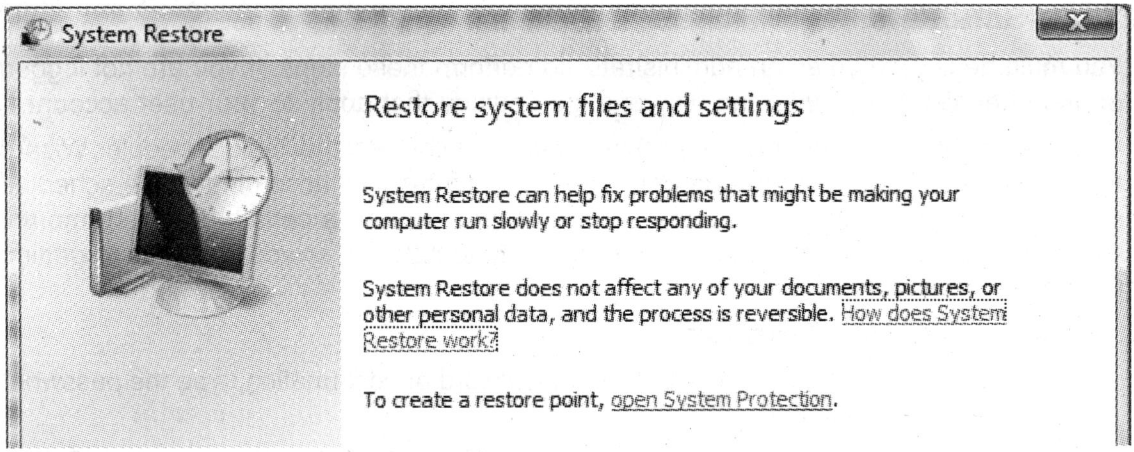

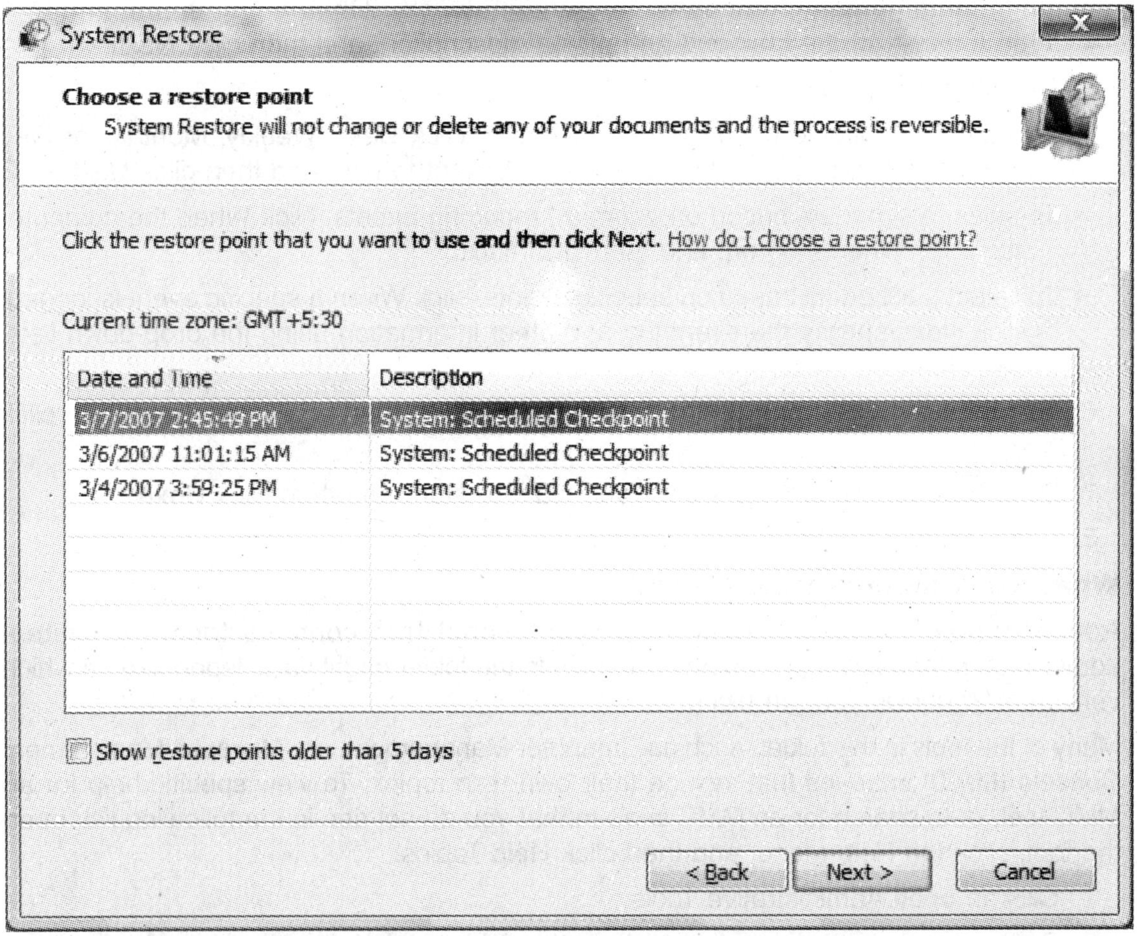

System Restore is not intended for backing up personal files, so it cannot help you recover a personal file that has been deleted or damaged. You should regularly back up your personal files and important data using a backup program.

Task Scheduler

You must be logged on as an administrator to perform these steps. If you are not logged on as an administrator, you can only change settings that apply to your user account.

If you use a specific program on a regular basis, you can use the Task Scheduler Wizard to create a task that opens the program for you automatically according to the schedule you choose. For example, if you use a financial program on a certain day each month, you can schedule a task that opens the program automatically so you don't risk forgetting to open it yourself.

1. Click to open Task Scheduler.
2. If you are prompted for an administrator password or confirmation, type the password or provide confirmation.
3. Click the Action menu, and then click Create Basic Task.
4. Type a name for the task and an optional description, and then click Next.
5. Do one of the following:
   - To select a schedule based on the calendar, click Daily, Weekly, Monthly, or One time, click Next, specify the schedule you want to use, and then click Next.
   - To select a schedule based on common recurring events, click When the computer starts, or When I log on, and then click Next.
   - To select a schedule based on specific events, click When a specific event is logged, click Next, specify the event log and other information using the drop-down lists, and then click Next.
6. To schedule a program to start automatically, click Start a program, and then click Next.
7. Click Browse to find the program you want to start, and then click Next.
8. Click Finish.

What are Administrative Tools?

Administrative Tools is a folder in Control Panel that contains tools for system administrators and advanced users. The tools in the folder might vary depending on which version of Windows you are using.

Many of the tools in this folder, such as Computer Management, are Microsoft Management Console (MMC) snap-ins that include their own help topics. To view specific help for an MMC tool, or to search for an MMC snap-in that you do not see in the following list, open the tool, click the Help menu, and then click Help Topics.

1. Click to open Administrative Tools.
2. Some common administrative tools in this folder include:
   - Computer Management. Manage local or remote computers by using a single, consolidated desktop tool. Using Computer Management, you can perform many tasks, such as monitoring system events, configuring hard disks, and managing system performance.

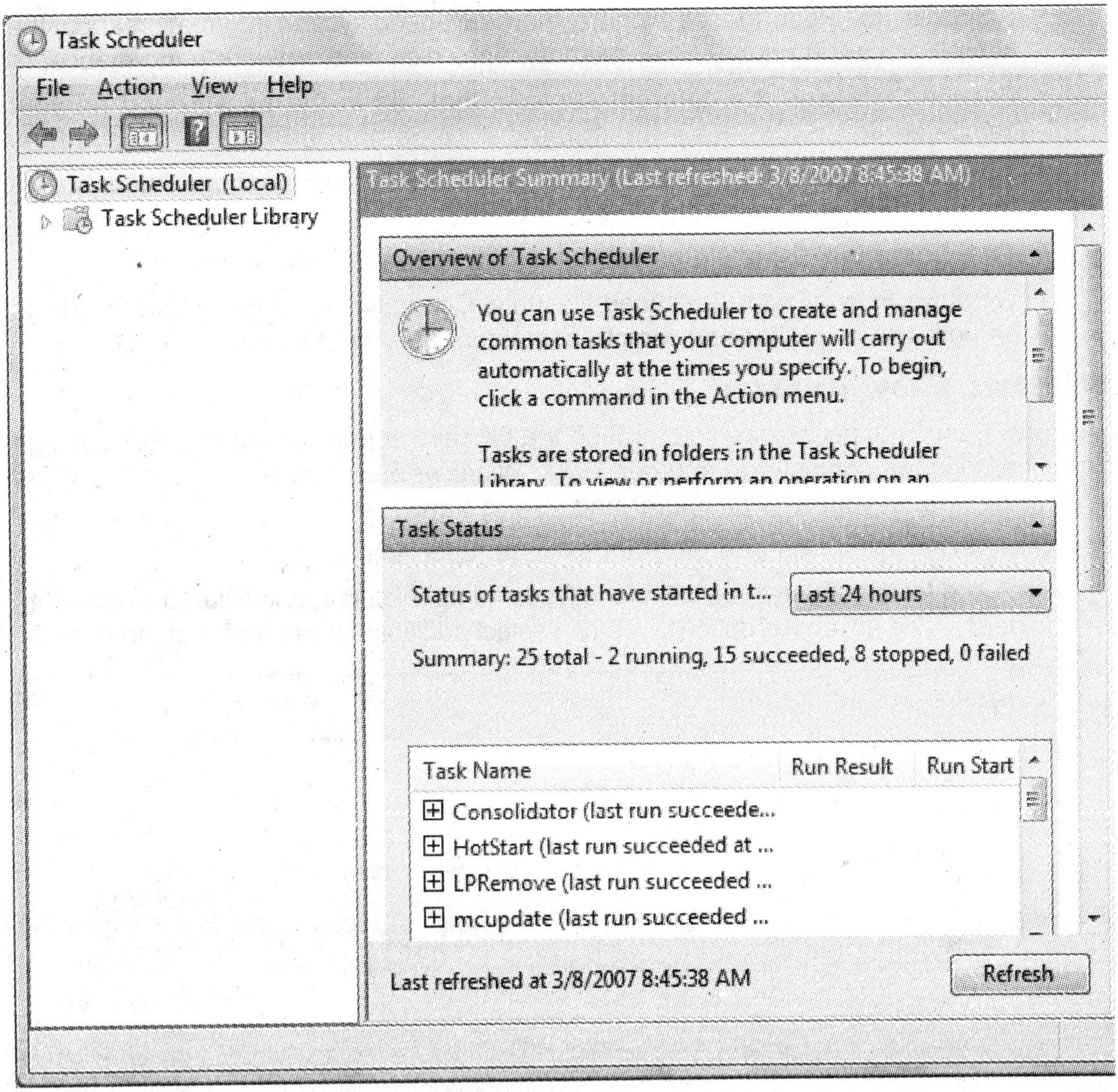

- Data Sources (ODBC). Use Open Database Connectivity (ODBC) to move data from one type of database (a data source) to another.
- Event Viewer. View information about significant events, such as a program starting or stopping, or a security error, that are recorded in event logs.
- iSCSI Initiator. Configure advanced connections between storage devices on a network.
- Local Security Policy. View and edit Group Policy security settings.
- Memory Diagnostics Tool. Check your computer's memory to see if it is functioning properly.
- Print Management. Manage printers and print servers on a network and perform other administrative tasks.

- Reliability and Performance Monitor. View advanced system information about the central processing unit (CPU), memory, hard disk, and network performance.
- Services. Manage the different services that run in the background on your computer.
- System Configuration. Identify problems that might be preventing Windows from running correctly.
- Task Scheduler. Schedule programs or other tasks to run automatically.
- Windows Firewall with Advanced Security. Configure advanced firewall settings on both this computer and remote computers on your network.

Windows Easy Transfer

Windows Easy Transfer guides you through the process of transferring files and settings from one Windows computer to another. Using Windows Easy Transfer, you can choose what to transfer to your new computer and how to transfer it.

You can transfer most files and program settings. Specifically:

- Files and folders. Everything within the Documents, Pictures, and Shared Documents folders. Using advanced options, you can select additional files and folders to transfer.

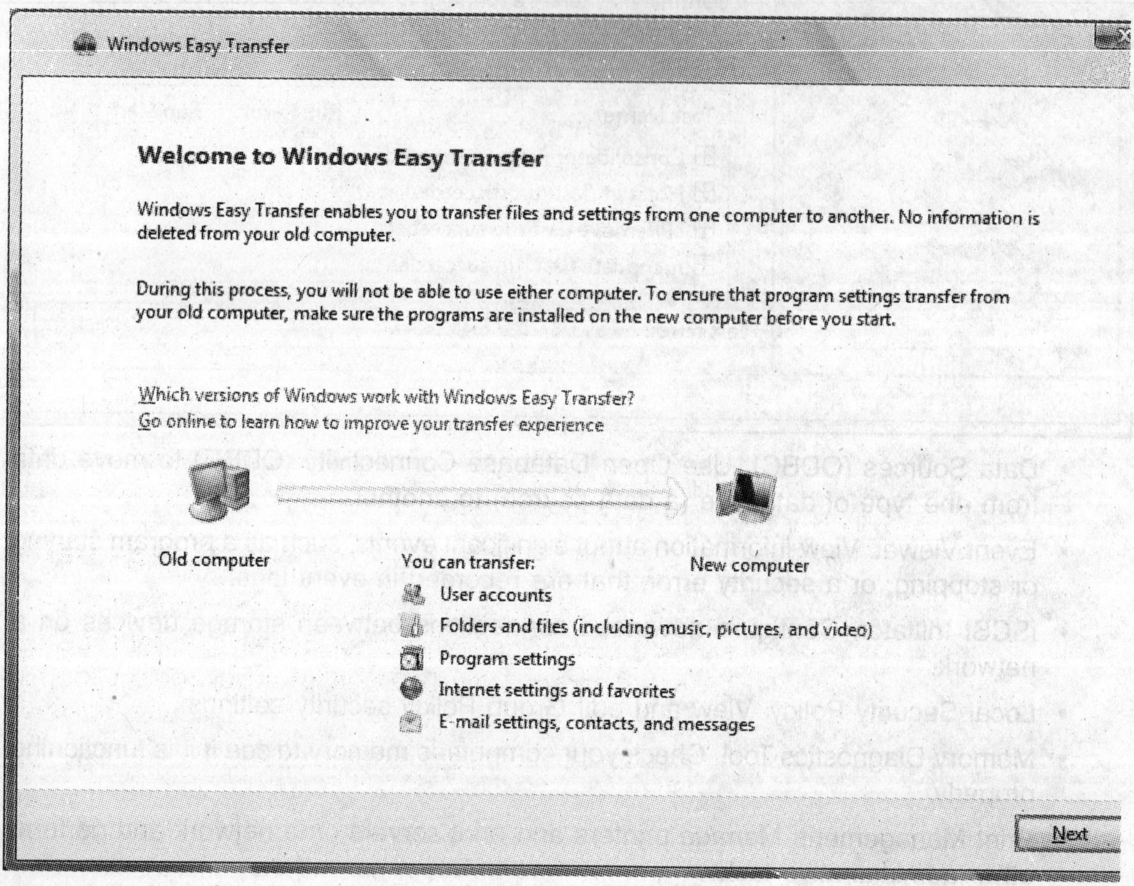

- E mail settings, contacts, and messages. Messages, account settings, and address books from Microsoft Outlook Express, Outlook, Windows Mail, and other e mail programs.
- Program settings. Settings that keep your programs configured as you had them on your old computer. You must first install the programs on your new computer, because Windows Easy Transfer does not transfer the programs themselves. Some programs might not work on this version of Windows, including security programs (which are often not compatible with all versions of Windows), antivirus programs, firewall programs (your new computer should already have a firewall running to help ensure safety during the transfer), and programs with software drivers (some are not compatible with all versions of Windows).
- User accounts and settings. Color schemes, desktop backgrounds, network connections, screen savers, fonts, Start menu options, taskbar options, folders, specific files, network printers and drives, and accessibility options.
- Internet settings and favorites. Internet connection settings, favorites, and cookies.
- Music. Electronic music files, playlists, and album art.
- Pictures and video. Pictures—which includes any visual file type (for example, .jpg, .bmp, .gif)—and personal videos.

Tablet PC

This is the next set of accessories. It includes: Sticky Notes, Tablet PC Input Panel and Windows Journal.

Sticky Notes

A Tablet PC accessory that you can use to create short handwritten or voice notes. The small, yellow notes are arranged in a stack on the desktop, similar to paper sticky notes.

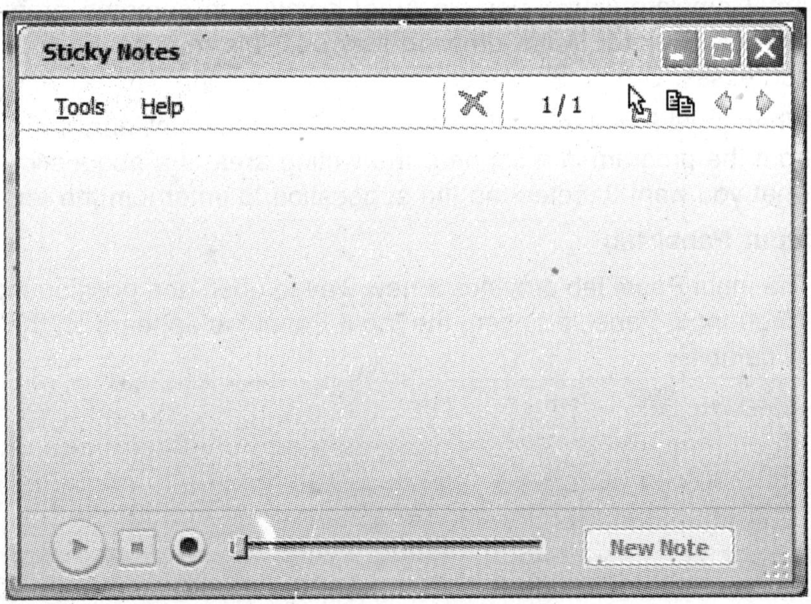

Open Sticky Notes

You can open Sticky Notes quickly by using the Start button, or specifying that Sticky Notes opens automatically when you start your computer. You can also keep Sticky Notes always visible on your desktop.

To open Sticky Notes

- On the Windows taskbar, tap the Start button , point to All Programs, and then tap Sticky Notes.

To make Sticky Notes open automatically at startup

- Tap the Tools menu, point to Options, and then tap Open at Startup.

To keep Sticky Notes always visible on the desktop

- Tap the Tools menu, point to Options, and then tap Always on Top.

To close Sticky Notes

- On the title bar, tap the Close button.

Your notes are automatically saved when you close Sticky Notes.

Tablet PC Input Panel

You can use Tablet PC Input Panel to enter text without using a standard keyboard. Use the writing pad or the character pad to convert your handwriting into typed text, or use the on-screen keyboard to enter characters.

What's new in Input Panel?

Input Panel has a new look and several new features. These new features include:

- AutoComplete
- Input Panel tab
- Back-of-pen erase
- New scratch-out gestures

AutoComplete

AutoComplete works just like AutoComplete in common programs, such as Microsoft Internet Explorer. AutoComplete lists possible matches in Input Panel, such as e-mail addresses, URLs, file names, and other items that you've entered before.

When Input Panel recognizes your handwriting, AutoComplete displays possible matches from the program in a list near the writing area. If a suggestion in the list of matches is what you want to enter, tap the suggestion to enter it in the text entry area.

Input Panel tab

The Input Panel tab provides a new way to open and position Input Panel on the screen. When Input Panel is closed, the Input Panel tab appears on the left edge of your screen by default.

To open Input Panel, simply tap the Input Panel tab, and Input Panel will slide out from the edge of your screen. When you close Input Panel, it slides back to the edge of the screen.

You can move the Input Panel tab by dragging it up or down along the edge of the screen. Then, when you tap it, Input Panel opens at the same horizontal location on the screen that the tab appears.

When you open Input Panel by using the Input Panel tab, it floats over any open windows and stays open until you close it.

- Use the Input Panel tab to open Input Panel when you're running a program that uses the entire the screen, such as Remote Desktop.

Back-of-pen erase

If your tablet pen has an eraser, you can use it to delete writing and recognized text from Input Panel. It works in the writing pad, the character pad, and the correction area.

Scratch-out gestures

Windows includes new, more tolerant scratch-out gesture to delete your handwriting or recognized text in Input Panel. These scratch-out gestures are intended to work better with your personal style of crossing out text in Input Panel. The new scratch-out gestures include, but are not limited to:

- Strikethrough, a horizontal line drawn across a word
- Vertical scratch-out, in the pattern of an M or W
- Circular scratch-out
- Angled scratch-out

You can still use the Z-shaped scratch-out gesture that was available in Microsoft Windows XP Tablet PC Edition.

If your handwriting is sometimes accidentally deleted by one of the new scratch-out gestures, you can adjust your settings to use only the Z-shaped scratch-out gesture.

Text entry

You can use the writing pad, the character pad, or the on-screen keyboard to enter text. The writing pad and the character pad convert your handwriting into typed text. The on-screen keyboard works just like a standard keyboard except that you enter text by tapping keys with your tablet pen. The following table describes the different choices for using Input Panel.

- With the writing pad, you can write continuously, as if you were writing on a lined piece of paper.
- The character pad converts your handwriting to typed text, one letter, number, or symbol at a time.
- The on-screen keyboard is similar to a standard keyboard.

The writing pad and character pad have a number pad, a symbol pad, and web quick keys to help you quickly and accurately enter these types of text. These quick keys are hidden when you start to write, but appear after you insert or delete your writing.

- If the password security settings are turned on, Input Panel automatically switches to the on-screen keyboard when you place the insertion point in a text input area where you enter a password.

Text correction

Input Panel provides you with several ways to easily correct the text that you enter.

You can correct your handwriting recognition results directly in the writing pad or the character pad before you insert the text.

To erase a word or a character, use a scratch-out gesture or the back-of-pen erase to remove the word or character, and then start over.

In the writing pad for Western languages, you can use the correction area to fix incorrectly recognized text. You can select an alternate word that Input Panel suggests, or rewrite letters to correct the word in the correction area. To access the correction area, tap the recognized text for the word that you want to correct.

In the character pad, you can write over an incorrectly recognized character or use the drop-down menu to select from a list of characters that the handwriting recognizer has identified as alternates.

If you've already inserted the text in a program, you can select the text that you want to correct, and then either select an alternate word that Input Panel suggests or use the correction area to correct the word.

Tips for using Input Panel

Use the following tips to become more efficient with using Input Panel.

- Use the number pad to insert numbers. To open the number pad, tap the Num button on the writing pad or the character pad.
- Use the symbol pad to insert symbols. To open the symbol pad, tap the Sym button on the writing pad or the character pad.
- Use web quick keys to enter URLs more quickly. To open the web quick keys, tap the Web button on the writing pad or the character pad.
- Use gestures to perform common keystroke actions.
- Do not hyphenate a word if it doesn't fit on one line in the writing pad. Write the entire word on a new line instead.

Windows Journal

It is an accessory that enables users who do not have a computer running Windows Journal to view files that were created with Windows Journal.

Tips for working efficiently in Journal

In Windows Journal, you can handwrite by using your tablet pen. You can save your

handwriting in a note, convert the writing to typed text, and then enter typed text into your notes. Or, you can just leave your handwriting as ink in a note. You can also create drawings and insert pictures in your notes.

Use the following information to help you work with Journal quickly and efficiently.

Using shortcut menus

The fastest way to do many tasks is to use a right-click equivalent with your tablet pen. The following is a list of places where you can use right-click equivalents:

- Ink on a page
- An empty space on a page
- A picture or a flag
- The area inside a text box
- A text box border
- A column header in the find pane or the note list pane
- A note title in the find pane or note list pane
- A toolbar

- The vertical and horizontal scroll bars on a page

Using keyboard shortcuts

Many of the toolbar buttons and menu commands in Journal have corresponding keyboard shortcuts. You can use these keyboard shortcuts instead of your tablet pen to do things such as create or save notes, open or close recently used notes, and print notes.

The following table shows the various keyboard shortcuts available in Journal.

Action	*Keyboard shortcut*
Start a new note	CTRL+N
Open a recently used note	CTRL+O
Save changes to a note	CTRL+S
Move a note to a specific folder	CTRL+SHIFT+V
Print a note	CTRL+P
Close a note and its Journal window	ALT+F4
Undo a change	CTRL+Z
Redo a change	CTRL+Y
Select all items on a page	CTRL+A
Cut a selection	CTRL+X
Copy a selection to the Clipboard	CTRL+C
Paste a selection from the Clipboard	CTRL+V
Cancel a selection	ESC
Delete a selection	DEL
Start a basic find	CTRL+F
Go to a page	CTRL+G
Refresh find results	F5
Refresh the note list	F5
Toggle between a note list and a note	F6
Display a shortcut menu for column headings in a note list	CTRL+SHIFT+C
View a note in full-screen mode	F11
Open Journal Help	F1

Create and save a Journal note

You can create, save, open, and close notes in Windows Journal. You can export a note to a different file format for a colleague who doesn't have Journal. Journal can also help you to recover note content if a note closes unexpectedly.

To create a note

You should give each new note a note title. When you save a new note, Journal suggests a file name based on the note title that you write. Also, when you view a list of notes in the find pane or the note list pane, you can see the note titles written in your own handwriting.

Journal can suggest a file name based on your note title only when you have enabled handwriting recognition. You can do this on the Other tab in the Options dialog box. (Tap Tools, tap Options, and then tap the Other tab.)

1. On the Standard toolbar, tap New Note.
2. To create a note title, write a note title in the title area at the top of the first page of your note.
3. You can control the appearance of the title area on the Background and Title Area tab in the Page Setup dialog box. (Tap File, tap Page Setup, and then tap the Background and Title Area tab.)

To save a note

Journal notes are saved by default in Journal note format (.jnt). If you want to save a note as a template, you can also save it in Journal template format (.jtp).

1. On the Standard toolbar, tap Save.
2. In the Save in box, browse to the folder in which you want to save your note.
3. In the Save as type list, tap the format that you want.
4. In the File name box, enter a name for your note.
   - How do I enter text without a standard keyboard?
   - To open Input Panel, tap the Input Panel tab, which appears by default on the left edge of the screen.
   - Tap the On-Screen Keyboard button.
   - Make sure that the insertion point is in the File name box, and then use the on-screen keyboard to enter the text.
5. Tap Save.

To save changes to a note

- On the Standard toolbar, tap Save.

To export a note

1. Tap the File menu, and then tap Export As.
2. In the Export dialog box, in the Save in box, browse to the folder to which you want to export your note.
3. In the Save as type list, tap the format that you want.
4. In the File name box, enter a name.

- How do I enter text without a standard keyboard?
- To open Input Panel, tap the Input Panel tab, which appears by default on the left edge of the screen.
- Tap the On-Screen Keyboard button.
- Make sure that the insertion point is in the File name box, and then use the on-screen keyboard to enter the text.

5. Tap Export.

3 Control Panel of Windows Vista

Introduction

Like all the earlier versions of Windows, this Windows version too has a control panel. It is a group of icons which when selected invoke applications which allow you to change the settings of the Windows. In this chapter we will study about the various options available in the control panel.

Accessing Control Panel

Control panel can be accessed from two places: **Control Panel** in **My Computer** icon and from **Start** button on the on the desktop. When you click **Start** button, you see the different options. **Control Panel** is one of them.

Control Panel can be seen in Alphabetic order of the programs or Control Panel Home view which shows the programs subjec wise. Both views are shown here.

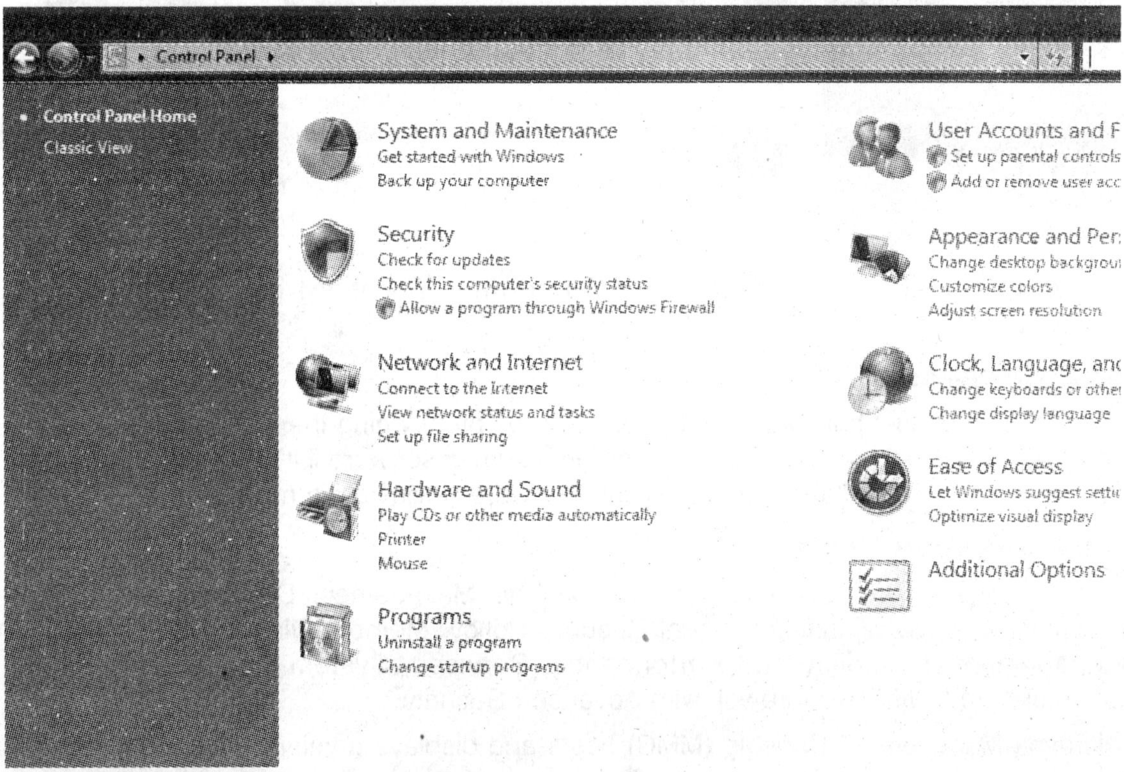

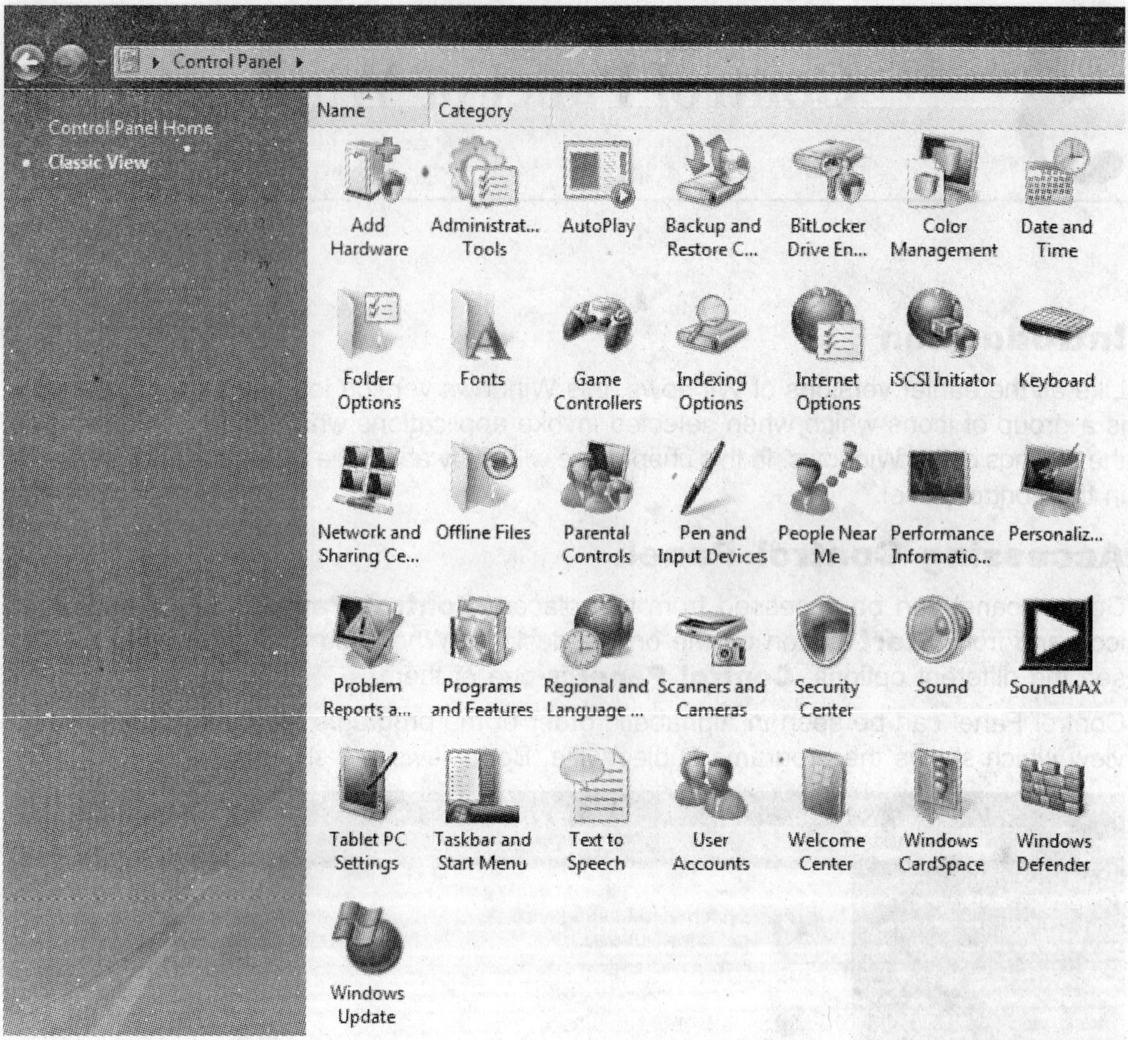

Let us see what function each of them performs. For this I am going through it alphabetically.

Add Hardware

You can install most hardware or portable devices by plugging them into your computer. Windows will automatically install the appropriate driver software if it's available, or prompt you to insert the disc that came with your hardware device if it's not.

Adminstrative Tools

It has the different tools under it, they are: Computer Management, Data Sources (ODBC), Event Viewer, iSCSI Initiator, Local Security Policy, Memory Diagnostics Tool, Print Management, Reliability and Performance, Services, System Configuration, Task Scheduler and Windows Firewall with Advanced Security.

Microsoft Management Console (MMC) hosts and displays administrative tools created

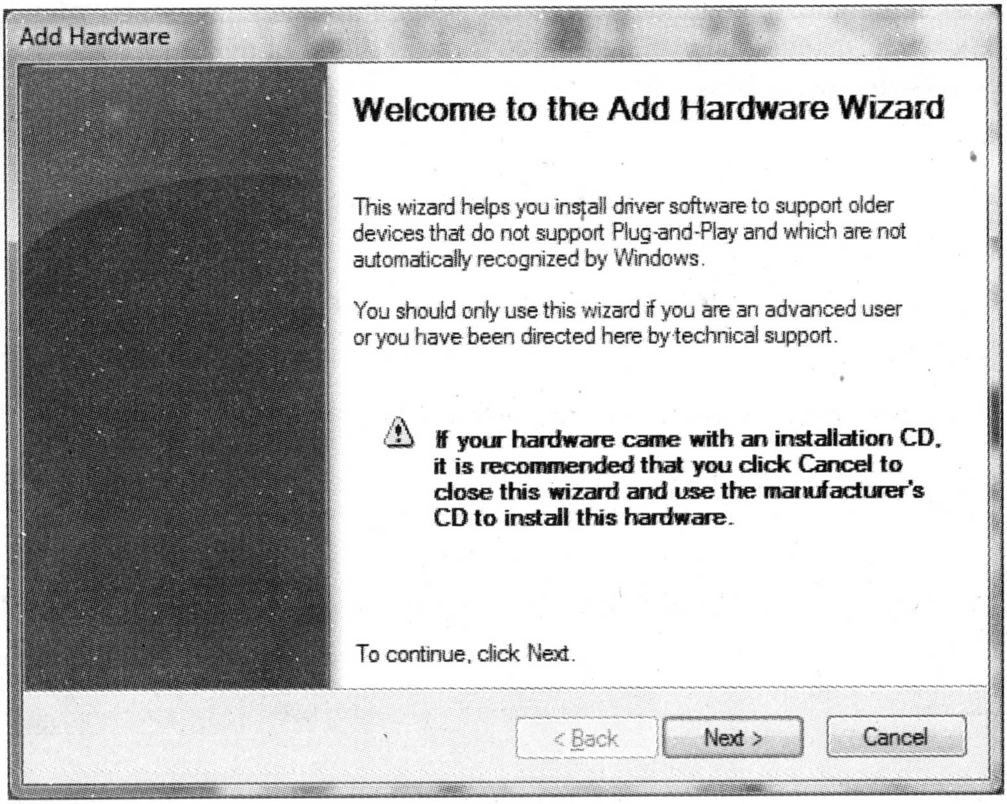

by Microsoft and other software vendors. These tools are called snap-ins, and they are used for managing the hardware, software, and network components of Windows. Several of the tools in the Administrative Tools folder, such as Computer Management, are MMC snap-ins.

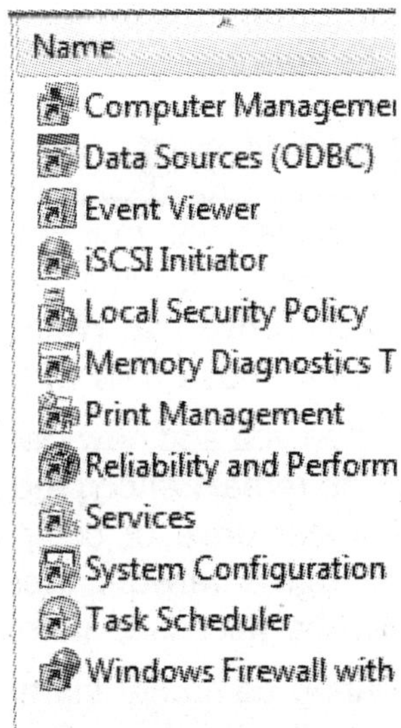

AutoPlay

AutoPlay, new to Vista, gives you a single place to configure how you would like your CDs and DVDs (and memory cards, flash drives, and cameras) to be run. And you can specify how audio CDs are handled, versus enhanced audio CDs.

Backup and Restore Centre

It allows you backup your drive and then restore it.

BitLocker Drive Encryption

Turning on BitLocker Drive Encryption (BitLocker) protects all files stored on the drive Windows is installed on. Unlike Encrypting File System (EFS), which enables you to encrypt individual files, BitLocker encrypts the entire system drive, including the Windows system files necessary for startup and logon. You can log on and work with your files normally, but BitLocker can help block hackers from accessing the system files they rely

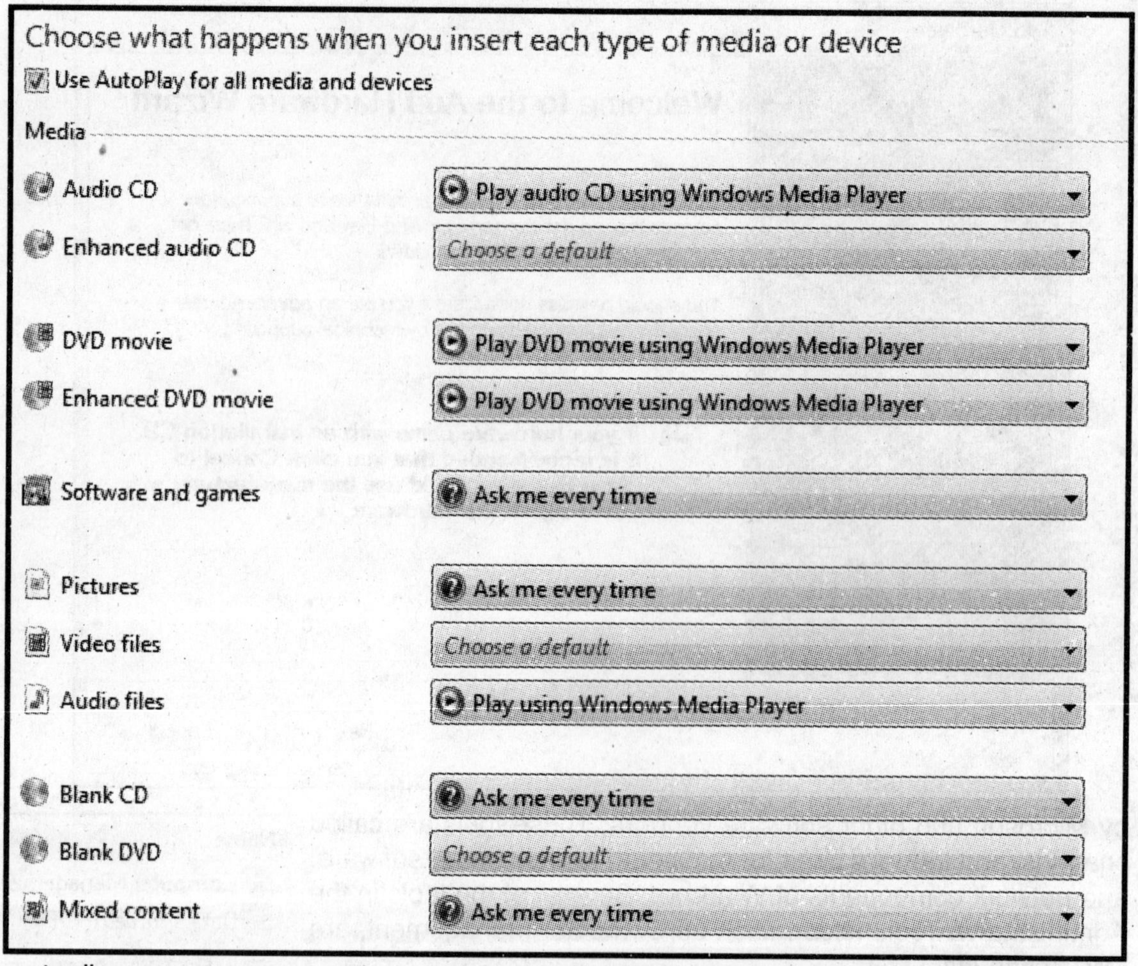

on to discover your password, or access your hard disk by removing it from your computer and installing it in a different computer. BitLocker can only help protect files that are stored on the drive that Windows is installed on. If you store files on other drives, you can help protect those files with EFS.

When you add new files to the drive with BitLocker, BitLocker encrypts them automatically. Files remain encrypted only while they are stored in the encrypted drive. Files copied to another drive or computer are decrypted. If you share files with other users, such as through a network, these files are encrypted while stored on the encrypted drive, but they can be accessed normally by authorized users.

During computer startup, if BitLocker detects a system condition that could represent a security risk (for example, disk errors, a change to the BIOS , or changes to any startup files), it will lock the drive and require a special BitLocker recovery password to unlock it. Make sure that you create this recovery password when you turn on BitLocker for the first time; otherwise, you could permanently lose access to your files.

You can turn off BitLocker at any time, either temporarily by disabling it, or permanently by decrypting the drive.

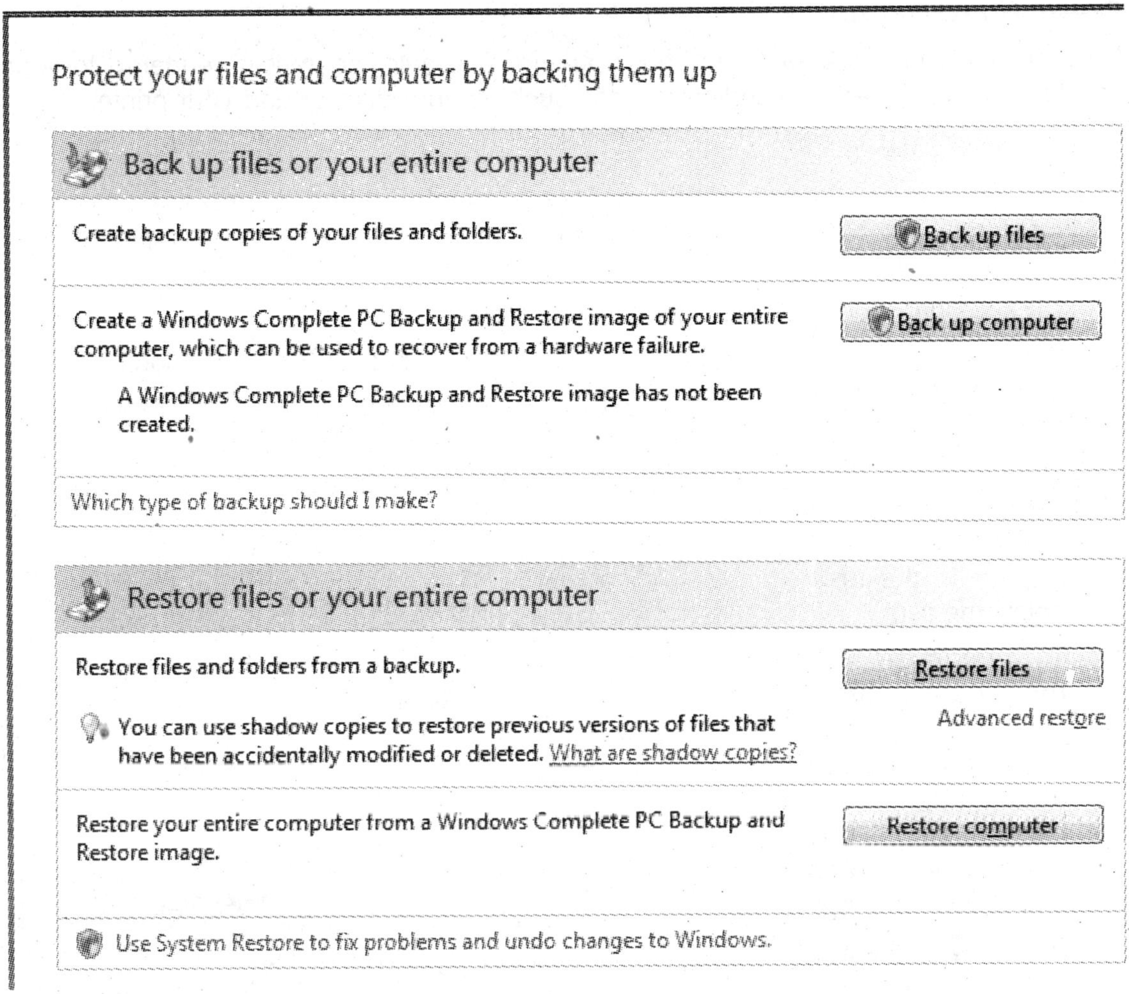
Protect your files and computer by backing them up
Back up files or your entire computer
Create backup copies of your files and folders.
Back up files
Create a Windows Complete PC Backup and Restore image of your entire computer, which can be used to recover from a hardware failure.
Back up computer
A Windows Complete PC Backup and Restore image has not been created.
Which type of backup should I make?
Restore files or your entire computer
Restore files and folders from a backup.
Restore files
You can use shadow copies to restore previous versions of files that have been accidentally modified or deleted. What are shadow copies?
Advanced restore
Restore your entire computer from a Windows Complete PC Backup and Restore image.
Restore computer
Use System Restore to fix problems and undo changes to Windows.

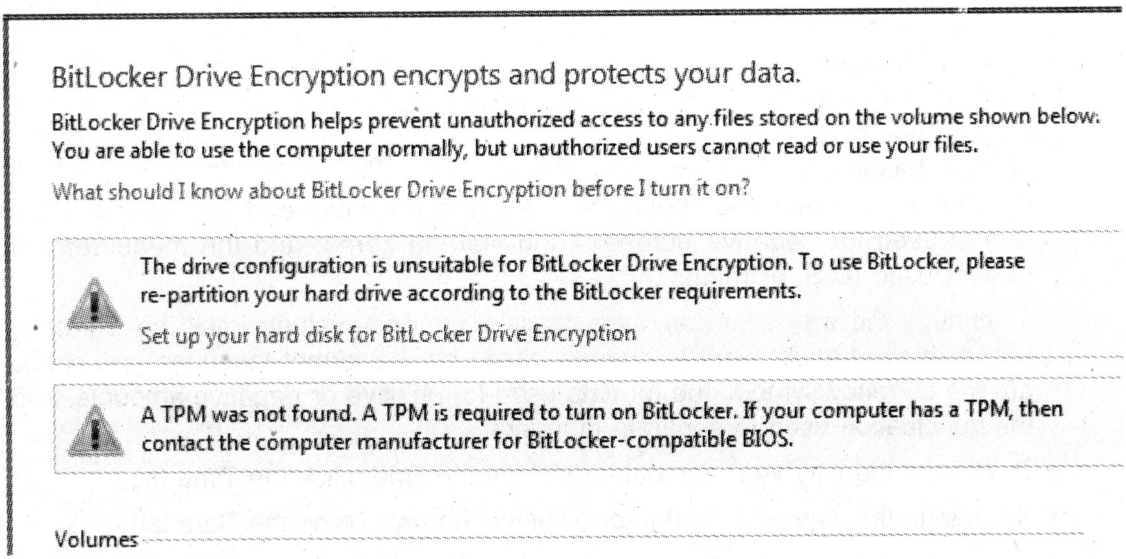
BitLocker Drive Encryption encrypts and protects your data.
BitLocker Drive Encryption helps prevent unauthorized access to any files stored on the volume shown below. You are able to use the computer normally, but unauthorized users cannot read or use your files.
What should I know about BitLocker Drive Encryption before I turn it on?
The drive configuration is unsuitable for BitLocker Drive Encryption. To use BitLocker, please re-partition your hard drive according to the BitLocker requirements.
Set up your hard disk for BitLocker Drive Encryption
A TPM was not found. A TPM is required to turn on BitLocker. If your computer has a TPM, then contact the computer manufacturer for BitLocker-compatible BIOS.
Volumes

Color Management

Color management is a system used to ensure that color content is rendered to your satisfaction everywhere—including devices such as your display and your printer.

Date and Time

You can change the format Windows uses to display dates, times, currency, and measurements. You can also change the sorting order of text to match sorting rules used in a specific country or region.

1. Click to open Regional and Language Options.
2. Click the Formats tab, and then, in the Current format list, select the locale to use for the display of the date, time, currency, and measurements.

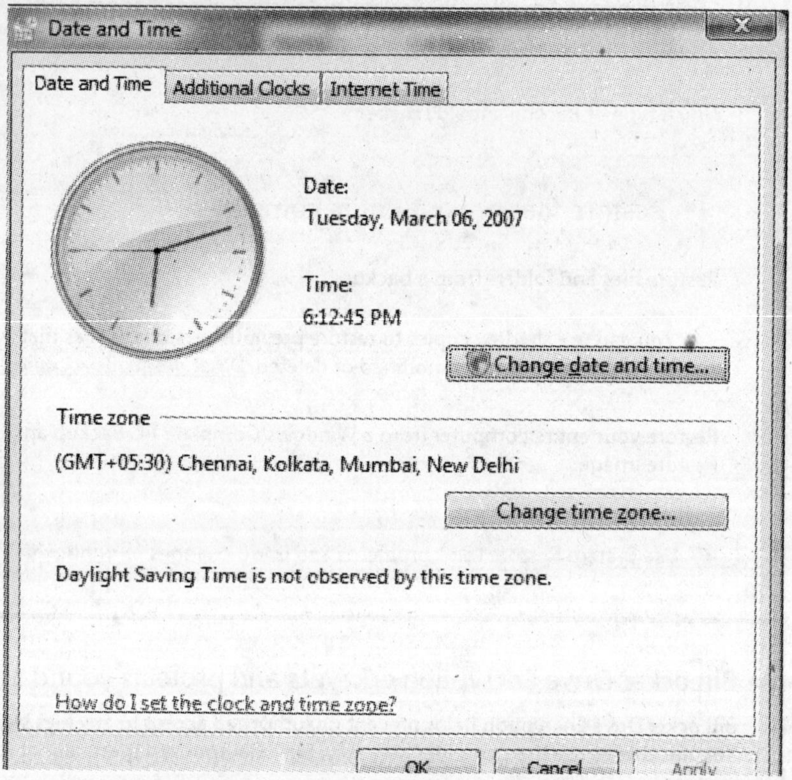

3. You can see how these items will appear in the area below the list.
4. To customize how the date, time, currency, and measurements are displayed, click Customize this format, and then do one of the following:
   - To change the way your computer displays numbers, click the Numbers tab. Items you might want to change based on the format language you chose are the decimal symbol and list separator, the format used for negative numbers and leading zeros, and the measurement system used (U.S. or metric).
   - To change the way your computer displays currency values, click the Currency tab. Items you might want to change based on the format language you chose are the currency symbol, the formats used for positive or negative amounts, and the punctuation used to separate numbers.
   - To change the way your computer displays the time, click the Time tab.
   - To change the way your computer displays the date, click the Date tab.

Default Programs

Set Program Access and Computer Defaults makes it easy for you to change the default program used for certain activities, such as web browsing, sending e mail, playing audio and video files, and using instant messaging.

You can also specify which of these default programs are displayed on the Start menu, on the desktop, and in other locations.

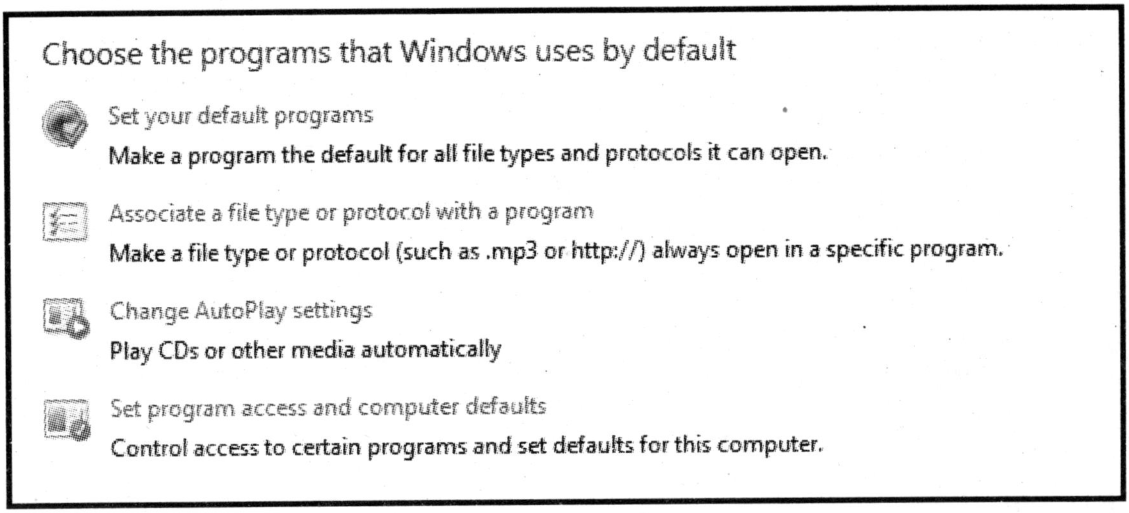

Device Manager

The device manager console shows you where all your hardware money was spent. Here, you or your tech-support person can troubleshoot a flaky device, disable and enable devices, and manage device drivers.

Ease of Access

It is the enhanced version of Accessability Options of the earlier version. It is designed to make computing easier for people with disabilities, though some of the options here can benefit anyone.

Folder Options

Using Folder Options in Control Panel, you can change the way your files and folders function, as well as how the content in your folders is displayed.

Click to open Folder Options.

Change the way folders are displayed

You can change the way your folders look and work to suit your needs. For example, you can open all files and folders with one click (like links in a webpage) instead of the usual double-click. Here is an overview of the settings you can change:

To	***Do this***
Turn off the Details pane and the Preview pane in all folders. This setting gives you	Click the General tab, and then click Use Windows classic folders. (To turn the panes

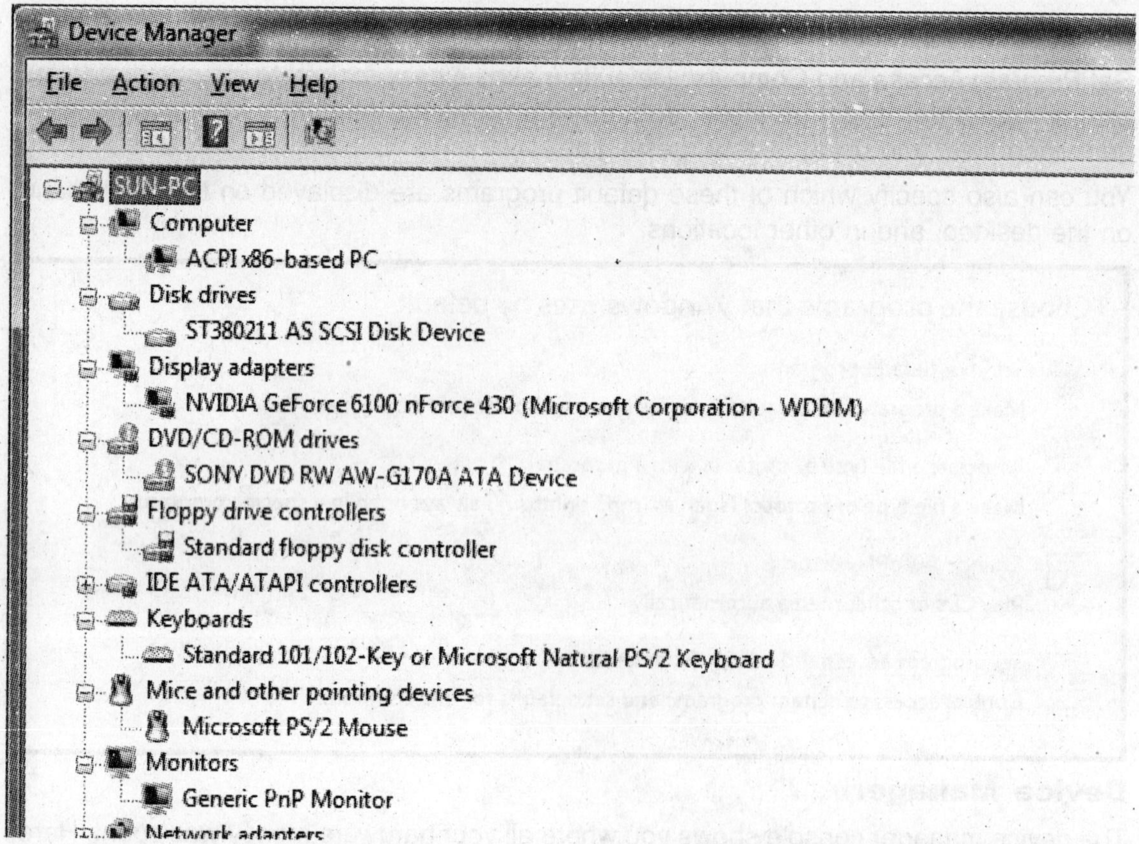

more room to display files by hiding panes you might not need.	back on, click Show preview and filters.)
Open every new folder in its own folder window. This can be convenient if you want to keep all the folders you are working with on the screen at the same time.	Click the General tab, and then click Open each folder in its own window. (To make each new folder replace the previous folder window, click Open each folder in the same window.)
Open an item with a single click. Use this setting if you want files and folders to open with one click, just like links in a webpage.	Click the General tab, and then click Single-click to open an item. (To switch back to the standard double-click, click Double-click to open an item.)

Change advanced file and folder settings

You can make additional changes to the appearance and behavior of your files and folders by using the advanced settings of Folder Options in Control Panel. Here is an overview of the advanced settings that you can change:

To	*Do this*
Always show static icons of files and never show thumbnail previews of files.	Click the View tab, and then select the Always show icons, never thumbnails

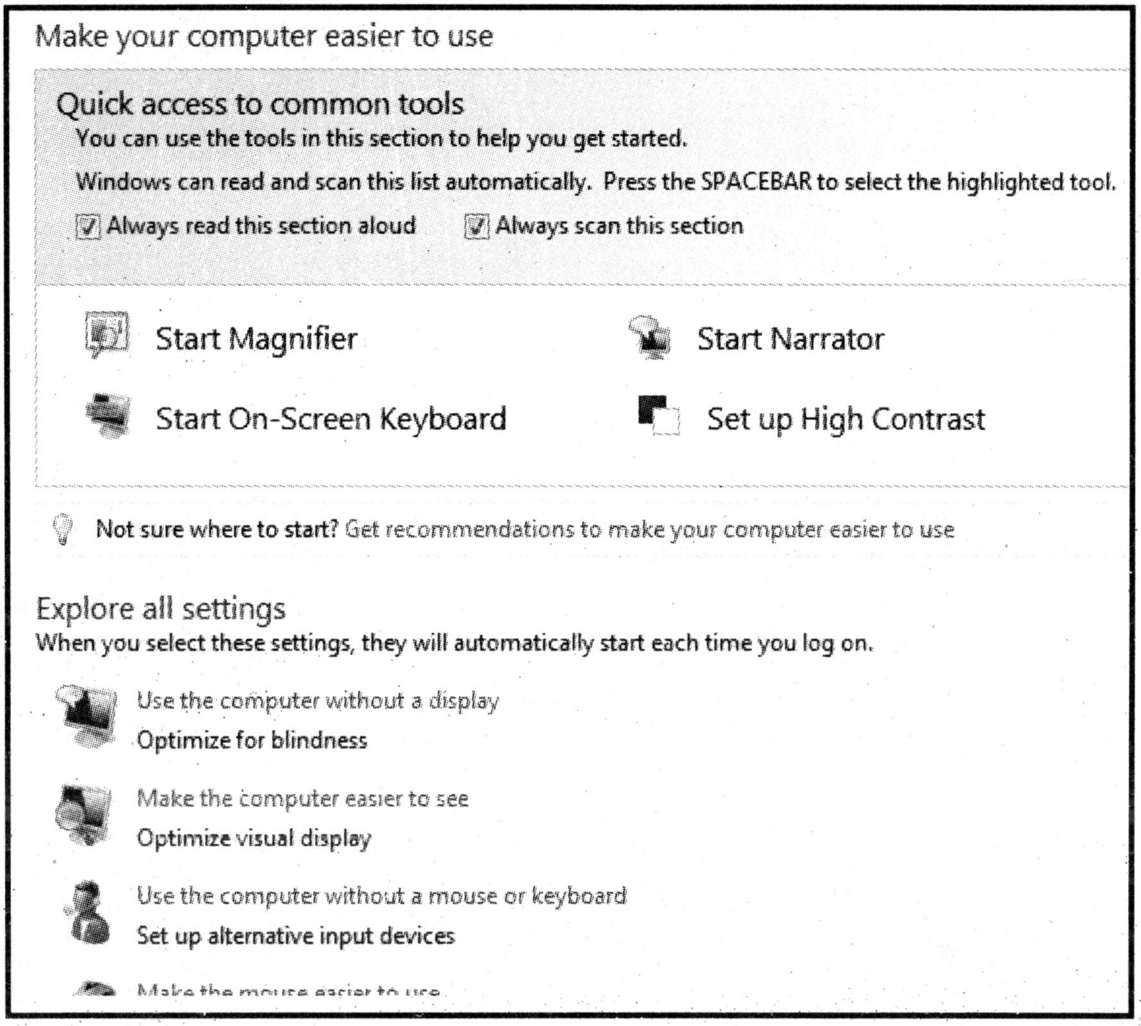

Use this setting if the thumbnail previews are slowing down your computer. You'll get better performance by using static icons.	check box.
Always show the menus above the toolbar. Use this setting if you prefer to have access to the Classic menus, which are hidden by default.	Click the View tab, and then select the Always show menus check box.
See the size of a folder in a tooltip when you rest your mouse pointer over the folder. Use this setting if you frequently need to know the total size of the contents of a folder and would like to see this information by resting the mouse pointer over the folder.	Click the View tab, and then select the Display file size information in folder tips check box.

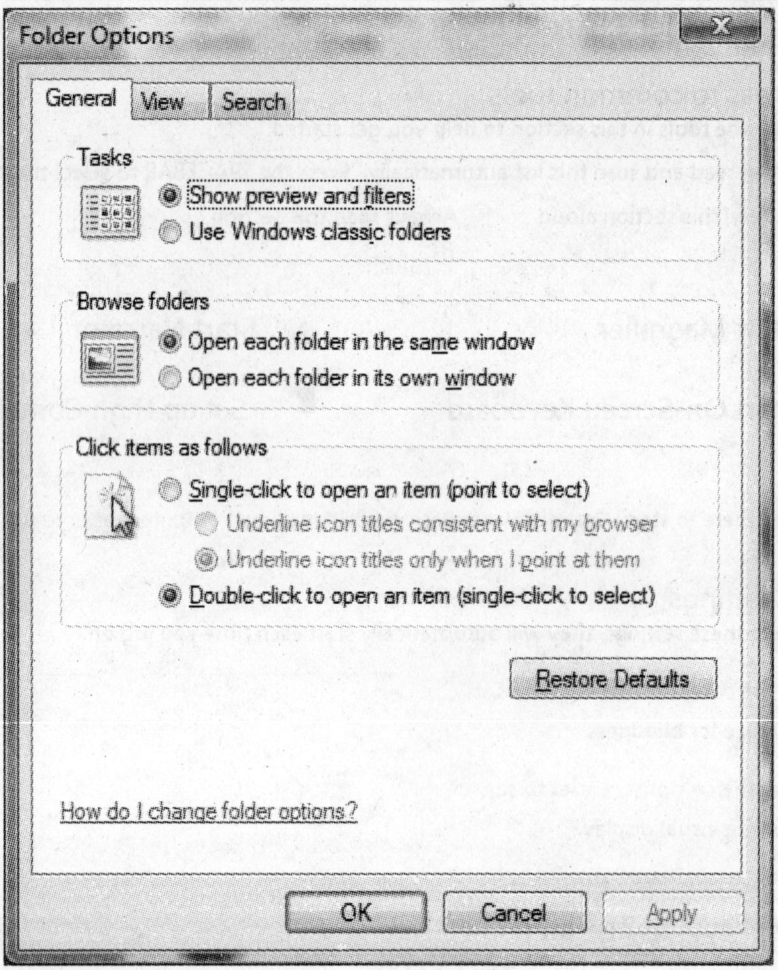

See files and folders marked as hidden. Use this setting if you need to work with files that are usually hidden from view, such as user files that have been marked as hidden.	Click the View tab, and then click Show hidden files and folders.
See folders with lines that connect folders and subfolders.	Click the View tab, and then clear the Display simple folder view in Navigation pane check box.
See file name extensions as a part of file names. This is a good way to ensure that files are not malicious software disguised as common files.	Click the View tab, and then clear the Hide extensions for known file types check box.
See all system files that are usually hidden from view.	Click the View tab, and then clear the Hide protected operating system files check box.
Increase the stability of Windows by	Click the View tab, and then select the

opening every folder in a separate part of memory. Use this setting if your computer frequently crashes, and you are trying to minimize problems or troubleshoot. Be aware, however, that doing this could slow down the performance of your computer.	Launch folder windows in a separate process check box.
Ignore custom view settings for every folder and have every folder open using default settings instead. Use this setting to force all folders to stop using display settings you have specified.	Click the View tab, and then clear the Remember each folder's view settings check box.
Automatically open the folders that you were using when you last shut down Windows whenever you start your computer. Use this setting to help you preserve your work from session to session.	Click the View tab, and then select the Restore previous folder windows at logon check box.
Hide the drive letter of each drive or device in the Computer folder. Use this setting if you don't want to see drive letters displayed on your computer and prefer to see only the friendly name of each drive.	Click the View tab, and then clear the Show drive letters check box.
Display encrypted or compressed NTFS files as ordinary files, without any unique color coding to identify them. Use this setting if you have encrypted or compressed NTFS files and do not want to see them represented differently than other files on your computer.	Click the View tab, and then clear the Show encrypted or compressed NTFS files in color check box.
Turn off the tooltips that appear when you rest your mouse pointer over files. Use this setting if you don't want to see the file information that appears in tooltips when you rest the pointer over files and folders.	Click the View tab, and then clear the Show pop-up descriptions for folder and desktop items check box.
Never show the contents of files in the Preview pane. Use this setting to improve the performance of your computer, or if you don't want to use the Preview pane.	Click the View tab, and then clear the Show preview handlers in preview pane check box.

Add check boxes to file views to make it easier to select several files at once, which can be useful if it is difficult for you to hold the CTRL key while clicking to select multiple files.	Click the View tab, and then select the Use check boxes to select items check box.

Fonts

It shows all the fonts available in the hard disk.

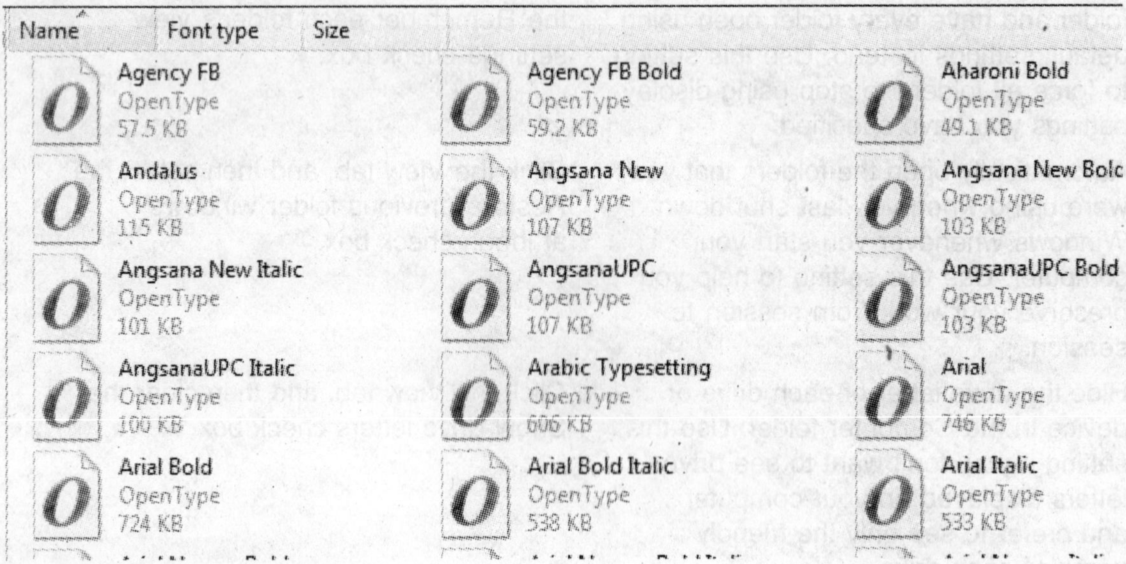

Game Controllers

If you are a serious gamer, this would interest you. You use it to configure and control the joysticks, steering wheels, game pads, flight yokes, and other controllers you have attached to your PC. Afterall, if your joysticks and controllers are not installed and confgured properly, you can't pulverize alients to full capacity.

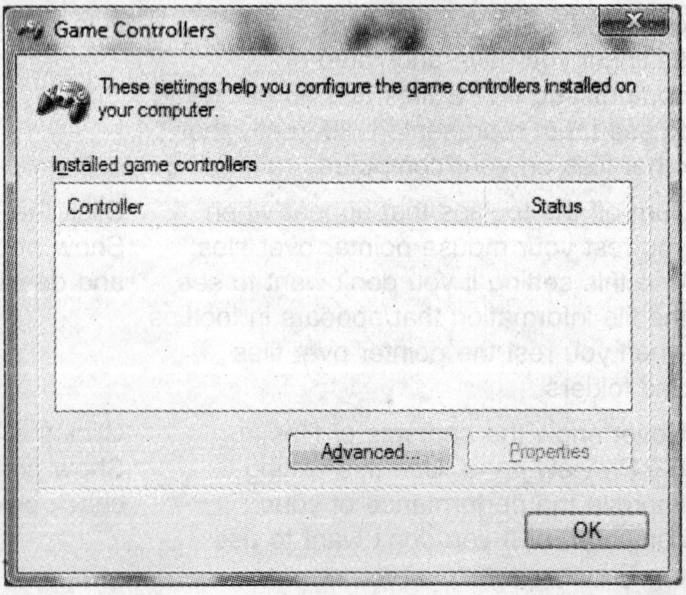

To get started, install the driver software that came you gaming device. If it's a modern, USB, Vista-compatible gadget, you may not even need to do that much. Just plug the device and watch the notifification area for a message that Vista has detected it and installed the correct driver.

Indexing Options

Similar to the way the index in a book helps you to keep track of its contents, the index in Windows keeps track of the files on your computer. The index stores information about files, including the file name, date modified, and properties like author, tags, and rating. You will never see the index, but it is used by Windows to perform very fast searches of the most common files on your computer.

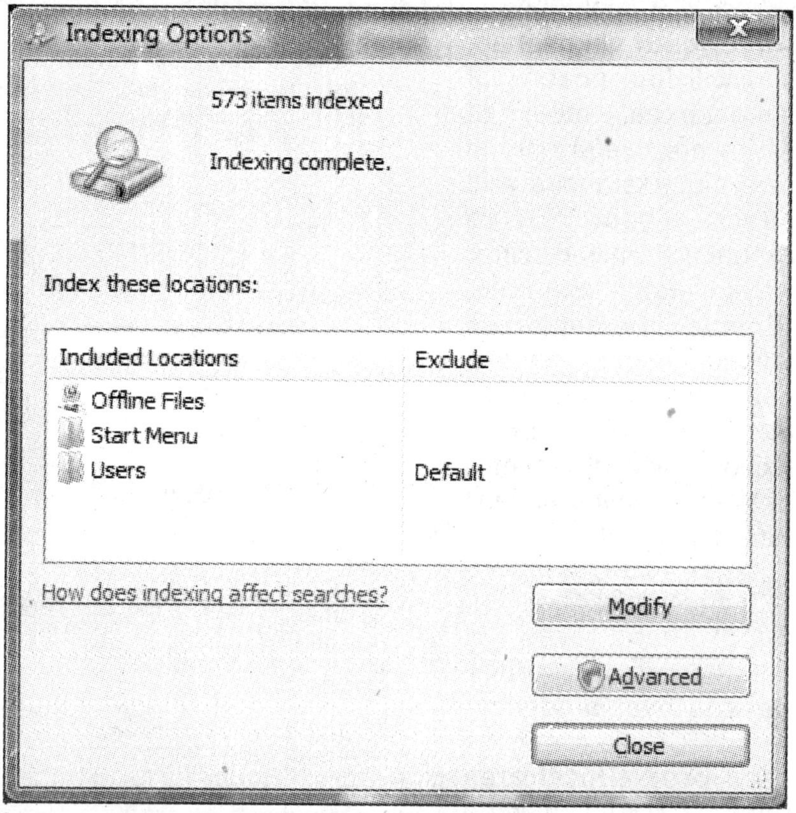

The index is used to make searching for files much faster. Instead of looking through your entire hard disk for a file name or file property, Windows scans the index, which allows most results to appear in a small fraction of the time that a search without the index would take.

By default, all of the most common files on your computer are indexed. Indexed locations include all of the files in your personal folder (such as Documents, Pictures, Music, and Videos), as well as e mail and offline files. Files that are not indexed include program files and system files. The locations that contain those files are not indexed because you rarely need to search those files, and so not including them in the index makes your searches perform faster.

Internet Options

As can be seen from the figure next, it has the following tabs:

General, Security, Private and Content: These tabs control your home page, cache files, search field defaults, and history list. They also let you define certain Web pages as off-limits for your kids and manage RSS feeds, as well as block pop-up windows.

Connections: Controls when your PC modem dials.

Programs: Use this tab to manage browser add-ons, decide whether or not Internet Explorer should warn you whenever it is not the default browser (for your protection, of course), or choose the default programs that open, should you click a link to email someone, open a media file, or view the HTML source of a Web page.

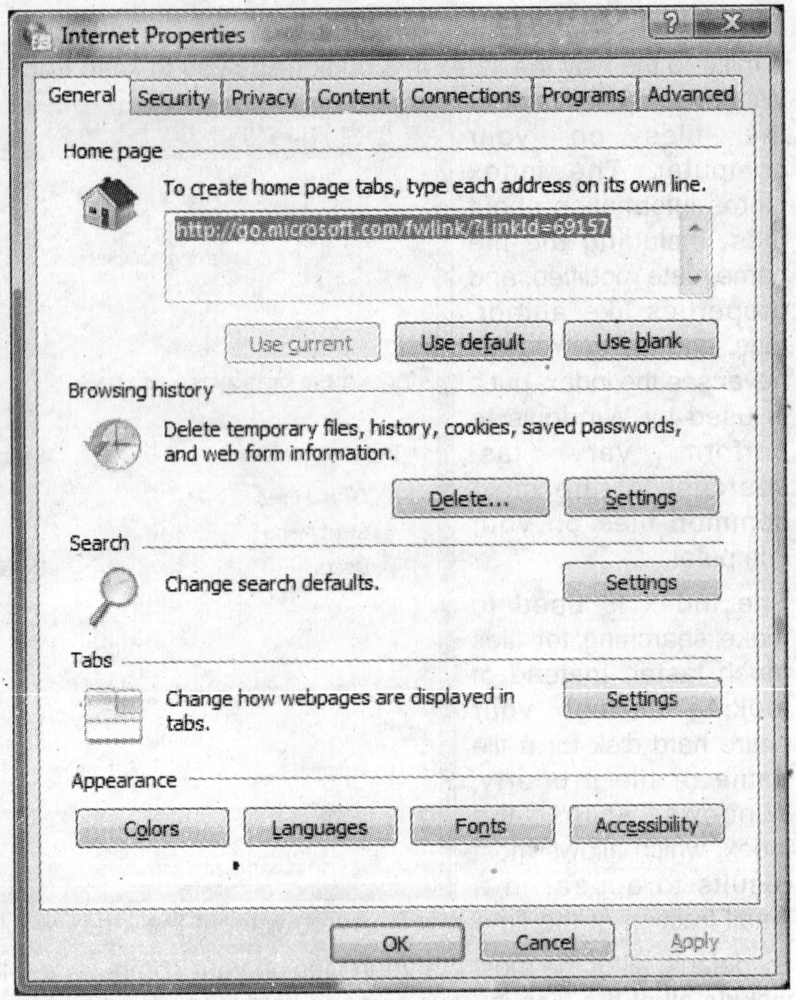

Advanced: On this tab, you will find dozens of checkboxes, most of which are useful only in rare circumstances and affect your Web experience only in mirror ways. For example, "Enable personalized favorites menu" shortens your list of bookmarks over time, as Internet Explorer hides the names of Web sites you haven't visited in a while.

iSCSI Initiator

iSCSI is a way of connecting storage devices over a network using TCP/IP. It can be used over a local area network (LAN), a wide area network (WAN), or the Internet.

iSCSI devices are disks, tapes, CDs, and other storage devices on another networked computer that you can connect to. Sometimes these storage devices are part of a network called a storage area network (SAN).

In the relationship between your computer and the storage device, your computer is called an initiator because it initiates the connection to the device, which is called a target.

Keyboard

You can customize how long you must press a key before the keyboard character starts repeating, the speed at which keyboard characters repeat, and the rate at which the cursor blinks.

To change the delay before keyboard characters repeat

1. Click to open Keyboard Properties.
2. Under Character repeat, move the Repeat delay slider to the left to increase the amount of time you must hold down a key before the keyboard character repeats.

Move the slider to the right to decrease the amount of time before characters repeat.

To change the speed at which keyboard characters repeat

1. Click to open Keyboard Properties.
2. Under Character repeat, move the Repeat rate slider to the left to make keyboard characters repeat more slowly, or to the right to make them repeat faster.

To change the cursor blink rate

1. Click to open Keyboard Properties.
2. Move the Cursor blink rate slider to the right to increase the cursor blink speed. If you move the slider all the way to the left, the cursor will stop blinking.

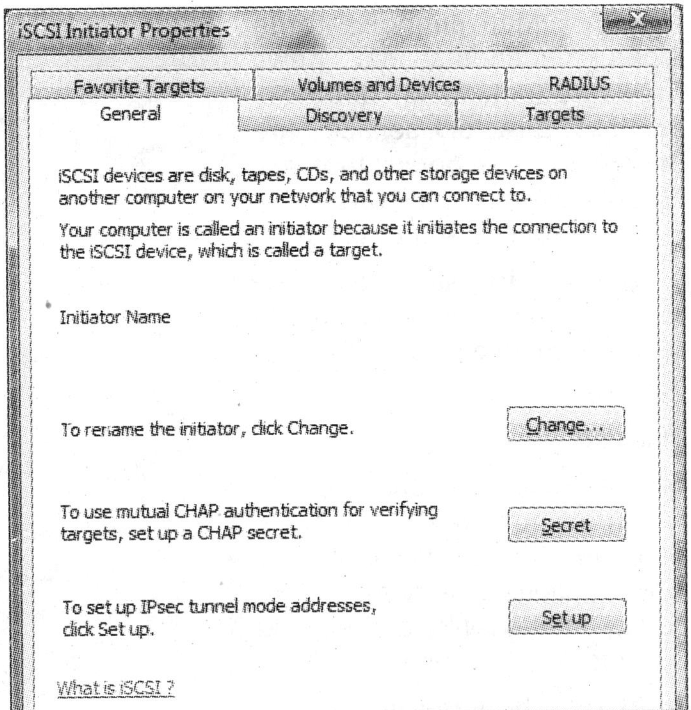

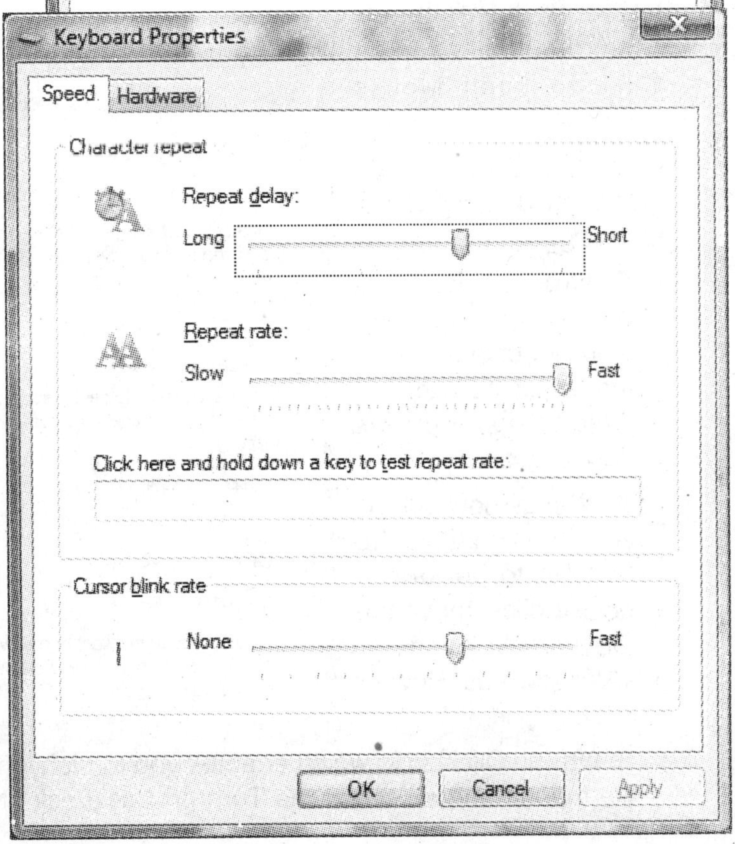

Mail

Windows Mail has the tools you need to exchange e mail with colleagues and friends, or join newsgroups to trade ideas and information.

Add or remove a Windows Mail account

You can set up a variety of different accounts using Windows Mail. You can set up a single personal e mail account, or you might also add your work e mail account and some newsgroups as well. Windows Mail makes managing multiple accounts easy by putting each account in its own folder.

Windows Mail supports three types of accounts: mail, news (newsgroups), and directory services. Directory services are online address books that are typically offered by organizations such as colleges and businesses.

Before you add an account, be sure that you have the logon and server information for your e mail account.

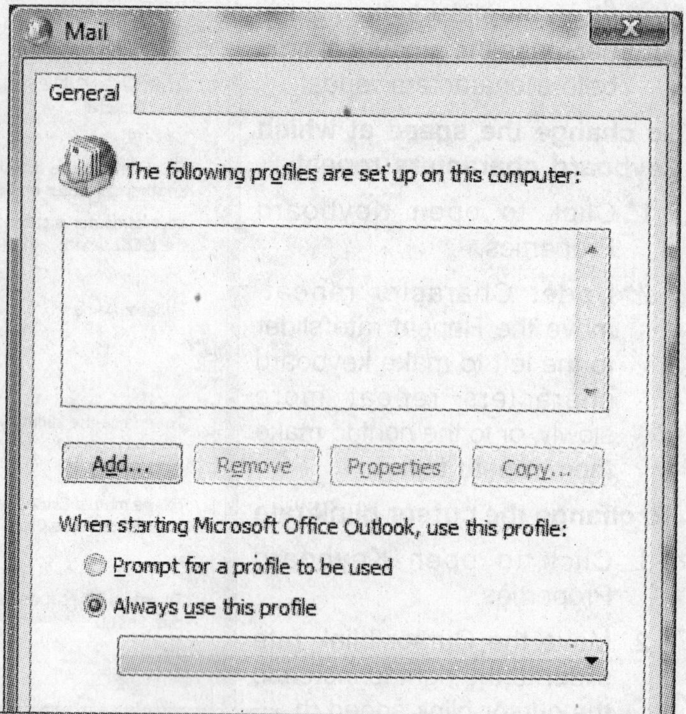

Mouse

You can customize your mouse in a variety of ways, such as swapping the functions of your mouse buttons, making the mouse pointer more visible, and altering the scroll wheel speed.

To change how the mouse buttons work

1. Click to open Mouse Properties.
2. Click the Buttons tab, and then do any of the following:
   - To swap the functions of the right and left mouse buttons, select the Switch primary and secondary buttons check box.
   - To change how quickly you must click the buttons to perform a double-click, move the Double-click speed slider towards Slow or Fast.

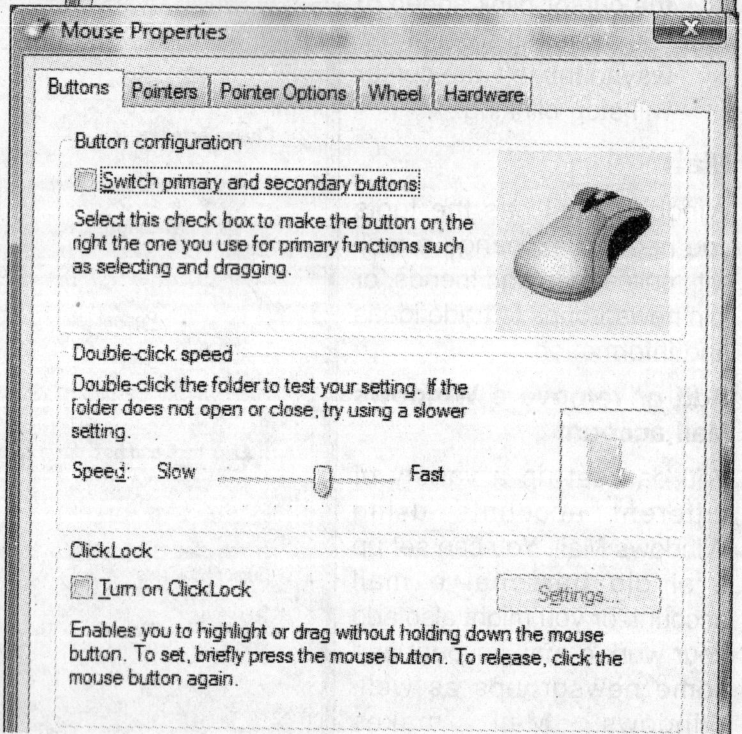

   - To turn on ClickLock, which enables you to highlight or drag without holding down the mouse button, select the Turn on ClickLock check box.

To change how the mouse pointer looks

1. Click to open Mouse Properties.
2. Click the Pointers tab, and then do one of the following:
   - To give all of your pointers a new look, click the Scheme list, and then click a new mouse pointer scheme.
   - To change an individual pointer, click the pointer you want to change in the Customize list, click Browse, click the pointer you want to use, and then click Open.

To change how the mouse pointer works

1. Click to open Mouse Properties.
2. Click the Pointer Options tab, and then do any of the following:
   - To change the speed at which the mouse pointer moves, move the Select a pointer speed slider towards Slow or Fast.
   - To make the pointer work more accurately when you're moving the mouse slowly, select the Enhance pointer precision check box.
   - To speed the process of selecting a choice when a dialog box appears, select the Automatically move pointer to the default button in a dialog box check box .
   - To make the pointer easier to find when you move it, select the Display pointer trails check box, and then move the slider towards Short or Long to decrease or increase the length of the pointer trail.
   - To ensure that the pointer doesn't block your view of the text you're typing, select the Hide pointer while typing check box.
   - To find a misplaced pointer by pressing the CTRL key, select the Show location of pointer when I press the CTRL key check box.

To change how the mouse wheel works

1. Click to open Mouse Properties.
2. Click the Wheel tab, and then do one of the following:
   - To set the number of lines the screen will scroll for each notch of mouse wheel movement, click The following number of lines at a time, and then enter the number of lines you want to scroll in the box.
   - To scroll an entire screen of text for each click of the mouse wheel, click One screen at a time.
   - If your mouse has a wheel that supports horizontal scrolling, in the Tilt the wheel to scroll the following number of characters at a time box, enter the number of characters you want to scroll horizontally when you tilt the wheel to the left or right.

Network and Sharing Centre

Windows provides two methods for sharing files directly from your computer. You can share files from any folder on your computer, or from the Public folder. Either method allows you to share files or folders with someone using your computer or another computer on the same network. Which method you use to share files with someone depends on where you want to store the shared files, who you want to share them with, and how much control you want to have over the files.

Share files from any folder on your computer

Follow these steps to share files from their current location without copying them to another location. Using this method, you can choose with whom you want to share files, regardless of whether they use this computer or another computer on the network.

1. Locate the folder with the files you want to share.
2. Click one or more files or folders that you want to share, and then, on the toolbar, click Share.
3. In the File Sharing dialog box, do one of the following:
   - Type the name of the person you want to share files with, and then click Add.
   - Click the arrow to the right of the text box, click the person's name in the list, and then click Add.
   - If you don't see the name of the person you want to share files with in the list, click the arrow to the right of the text box, and then click Create a new user to create a new user account so that you can share files with the person using this account.
4. The name of the person or group that you selected appears in the list of people you want to share files with.
5. Under Permission Level, click the arrow next to the permission level for that person or group, and then do one of the following to set sharing permissions:
   - Click Reader to restrict the person or group to viewing files in the shared folder.
   - Click Contributor to allow the person or group to view all files, add files, and change or delete the files that they add.
   - Click Co-owner to allow the person or group to view, change, add, and delete files in the shared folder.
   - If you are sharing a file instead of a folder, there is no option to set the permission level to Contributor.
6. When you are finished choosing the people or groups you want to share files with, click Share. If you are prompted for an administrator password or confirmation, type the password or provide confirmation.
7. After you receive confirmation that your folder is shared, you should send a link to your shared files to the people you are sharing them with, so they know the files are shared and how to access them. Do one of the following:
   - Click E mail Link to automatically open a Windows Mail e mail message with the link to your shared files.

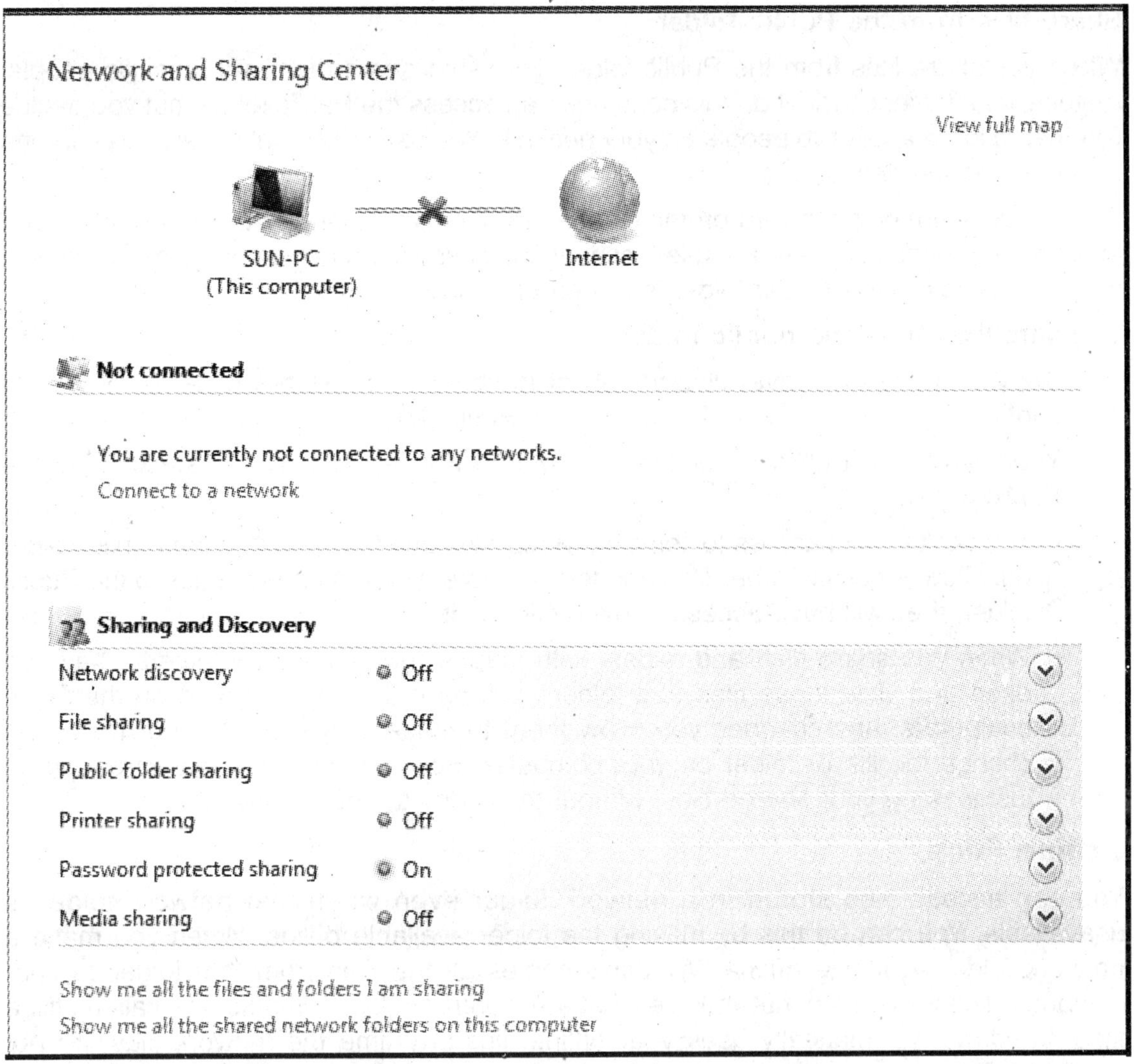

- Manually copy and paste the link displayed on this screen into an e mail message. Right-click the link and click Copy Link. Then open a new e mail message and paste in the link. You might want to do this if you don't use Windows Mail as your e mail program.

8. If you don't want to send an e mail message to the person you are sharing files with, click Done. They won't be able to find the shared files, however, until you give them the network location of the files.
   - You can give a shared folder a share name that makes it easier for someone else to find it on your computer. You can do this by using the Advanced Sharing dialog box for the folder. To access this dialog box, right-click a folder you have already shared, click Properties, click the Sharing tab, and then click Advanced Sharing. If you are prompted for an administrator password or confirmation, type the password or provide confirmation.

Share files from the Public folder

When you share files from the Public folder, you don't share them with specific people. Anyone with a user account on this computer can access the Public folder, but you decide whether to allow access to people on your network. You can only grant access to everyone or no one on the network.

You can also turn on password-protected sharing. This limits network access to the Public folder to only those people with a user account and password on your computer. By default, network access to the Public folder is turned off unless you enable it.

To share files from the public folder:

1. Copy or move whichever files you want to share to the Public folder or one of its subfolders, such as Public Documents or Public Music.
2. Your files in the Public folder are now shared with anyone who has access to the Public folder.
   - You can't restrict access to some individual files and folders within the Public Folder but allow access to other files and folders there. If users have access to the Public folder, they will have access to everything in it.
   - When you share files and folders with people using other computers, they can open and view those files and folders just as if they were stored on their own computers. Any changes you allow them to make to a shared file or folder will change the file or folder on your computer. However, you can restrict people to just viewing your shared files, without the ability to change them.

Offline Files

You can access files stored in a network folder even when that network folder is unavailable. You can do this by making the folder available offline. When you make a network folder available offline, Windows copies all the files from that folder to your computer. These copies of network files that are stored on your computer are called offline files. Windows automatically uses your offline files any time the network files are not available. This way you can keep working on the network files without interruption, even if you lose your connection to the network folder. When you connect to the network folder again, Windows will automatically sync the files on your computer with the files in the network folder.

To make files and folders available offline

To be able to work with a file offline, you first need to make it available offline.

1. Locate the network file or folder that you want to make available offline.
2. Right-click the file or folder, and then click Always Available Offline.
3. The next time you try to access this file or folder, you will be able to open it even if the network version is unavailable.
   - To confirm that the file or folder is now available offline, right-click the file or folder again, and make sure that a check mark appears next to Always Available Offline.

- If you don't want a network file or folder to be available offline any longer, right-click the file or folder, and then click Always Available Offline to clear the check mark next to the command.

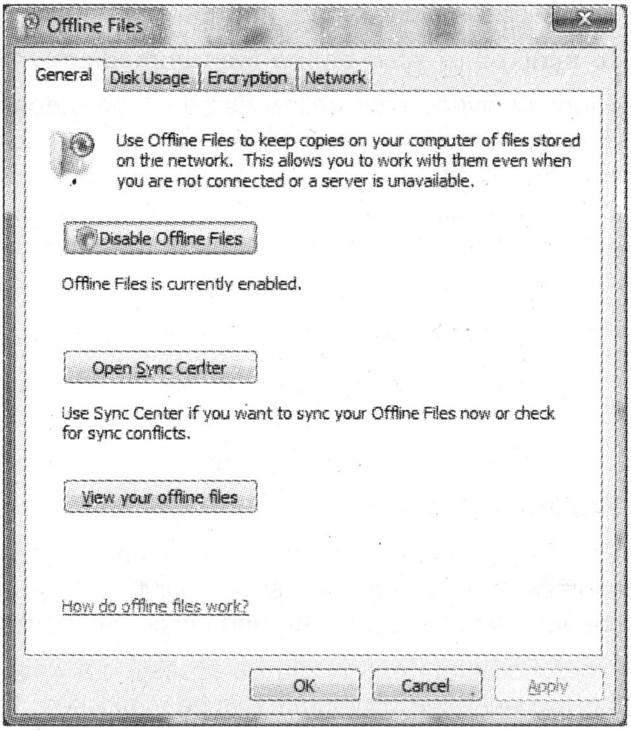

To enable offline files

Enable offline files if you want to work with files that are in a network folder. A copy of the file on your hard drive will be synchronized with the network copy as soon as you are back at work or you regain your network connection.

1. Click to open Offline Files.
2. Click the General tab, and then click Enable Offline Files.

To work offline

Sometimes you might want to work with the offline files stored on your computer rather than the files stored on the network. This can be a good idea if you have a slow network connection, for example.

1. Open the network folder that contains the files you have made available offline, and then, on the toolbar, click Work offline. This button appears only if you have already made this folder available offline.
2. When you are finished working with the files offline and want to begin working with the files in the network folder again, click Work online on the toolbar. This will sync any changes you have made offline with the files on the network.

To find out whether you're working offline

Offline files turn on automatically if you lose your network connection. A copy of your file is copied to your computer, and once your network connection is re-established, the two copies will be synchronized. To find out if you're working offline, do the following.

1. Open the network folder that contains the file you are working on.
2. Check the Details pane at the bottom of the window for the status. If the status is offline, you are working with a copy of the file on your computer. If the status in online, you are working with the file on the network.

To view all your offline files

If you work with offline files in many different folders, you may want to view all of them without opening each folder individually. Here's how to view all your offline files at once.

1. Click to open Offline Files.

2. Click the General tab, and then click View your offline files.

To sync all of your offline files immediately

Windows syncs your offline files for you automatically, so that when a network file is changed, the offline copy stored on your computer is also updated, and vice versa. But Windows does not sync your files continuously. Sometimes it is helpful to sync your offline files right away, such as if you are about to disconnect from a network and want to be sure you have the latest versions of files stored on the network.

1. Click to open Sync Center.
2. Click the Offline Files sync partnership, and then, on the toolbar, click Sync.
   - If you only want to sync the contents of a specific folder, open the folder that contains the files that you want to sync, and then, on the toolbar, click Sync. To sync an individual file, right-click the file, and then click Sync.

Parental Controls

You can use Parental Controls to help manage how your children use the computer. For example, you can set limits on your children's access to the web, the hours that they can log on to the computer, and which games they can play and programs they can run.

When Parental Controls blocks access to a webpage or game, a notification is displayed that the webpage or program has been blocked. Your child can click a link in the notification to request permission for access to that webpage or program. You can allow access by entering your account information.

Before you get started, make sure that each child that you want to set up Parental Controls for has a standard user account because Parental Controls can only be applied to standard user accounts. To set up Parental Controls for your child, you'll need an Administrator user account. Parental Controls cannot be applied to an Administrator user account.

To turn on Parental Controls for a standard user account

1. Click to open Parental Controls. If you are prompted for an administrator password or confirmation, type the password or provide confirmation.
2. Click the standard user account for which you want to set Parental Controls.
3. Under Parental Controls, click On.
4. Once you've turned on Parental Controls for your child's standard user account, you can adjust the individual settings that you want to control. You can control the following areas:
   - Web restrictions. You can restrict the websites that children can visit, make sure children only visit age-appropriate websites, indicate whether you want to allow file downloads, and set up which content you want the content filters to block and allow. You can also block or allow specific websites.
   - Time limits. You can set time limits to control when children are allowed to log on to the computer. Time limits prevent children from logging on during the specified

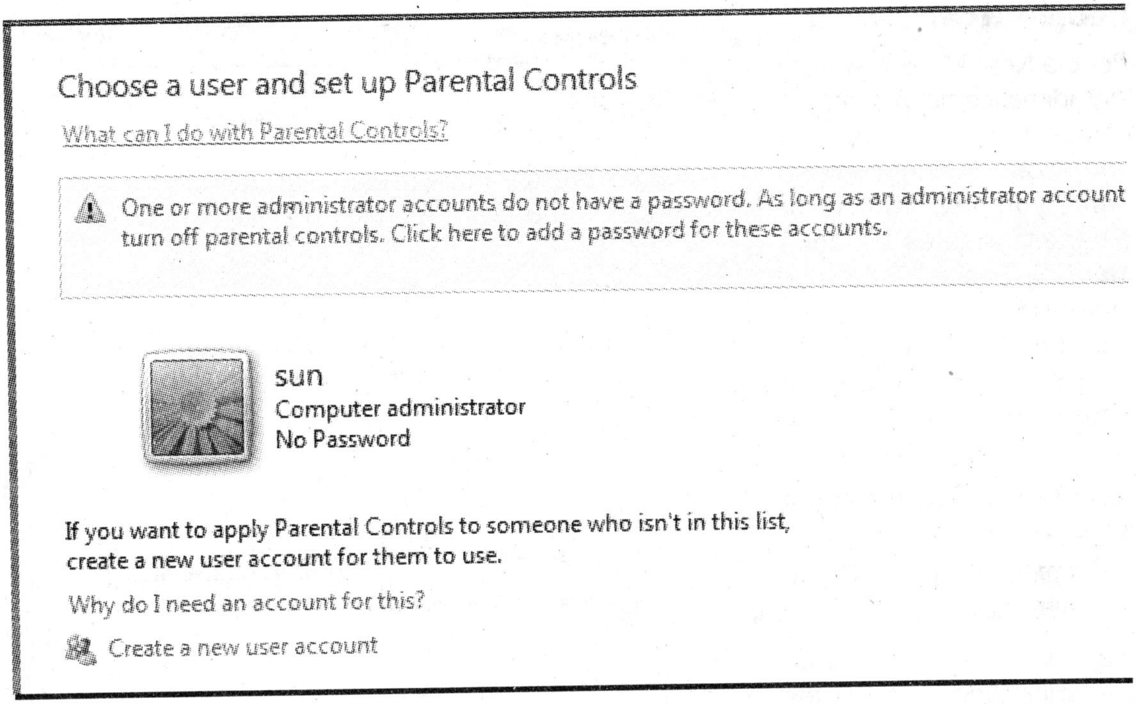

hours and, if they are already logged on, they will be automatically logged off. You can set different logon hours for every day of the week.

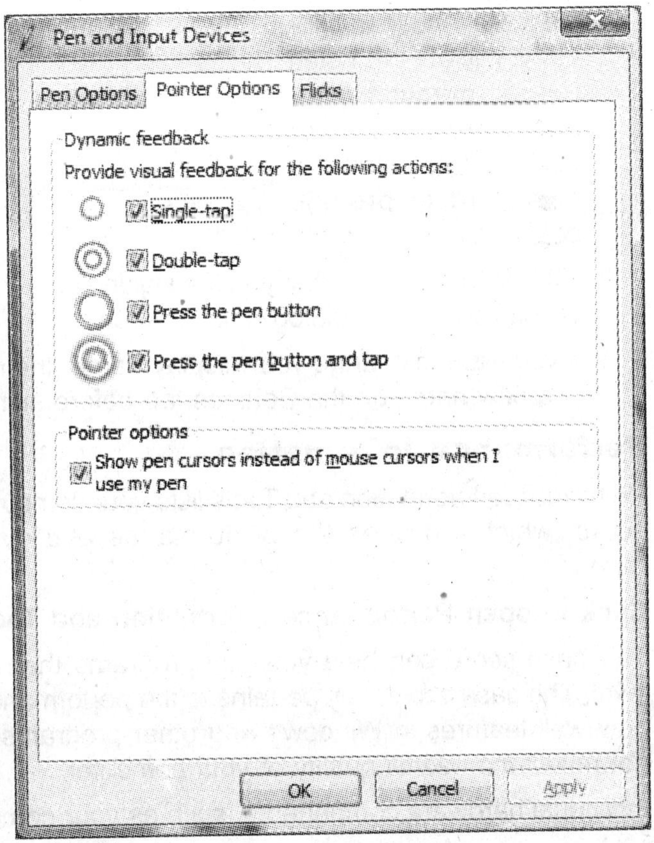

- Games. You can control access to games, choose an age rating level, choose the types of content you want to block, and decide whether you want to allow or block unrated or specific games.
- Allow or block specific programs. You can prevent children from running programs that you don't want them to run.

Pen and Input Devices

This applet opens up a dialog box where you can configure how your stylus (pen) interacts with the desktop and windows.

People Near Me

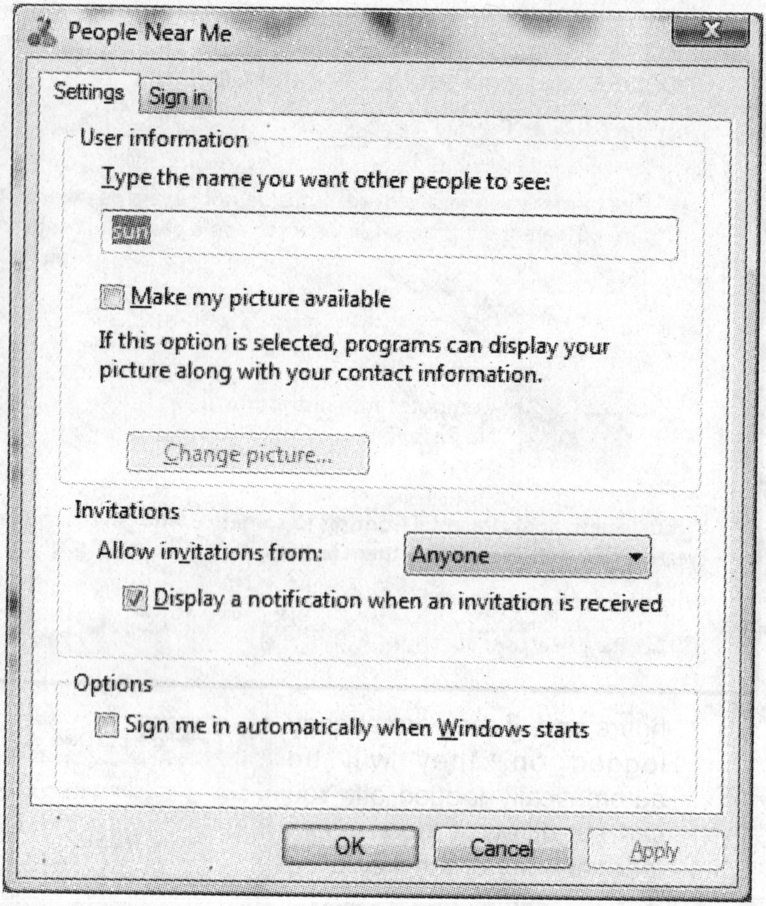

People Near Me is a service that identifies people nearby who are using computers and allows those people to send you invitations for programs such as Windows Meeting Space. They can only invite you to participate in programs that are installed on your computer. To use People Near Me, you have to sign in to the service.

How to sign in to People Near Me?

1. Click to open People Near Me.
2. Click the Sign in tab, click Sign in to People Near Me, and then click OK. If you are prompted for an administrator password or confirmation, type the password or provide confirmation.
3. If this is the first time that you are signing in to People Near Me, you'll see an additional dialog box. In that dialog box, click OK.

- If you want to change your display name (the name that other people will see), type a new name on the Settings tab before signing in.

Performance Information

Performance Information and Tools lists your computer's Windows Experience Index base score, which indicates the performance and overall capability of your computer's hardware.

Click to open Performance Information and Tools.

The base score can help you buy programs that match your computer's performance level. The base score only pertains to the performance aspects of the computer that affect how well features in Windows and other programs will run on this computer, and does not reflect the overall quality of your computer.

Individual hardware components, such as your computer's central processing unit (CPU)

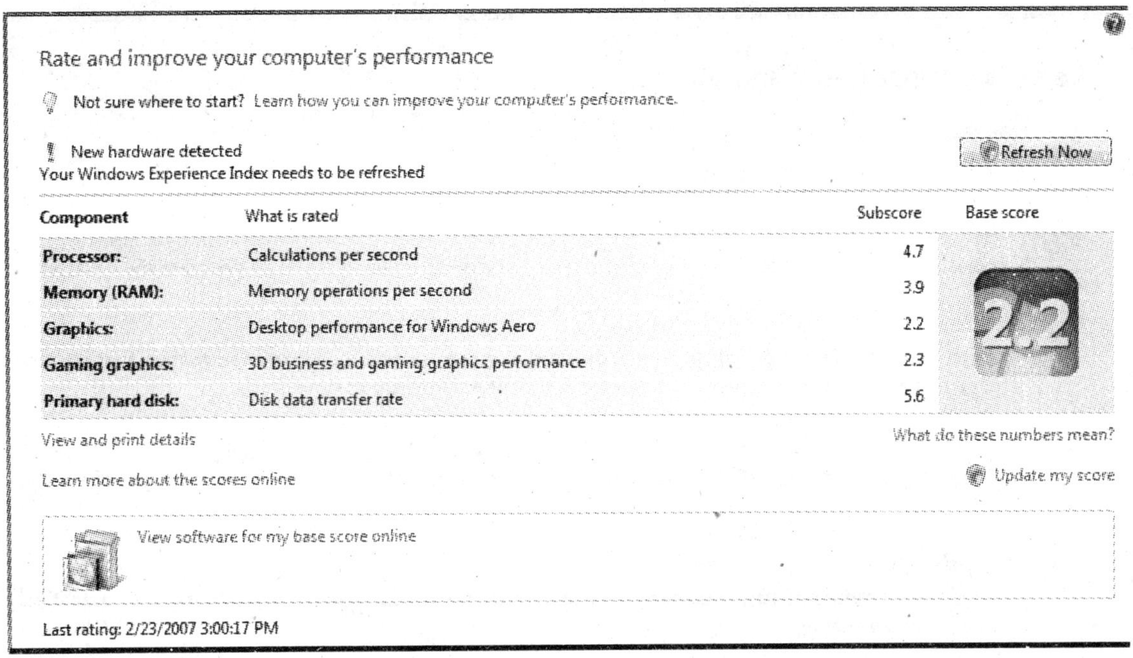

and random access memory (RAM), are tested and receive a subscore. Your computer's base score is determined by the lowest subscore. For example, if the lowest subscore of an individual hardware component is 2.6, then the base score is 2.6. The base score is not an average of the various subscores.

If you install new hardware and want to see if your score has changed, click Update my score. To view additional details about your computer's hardware, click View and print details.

Personalize

You can add a personal touch to your computer by using themes, changing the computer's colors and sounds, and choosing your own desktop background, screen saver, and user account picture.

Themes

A theme is a collection of visual elements that can affect the style of windows, icons, fonts, colors, and sometime sounds. For example, a nature-based theme might include a desktop background with plants, a pointer that looks like a leaf, and system sounds that mimic bird chirps.

Color

Windows Aero is the premium visual experience of this version of Windows. It features a transparent glass design with subtle window animations and new window colors. Click the Start button, click Control Panel, click Appearance and Personalization, click Personalization, and then click Window Color and Appearance.

- If you see the Appearance Settings dialog box instead of the Window Color and

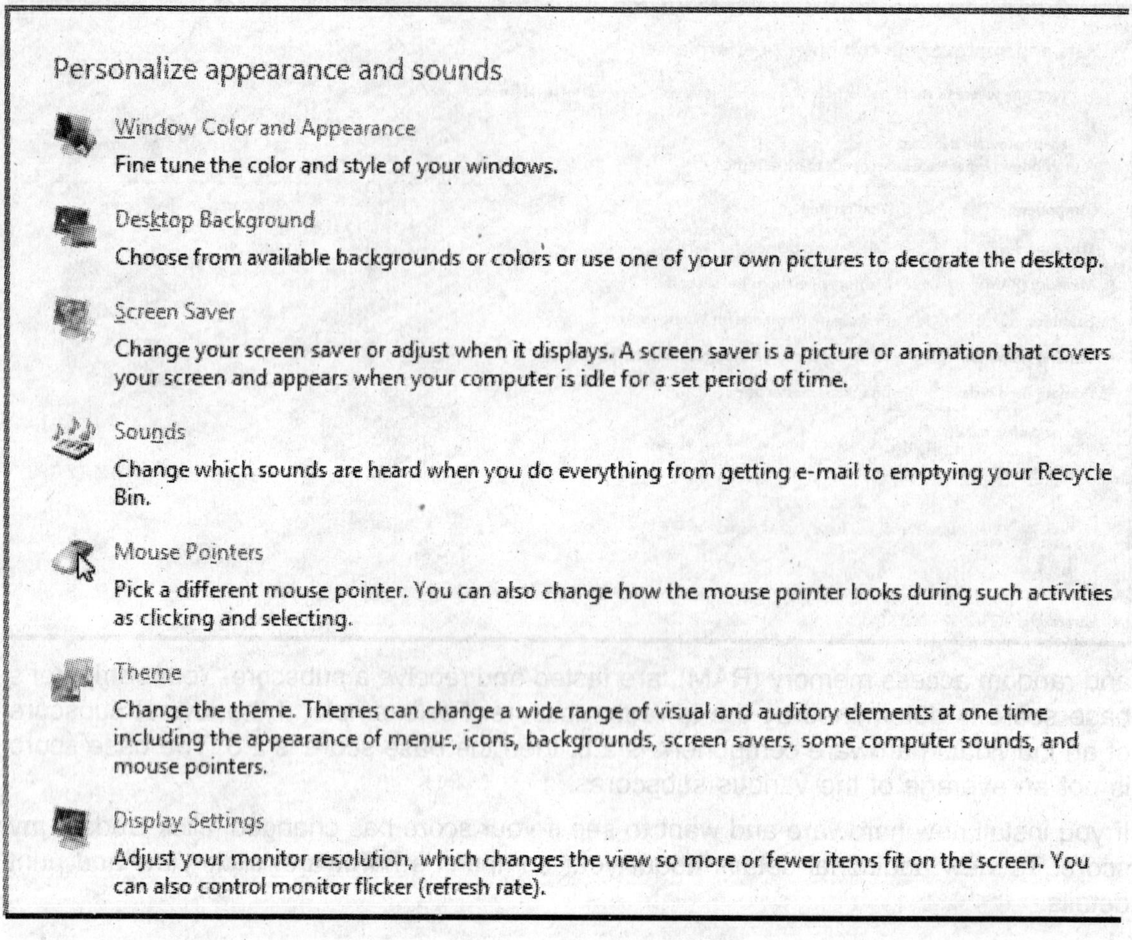

Appearance window, the theme might not be set to Windows Vista, the color scheme might not be set to Windows Aero, or the computer might not meet the minimum hardware requirements for running Windows Aero.

Sound

You can change the sound your computer makes when you receive e mail, start Windows, or shut down your computer.

Desktop background

The desktop background, also called wallpaper, is a picture or design on the desktop. It provides a backdrop to your open windows.

Screen saver

A screen saver is a picture or animation that appears on the screen when you haven't used the mouse or keyboard for a set period of time. Windows includes a variety of screen savers to choose from.

You can create a personalized screen saver by displaying selected pictures and videos as a slide show.

To use pictures as a slide show

1. Click to open Screen Saver Settings.
2. Click the Screen saver list, and then click Photos.
3. If you want to specify a location for the pictures you want to use in your screen saver, modify the slide show speed, or configure any other screen saver settings, click Settings. After you make your changes, click Save.
4. Click OK.

User account picture

A user account picture helps identify your account on a computer. The picture is displayed on the Welcome screen and on the Start menu. You can change your user account picture to one of the pictures included with Windows, or you can use your own picture.

Windows Sidebar

Windows Sidebar provides a way to organize the information, games, and tasks that you want to access quickly without cluttering your workspace. It's made up of gadgets, which are customizable mini-programs that can display continuously updated headlines, a picture slide show, contacts, and more, without having to open a new window.

Phone and Modem Options

The following are descriptions of the settings on the Dialing Rules, Modems, and Advanced tabs in Phone and Modem Options.

Click to open Phone and Modem Options.

If you haven't opened Phone and Modem Options before, a dialog box will be displayed, prompting you to type your area code and other access codes.

Dialing Rules tab

The Dialing Rules tab lists all currently defined dialing locations (sets of rules applied to outgoing phone calls from your computer's modem). Use this tab to add, delete, or configure dialing locations. When you specify the destination phone number, the rules associated with the dialing location determine whether the area code must be included, whether a calling card should be used, and so on.

The following table describes the options on the Dialing Rules tab.

Control	*Description*
Locations	Lists all of the currently defined locations on your computer. The currently selected location appears in bold text, and its rules apply to any phone calls made from your computer. Double-clicking a location opens the Edit dialog box, where you can make changes to the rules associated with that location.
New	Allows you to create a new location and specify the rules associated with that location.
Edit	Allows you to edit the rules for the currently selected location.

Delete — Removes the currently selected location and all rules associated with it. It does not remove any existing calling card definitions.

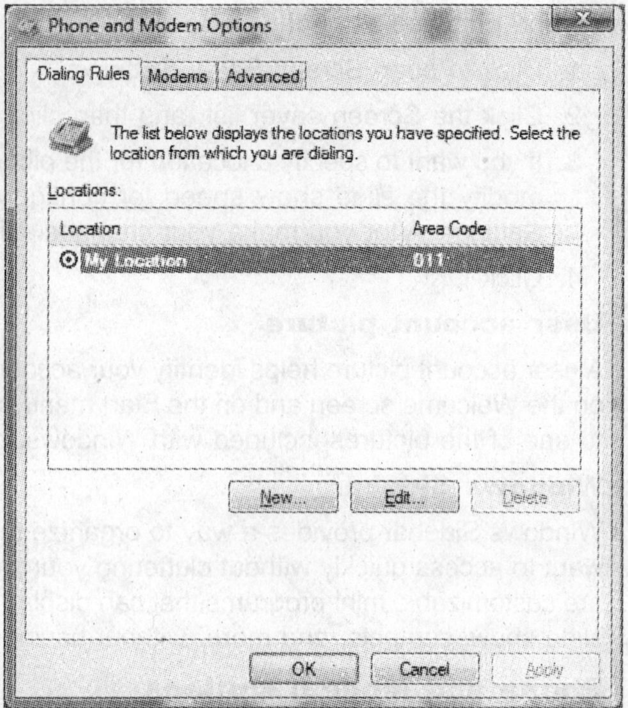

Modems tab

The Modems tab lists all modems currently installed on your computer. Use this tab to add, remove, and configure modems.

The following table describes the options on the Modems tab.

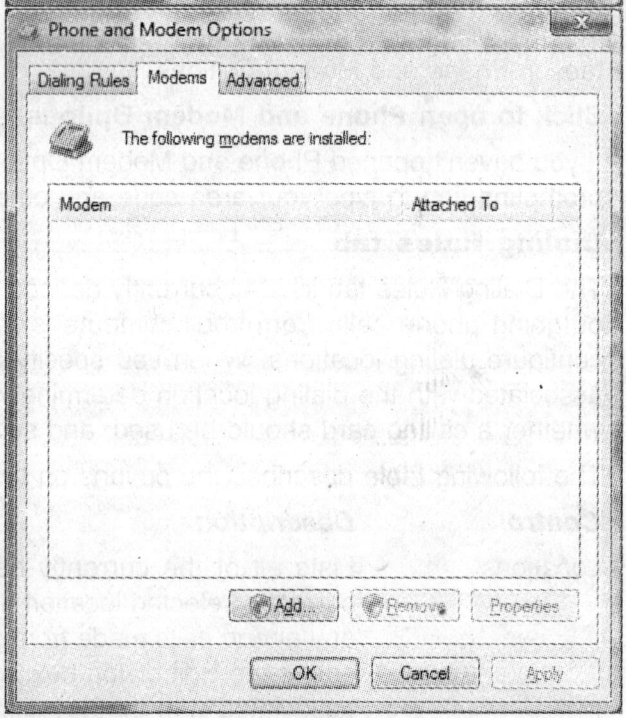

Control	***Description***
The following modems are installed	Lists the modems currently installed on your computer, and the communications port your computer uses to communicate with each modem.
Add	Allows you to install a new modem on your computer. If the drivers for your new modem are not already installed on your computer, you will be asked to install the drivers provided by the modem manufacturer.
Remove	Uninstalls the currently selected modem from your computer. You should unplug or remove the modem from your computer after uninstalling it, or it could be detected and reinstalled the next time you start your computer.

Properties	Allows you to view or change the configuration of the currently selected modem. The options available depend on the make and model of the modem.

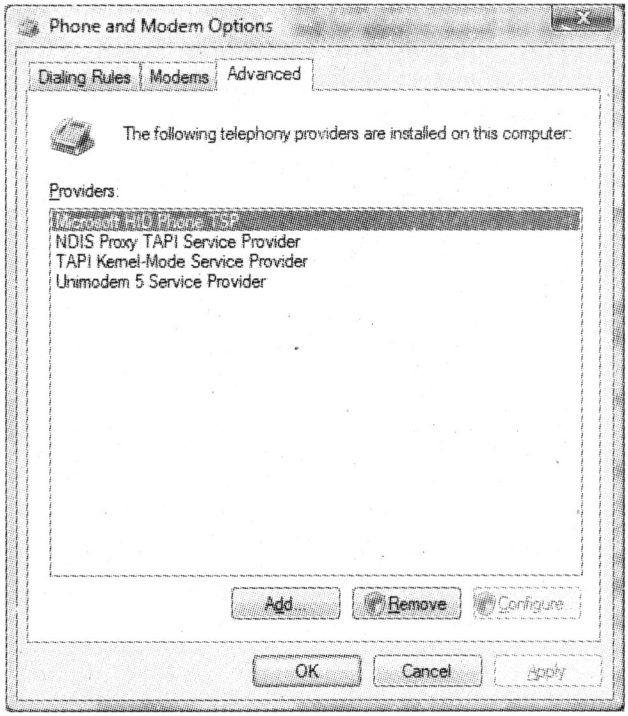

Advanced tab

The Advanced tab lists the telephony providers (software used to communicate with telephony hardware, such as modems) currently installed on your computer. Use this tab to add, remove, and configure providers.

The following table describes the options on the Advanced tab.

Control	***Description***
Providers	Lists the telephony providers currently installed on your computer.
Add	Allows you to add a Telephony Application Programming Interface (TAPI) service provider to the list and make it available to telephony programs. To do this, you must have the drivers for the TAPI-supported telephony hardware already installed on your computer.
Remove	Removes the selected TAPI service provider from the list. Removing a TAPI service provider makes it unavailable to telephony programs. It does not delete any files from your computer.
Configure	Allows you to view or change the properties of the selected TAPI service provider. If this is unavailable, there are no configurable properties for the service provider.

Power Options

The Power Options program manages the power consumption of your computer. That's a big deal when you are running off a laptop's battery, of course, but it's also important if you'd like to save money (and the environment) by cutting down on the juice consumed by your desktop PC.

In Vista, Microsoft has tried to simplify the business of managing the electricity/speed tradeoff in two ways. First, it has abandoned the old name power scheme and adopted a new one: power plan.

Printers

You can print almost any document, picture, webpage, or file that you can view on your computer. If you're new to printing, this article can help you understand printer types, how to connect a printer to your computer, and common print options.

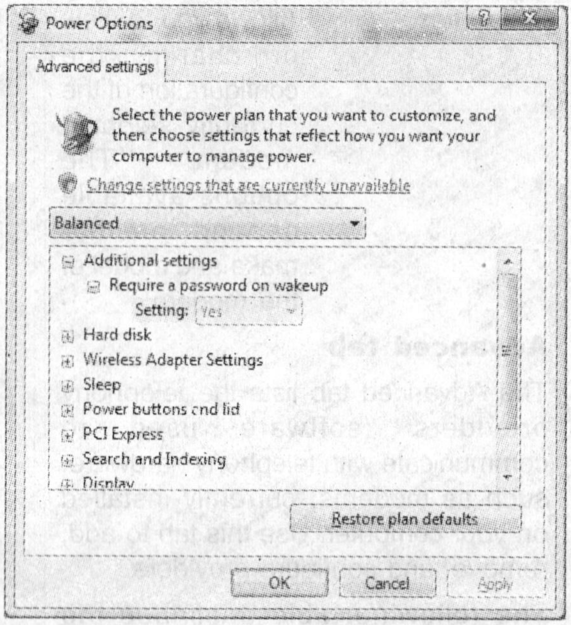

Understanding printer types and technologies

Printers are categorized by the way that they reproduce text and graphics on paper. Each type of printer offers different advantages.

Inkjet printers

Inkjet printers print by placing small dots of ink on a page to reproduce text or graphics. Inkjet printers can print in color or black ink. Although ink cartridges must be periodically replaced, inkjet printers are often purchased for home use because they can be relatively inexpensive. Some inkjet printers can reproduce high-quality pictures and detailed graphics.

Laser printers

Laser printers use toner, which is a fine, powdery substance, to reproduce text and graphics on paper. Laser printers can print in color or black ink, although color laser printers are usually more expensive. A laser printer that can print using only black ink is sometimes referred to as a monochrome printer.

Laser printers typically have high–capacity paper trays, so you don't need to add paper as often as you would for an inkjet printer. They also can print more pages per minute than most inkjet printers and can print more pages per cartridge. If you print in large volumes, this means that a laser printer can cost less for each page that you print.

Multifunction printers

Inkjet or laser printers that also allow you to fax, photocopy, or scan documents are referred to as multifunction printers. A single multifunction printer can more convenient to connect to your computer than multiple devices. You might also be able to use some features of a multifunction printer without turning on your computer.

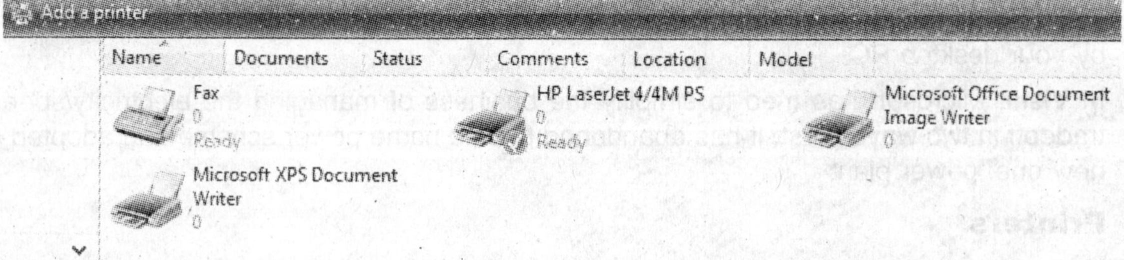

Connecting a printer

Some printers allow you to print without using your computer—for example, to print photos directly from a digital camera's memory card. However, connecting a printer to your computer allows you to print documents, files, pictures, webpages, and more. For more information about how to connect a printer, see Add or remove a printer.

When you add a printer, Windows will automatically install the software that allows it to work with your computer. You can add a printer using either a wired or wireless connection.

Wired printers

A wired printer is any printer that connects to a computer using a cable and a port on the computer. Most printers use a universal serial bus (USB) cable. When you connect a wired printer to your computer and power it on, Windows will automatically try to install the printer for you. If Windows can't detect the printer, you can find and add the printer manually.

Wireless printers

A wireless printer is any printer that connects to a computer using either Bluetooth or another wireless technology, such as 802.11a, 802.11b, or 802.11g.

Bluetooth technology uses radio transmissions to enable a printer to communicate with your computer over a short distance. To connect a Bluetooth printer, you need to add a Bluetooth adapter to your computer. Most Bluetooth adapters plug into a USB port on your computer. When you plug in the adapter and turn on the Bluetooth printer, Windows will try to install it automatically, or prompt you to install it. If Windows can't detect the printer, you can find and add it manually.

To connect a printer using a wireless technology other than Bluetooth, both your computer and the printer must first be connected to a wireless network. Check the information that came with your printer to see if it has a wireless network adapter. If not, you need to add one before you can connect the printer to your wireless network. To prevent interference between a wireless printer and your computer, try not to locate cordless phones or other wireless appliances near the printer.

Making sure your printer is ready to print

After you've added a printer, it's a good idea to print a test page to make sure that the printer is working correctly. A test page prints sample text and graphics in color or in black and white, depending on what type of printer you're using. It might also print information about the printer, such as the printer driver name and version, that can help you troubleshoot problems if the printer is not working correctly.

If you add one printer only, it becomes your default printer. This means the printer will be selected automatically when you print a document or file. If you add more than one printer, you can choose which printer to use by default. Choose the printer that you will use most often.

Print using Windows

The quickest way to print a document or file is to print using Windows. You don't need to open the file, choose print options, or change printer settings. Windows will print the document to your default printer.

1. Click to open Documents.
2. Locate the file that you want to print.
3. Right-click the file, and then click Print. Windows will print it using your default printer settings.

Print using a program

To print using a program, open the document, picture, or file that you want to print. After you open the document in a program, you can choose print options.

Common print options

Most print options are located in the Print dialog box, which you can access from the File menu in a program. The options that are available to you will depend on the program and the printer that you're using. To access some options, you might need to click a "Preferences," "Properties," or "Advanced Options" link or button within the Print dialog box.

Print dialog box in WordPad

Common print options for a program include:

- Printer selection. Allows you to choose a printer from a list of printers that are connected to your computer.
- Page range. Allows you to print specific pages or sections of a document. To select individual pages or a sequence (range) of pages, you can typically type the page numbers separated by commas or hyphens. For example, if you type 1,4,5-7, only pages 1 and 4, and then pages 5 through 7, will be printed.
- Number of copies and Collate. Allows you to print more than one copy of a document, picture, or file at a time. Use the collate option to print all pages in a document at once, in order, before printing more copies of the document.
- Page orientation. Also referred to as the paper layout, this option allows you to print content as a tall page (Portrait) or wide page (Landscape).
- Paper size. If your printer can print on more than one size of paper, this option allows you to select the paper size that you have loaded in the printer.
- Output or paper source. Also referred to as output destination or paper tray, this option allows you to specify which paper tray the printer should use. That way, you can load and store different paper sizes in each tray.
- Double-sided printing. Also referred to as duplex or two-sided printing, this option allows you to print on both sides of a sheet of paper. This option is only available if your printer supports it.
- Print in color or black in. This option is only available if your printer supports it.

Use print preview

To see what the print copy will look like before you print it, open the document in a program that offers a print preview. Print preview is typically located on the File menu for a program. You should be able to preview each page of the document. In some programs, you can choose print options in the preview mode, and then print directly from the preview. In other programs, you might have to close the preview, change the document or your printer settings, and then print it.

Print preview in WordPad

If you preview or print a document and it doesn't look the way you intended, you might need to edit the document or change your print options. For example, if only part of your document fits on the printed page, you might need to reduce the font size, decrease the margins, or change the page layout, and then try printing it again.

Keeping track of your print jobs

When you send a document or any other type of file to a printer, it becomes a print job. Some printers have a screen that will display a warning if a problem such as low ink or a paper jam occurs. Many printers display a message in the notification area on your computer. To troubleshoot problems, you can review any information displayed on your printer screen, refer to the information that came with the printer, or go to the printer manufacturer's website.

Using Windows, you can view the print queue to keep track of your print jobs. The print queue displays information about documents that are waiting to print, such as the printing status, document owner, and number of pages to print. You can use the print queue to view, pause, resume, restart, and cancel print jobs.

To view the print queue

1. Click to open Printers.
2. To open the print queue, double-click the printer that you're using.

Problem Reports and Solutions

Ever try to install a program that worked on your old computer onto a new computer? Ever have the installation fail mysteriously? Ever experience a hang, freeze, or crash? In Vista, Microsoft continues its efforts to conduct a troubleshooting session on a worldwide scale.

Programs and Features

It is about managing the software you have installed, managing updates, and buying software online. It replaces the old Add/Remove Programs program. The Windows is useful for fixing, which might simply mean reinstalling, changing, and uninstalling existing programs, and is the only place you can go to turn on, or off, Windows features like Fax and Scan, Games, Meeting Space and more.

Regional and Language Options

You can change the format Windows uses to display information (such as dates, times,

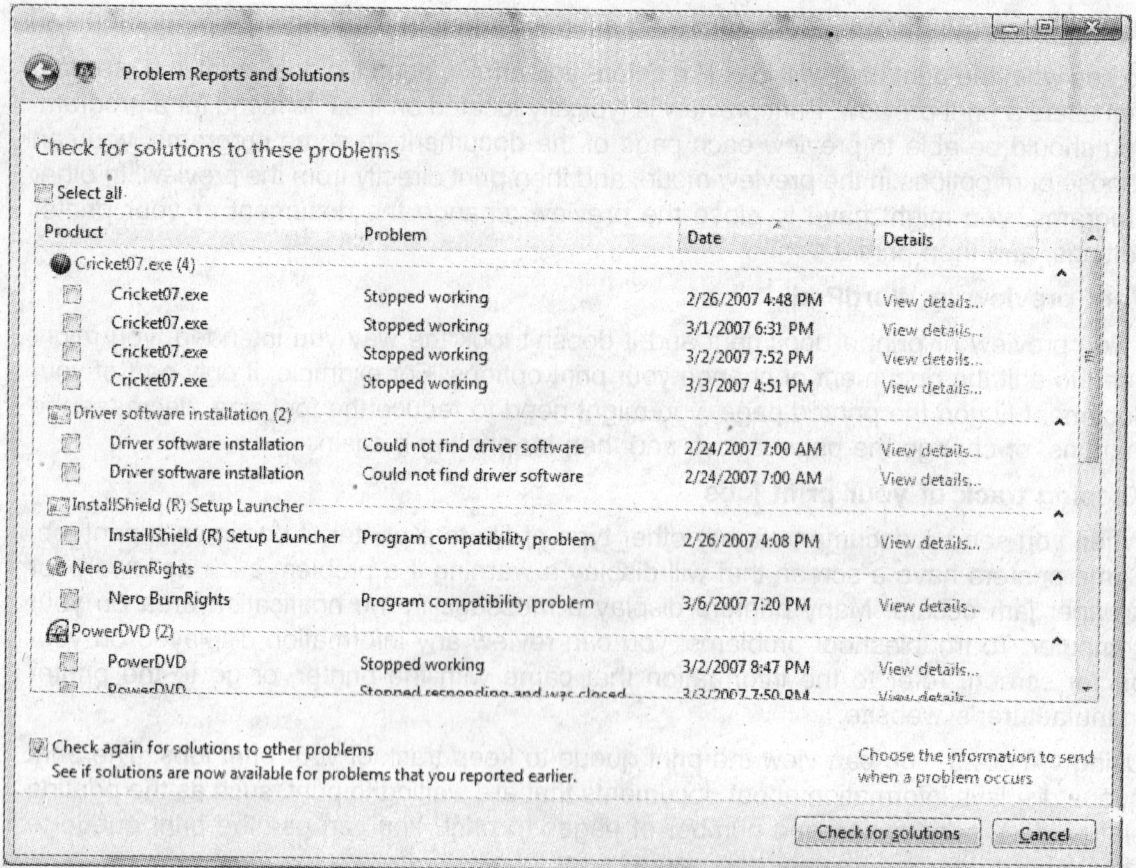
Problem Reports and Solutions
Check for solutions to these problems
Select all
Product
Problem
Date
Details
Cricket07.exe (4)
Cricket07.exe Stopped working 2/26/2007 4:48 PM View details...
Cricket07.exe Stopped working 3/1/2007 6:31 PM View details...
Cricket07.exe Stopped working 3/2/2007 7:52 PM View details...
Cricket07.exe Stopped working 3/3/2007 4:51 PM View details...
Driver software installation (2)
Driver software installation Could not find driver software 2/24/2007 7:00 AM View details...
Driver software installation Could not find driver software 2/24/2007 7:00 AM View details...
InstallShield (R) Setup Launcher
InstallShield (R) Setup Launcher Program compatibility problem 2/26/2007 4:08 PM View details...
Nero BurnRights
Nero BurnRights Program compatibility problem 3/6/2007 7:20 PM View details...
PowerDVD (2)
PowerDVD Stopped working 3/2/2007 8:47 PM View details...
Check again for solutions to other problems
See if solutions are now available for problems that you reported earlier.
Choose the information to send when a problem occurs
Check for solutions
Cancel

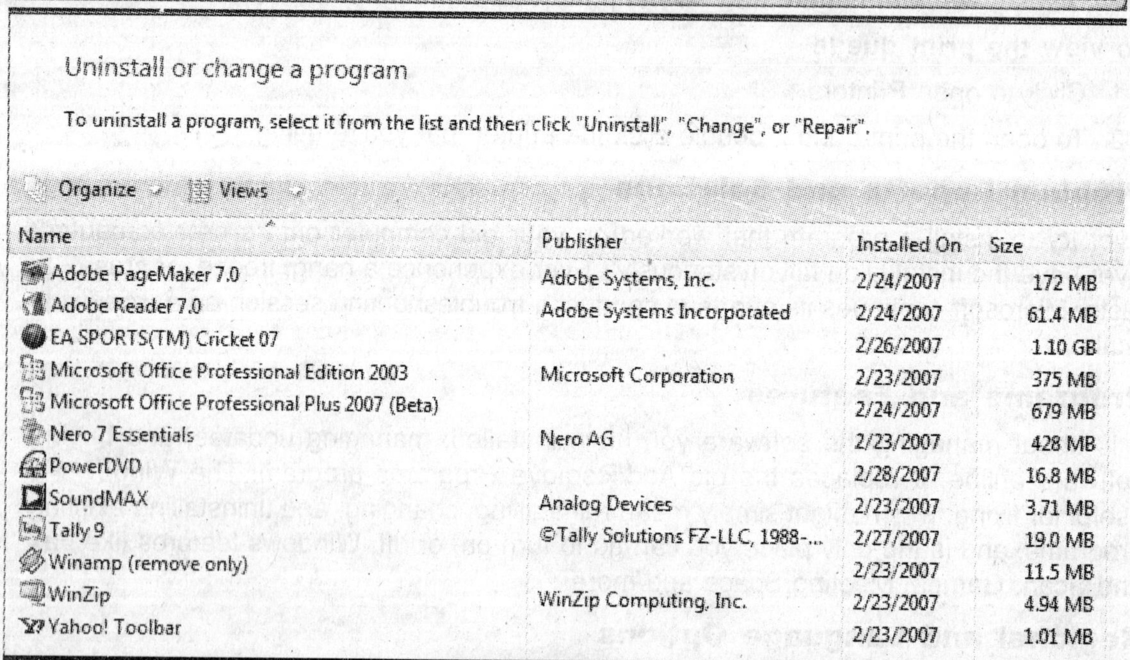
Uninstall or change a program
To uninstall a program, select it from the list and then click "Uninstall", "Change", or "Repair".
Organize
Views
Name
Publisher
Installed On
Size
Adobe PageMaker 7.0 Adobe Systems, Inc. 2/24/2007 172 MB
Adobe Reader 7.0 Adobe Systems Incorporated 2/24/2007 61.4 MB
EA SPORTS(TM) Cricket 07 2/26/2007 1.10 GB
Microsoft Office Professional Edition 2003 Microsoft Corporation 2/23/2007 375 MB
Microsoft Office Professional Plus 2007 (Beta) 2/24/2007 679 MB
Nero 7 Essentials Nero AG 2/23/2007 428 MB
PowerDVD 2/28/2007 16.8 MB
SoundMAX Analog Devices 2/23/2007 3.71 MB
Tally 9 ©Tally Solutions FZ-LLC, 1988-... 2/27/2007 19.0 MB
Winamp (remove only) 2/23/2007 11.5 MB
WinZip WinZip Computing, Inc. 2/23/2007 4.94 MB
Yahoo! Toolbar 2/23/2007 1.01 MB

currency, and measurements) so that it matches the standards or language used in the country or region where you are located. For example, if you work on documents in both French and English, you can change the format to French so that you can display currency in Euros or display dates in the day/month/year format.

If you need to type and edit documents in more than one language, you can add input languages. Many input languages support a variety of keyboard layouts, input method editors (IMEs), and speech and handwriting recognition programs. Deciding which of these options to use is usually a matter of personal preference. Experiment with the options to discover which work best for you. Even if you do most of your work in one language, you might want to try other keyboard layouts. For example, if you need to type accented letters in English, it might be easier to use the United States-International keyboard layout instead of the standard U.S. keyboard layout.

When you add input languages, keyboard layouts, input method editors, or speech or handwriting recognition programs, Windows displays the Language bar on your desktop. The Language bar provides a quick way to change the input language or keyboard layout from your desktop.

You can also change the display language—the language that the user interface text is displayed in—so that you can view wizards, dialog boxes, menus, and other items in the user interface in a different language. Some display languages are installed by default and others require you to install language files.

Formats tab

If you think 7/4 means July 4 and that 1,000 is the number of heads you have, skip this section. But, in some countries 7/4 means April 7, and 1,000 means one thousand. If your PC isn't showing numbers, times, currency, symbols, or dates in a familiar way, choose your country from the "Current format" button to rearrange the sequence of date elements.

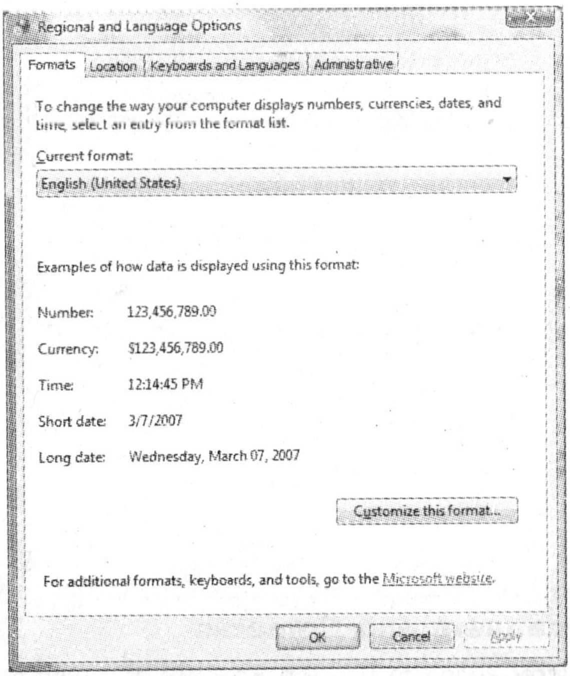

Location tab

This tab, new to Vista, identifies you computer's location. The point is so that when you go online to check local news and weather, you'll get the right news and weather—a handy feature if you're travelling with a laptop.

Keyboards and Languages tabs

The symbols you use when you're typing in English. Microsoft solved this problem by creating different keyboard layouts, one for each language, or more, like Qwerty or Dvorak for English. Each keyboard layout rearranges the letters that appear when you press the keys. For example, in the Swedish layout, pressing the semicolon key produces an Ö—not a simicolon(;).

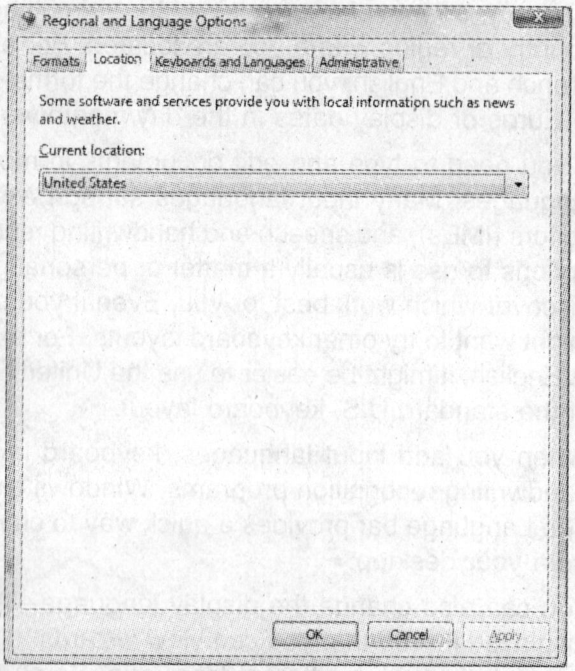

General tab

In order to even use Windows Vista, you must have an input language. The default is US English. If yours is different, then choose it from the drop-down list. This is the language that Vista will use to communicate with you, and the standard language for your keyboard.

Administrative tab

The "Change system locale" button this tab lets you specify—which language handles error messages and the occasional dialog box. The "Copy to reserved account" button lets the newly configured language settings apply to new user accounts, so anyone who gets a new account on this computer will have your language, format, and keyboard settings conveniently available to them.

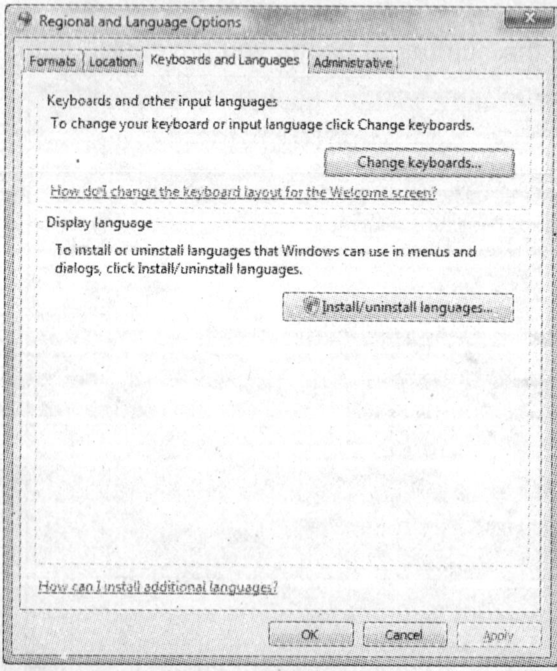

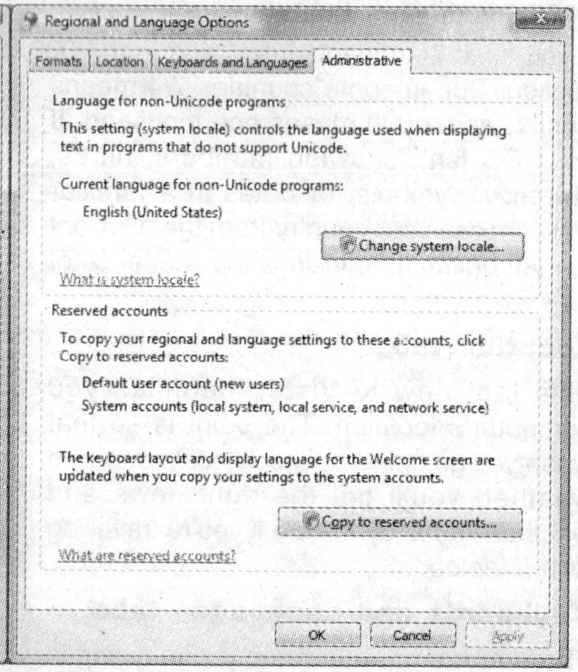

Scanners and Cameras

Before trying to use the Scanner and Camera Installation Wizard, you should first try connecting your scanner or camera to your computer and turning it on. If Windows recognizes your scanner or camera and installs the appropriate driver, you don't need to use the wizard. The Scanner and Camera Installation Wizard helps you to install driver software for older scanners and cameras—and some networked scanners—that are not automatically recognized by Windows.

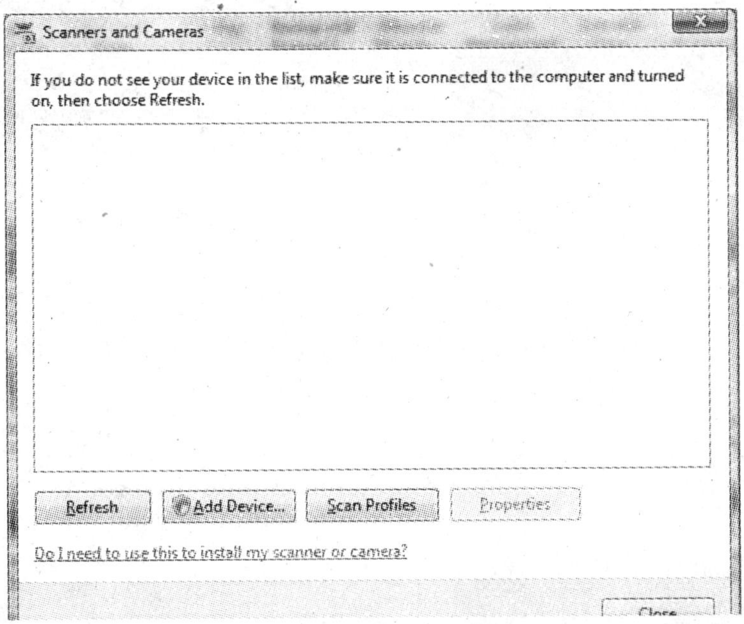

To start the Scanner and Camera Installation Wizard

1. Click to open Scanners and Cameras.
2. If you are prompted for an administrator password or confirmation, type the password or provide confirmation.
3. If you don't see your scanner or camera listed, ensure that it is connected to your computer and turned on, and then click Refresh.
4. If your device still isn't listed, click Add Device to start the Scanner and Camera Installation Wizard, and then follow the instructions to install the necessary driver software.
   - The wizard will ask you to select your scanner or camera from a list. If your scanner or camera isn't listed, you will need to obtain driver software for it, either from the manufacturer's website or from a disc provided by the manufacturer, and then click Have Disk when asked to choose your scanner or camera.

Security Center

Windows Security Center can help enhance your computer's security by checking the status of several security essentials on your computer, including firewall settings, automatic updates, anti-malware software settings, Internet security settings, and User Account Control settings. If Windows detects a problem with any of these security essentials (for example, if your antivirus program is out of date), Security Center displays a notification and places a Security Center icon in the notification area. Click the notification or double-click the Security Center icon to open Security Center and get information about how to fix the problem.

Firewall

A firewall can help prevent hackers or malicious software (such as worms) from gaining access to your computer through a network or the Internet. A firewall can also help stop

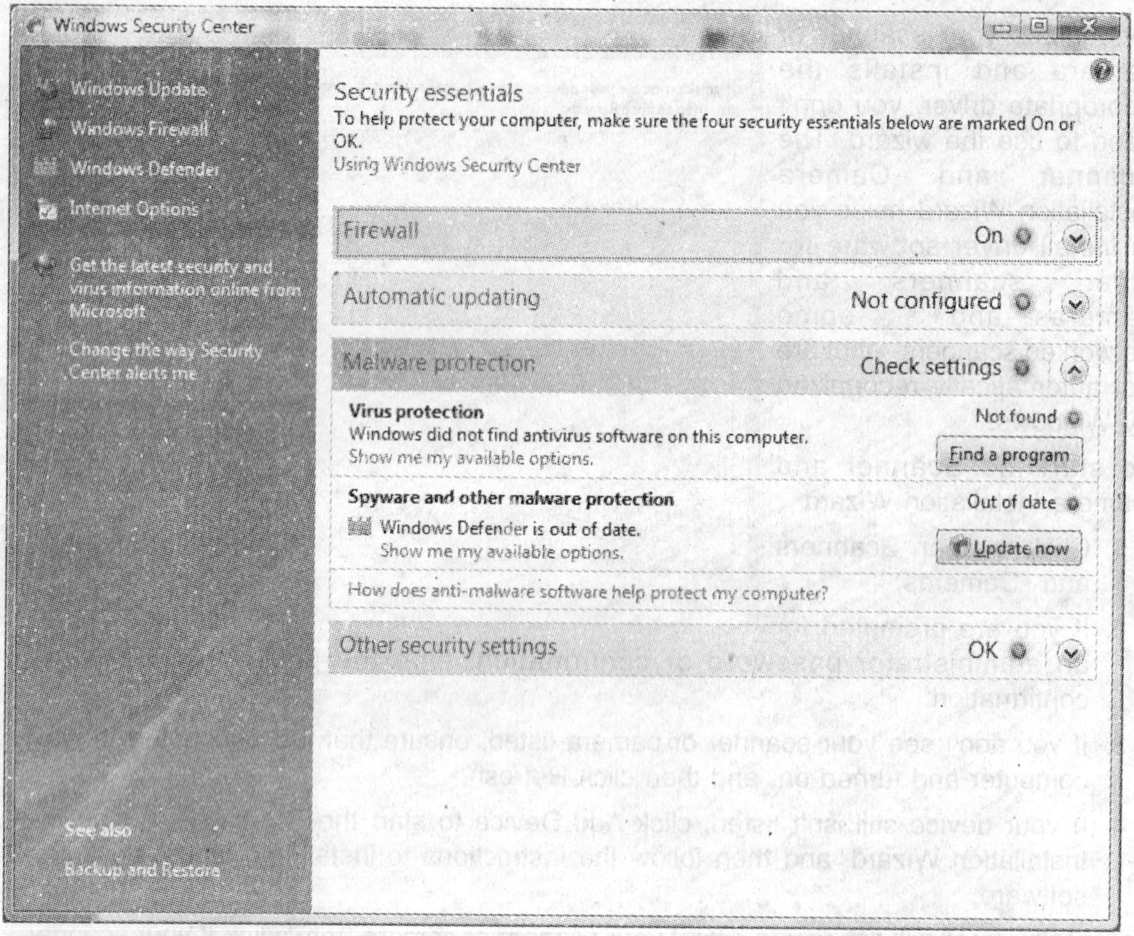

your computer from sending malicious software to other computers.Windows checks if your computer is protected by a software firewall. If the firewall is off, Security Center will display a notification and put a Security Center icon in the notification area.

To turn on Windows Firewall

1. Click to open Security Center.
2. Click Firewall, and then click Turn on now. If you are prompted for an administrator password or confirmation, type the password or provide confirmation.
3. If you have a firewall other than Windows firewall, check the information that came with the firewall or go to the manufacturer's website to find out how to turn it on.
4. Windows does not detect all firewalls. If you are sure that you have a firewall installed and turned on, you can click Show me my available options to stop receiving notifications from Security Center about your firewall. If you do this, Windows will not monitor your firewall status or alert you if it is off.

Automatic updating

Windows can routinely check for updates for your computer and install them automatically.

You can use Security Center to make sure Automatic updating is turned on. If updating is turned off, Security Center will display a notification and put a Security Center icon in the notification area.

To turn on automatic updating

1. Click to open Security Center.
2. Click Automatic updating, and then click Turn on now. If you are prompted for an administrator password or confirmation, type the password or provide confirmation.

Malicious software protection

Malicious software (malware) protection can help protect your computer against viruses, spyware, and other security threats. Security Center checks if your computer is using up-to-date antispyware and antivirus software. If your antivirus or antispyware software is turned off or out of date, Security Center will display a notification and put a Security Center icon in the notification area.

To install or update your anti-malware software

1. Click to open Security Center.
2. Click Malware protection, click the button under Virus protection or Spyware and other malware protection, and then choose the option that you want.
3. Windows does not detect all antivirus and antispyware software. If you are sure that you have anti-malware software installed, it is turned on, and it is up to date, you can click I have an antivirus program that I'll monitor myself or I have an antisypware program that I'll monitor myself to stop receiving notifications from Security Center about your anti-malware software. If you do this, Windows will not monitor your anti-malware software status or alert you if it is off.

Other security settings

Windows checks your Internet security settings and User Account Control settings to make sure they are set at the recommended levels. If your Internet or User Account Control settings are changed to a security level that is not recommended, Security Center will display a notification and put a Security Center icon in the notification area.

To restore Internet settings to recommended levels

1. Click to open Security Center.
2. Click Other security settings.
3. Under Internet security settings, click Restore settings.
4. Do one of the following:
    - To automatically reset the Internet security settings that are at risk to their default level, click Restore my Internet security settings now.
    - To reset the Internet security settings yourself, click I want to restore my Internet security settings myself. Click the security zone you want to change settings for, and then click Custom level.

To restore User Account Control settings to recommended levels

1. Click to open Security Center.
2. Click Other security settings.
3. Under User Account Control, click Turn on now. If you are prompted for an administrator password or confirmation, type the password or provide confirmation

Sound

In Vista, the Sound dialog box has been simplified. It now contains only three tabs that control every aspect of your microphone and speakers: Playback, Record, and Sounds.

Playback and Recording tabs

These tabs simply contain the icon for each attached sound device. To change a device's settings, select it, and then click Configure.

Sounds tab

Windows Vista comes with a new, freshly composed suite of little sound

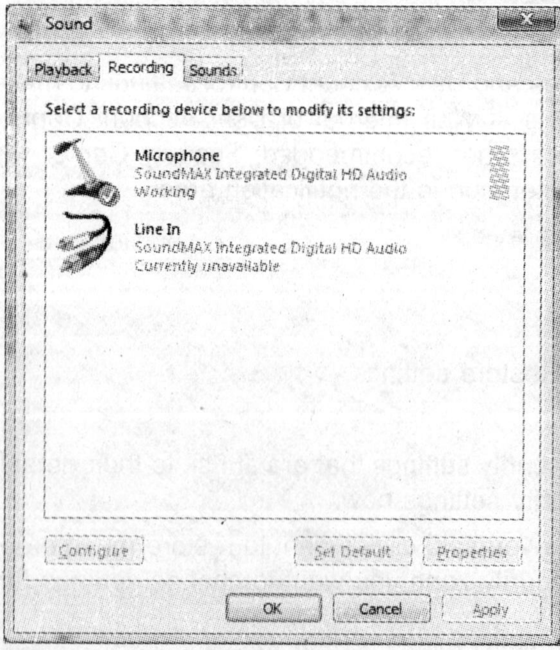

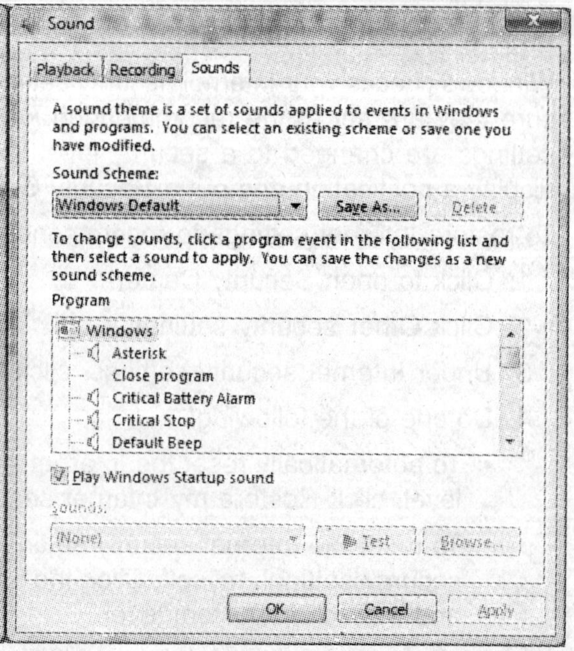

effects—beeps, musical ripples, and chords—that play when you turn on the PC, trigger an error message, empty the Recycle Bin, and so on. And if you like, you can hear them on many other occasions, such as when you open or exit a program, open a menu, restore a window, and so on. The tab lets you specify which sound effect plays for which situation.

SoundMAX

A sound card is a device installed in your computer that processes information from a computer program, such as a media player, and then sends a signal to your computer's speakers that you can hear. Some motherboards have sound capabilities built into them, but computers often have a dedicated sound card, which usually improves the quality of the sound the computer can produce.

Almost every computer is capable of playing sounds. Check the back or front of your computer for jacks to plug in a microphone, headphones, or external speakers. You can also use Device Manager to check for a sound card. You must be logged on as an administrator to perform these steps.

Click to open Device Manager. If you are prompted for an administrator password or confirmation, type the password or provide confirmation. Expand the Sound, video, and game controllers section to see the sound card that you have installed. If that section isn't displayed or no sound card is listed, either your computer doesn't have a sound card, or the driver for the sound card hasn't been properly installed.

Speech Recognition

To use Speech Recognition, the first thing you need to do is set it up on your computer. To learn how to do that, see Set up Speech Recognition. When you're ready to use Speech Recognition, you need to speak in simple, short commands. The tables below include some of the more commonly used commands.

1. Click to open Windows Speech Recognition.
2. Speech Recognition is not available in all languages.

Common Speech Recognition commands

The following table shows some of the most commonly used commands in Speech Recognition. Words in italic font indicate that you can say many different things in place of the example word or phrase and get useful results.

To do this	*Say this*
Click any item by its name	File; Start; View

Click item	Click Recycle Bin; Click Computer; Click File
Double-click item	Double-click Recycle Bin; Double-click Computer; Double-click File
Switch to an open program	Switch to Paint; Switch to WordPad; Switch to program name; Switch application
Scroll direction	Scroll up; Scroll down; Scroll left; Scroll right
Insert a new paragraph or new line in a document	New paragraph; New line
Select a word in a document	Select word
Select a word and start to correct it	Correct word
Select and delete specific words	Delete word
Show a list of applicable commands	What can I say?
Update the list of speech commands that are currently available	Refresh speech commands
Make the computer listen to you	Start listening
Make the computer stop listening	Stop listening
Move the Speech Recognition microphone out of the way	Move speech recognition
Minimize the microphone bar	Minimize speech recognition

Dictation

The following table shows commands for using Speech Recognition to work with text. Words in italic font indicate that you can say many different things in place of the example word or phrase and get useful results.

To do this	***Say this***
Insert a new line in the document	New line
Insert a new paragraph in the document	New paragraph
Insert a tab	Tab
Insert the literal word for the next command; for example, you can insert the word "comma" instead of the punctuation mark	Literal word
Insert the numeral form of a number	Numeral number
Put the cursor before a specific word	Go to word
Put the cursor after a specific word	Go after word
Do not insert a space before the next word	No space
Go to the start of the sentence that the cursor is in	Go to start of sentence
Go to the start of the paragraph the cursor is in	Go to start of paragraph
Go to the start of the document	Go to start of document

Go to the end of the sentence that the cursor is in	Go to end of sentence
Go to the end of the paragraph the cursor is in	Go to end of paragraph
Go to the end of the current document	Go to end of document
Select the word in the current document	Select word
Select the word range in the current document	Select word range; Select word through word
Select all text in the current document	Select all
Select the 1-20 words before the location of the cursor	Select previous 1-20 words; Select previous 10 words
Select the 1-20 words after the location of the cursor	Select next 1-20 words; Select next 10 words
Select the last text you dictated	Select that
Clear the selection on the screen	Clear selection
Capitalize the first letter of the word	Caps word
Capitalize all the letters of the word	All caps word
Make all the letters in the word lowercase	No caps word
Change the next number of words to uppercase	Change next number of words to uppercase
Change the next number of words to lowercase	Change next number of words to lowercase
Delete the previous sentence	Delete previous sentence
Delete the next sentence	Delete next sentence
Delete the previous paragraph	Delete previous paragraph
Delete the next paragraph	Delete next paragraph
Delete the selected or last dictated text	Delete that

Keyboard keys

The following table shows commands for using Speech Recognition to press keyboard keys. Words in italic font indicate that you can say many different things in place of the example word or phrase and get useful results.

To do this	***Say this***
Press any key on the keyboard	Press keyboard key; Press a; Press capital b; Press SHIFT plus a; Press CTRL plus a
Press certain keyboard keys without saying "Press" first	Delete; Backspace; Enter; Page Up; Page down; Home; End; Tab

- You can also use the ICAO\NATO phonetic alphabet to say the keyboard keys to press. For example, you can say "Press alpha" to press "a" or "Press bravo" to press "b."

- Using Speech Recognition to press keyboard keys will only work with Latin alphabets.

Punctuation marks and special characters

The following table shows commands for using Speech Recognition to insert punctuation marks and special characters. Words in italic font indicate that you can say many different things in place of the example word or phrase and get useful results.

To make this appear	*Say this*	*To make this appear*	*Say this*
,	Comma	;	Semicolon
.	Period; Dot; Full stop; Decimal point	:	Colon
“	Open double quote; Open quote; Open inverted commas		
”	Close double quote; Close quote; Close inverted commas		
‘	apostrophe	‘	Open single quote
’	Close single quote	>	Greater than sign
<	Less than sign	/	Forward slash
\	Backslash	~	Tilde
@	At sign	!	Exclamation mark; Exclamation point
?	Question mark	#	Number sign; Pound sign; Hash sign
$	Dollar sign	%	Percent sign
^	Caret	(	Open parenthesis; Open paren
)	Close parenthesis; Close paren	_	Underscore
-	Hyphen; Minus sign; Dash	–	En dash
—	Em dash; Double dash	=	Equal sign
+	Plus sign	{	Open brace; Open curly bracket
}	Close brace; Close curly bracket	[	Open bracket; Open square bracket
]	Close bracket; Close square bracket	|	Vertical bar
:-)	Press smiley face	:-(	Press frowny face
;-)	Press winky face	™	Trademark sign
¾	Three quarter sign	¼	One quarter sign
½	One half sign	£	Pound sterling sign; pound; pound sign
&	Ampersand; and sign	*	asterisk
//	Double slash	‘	Back quote
<	Open angle bracket	>	Close angle bracket
±	Plus or minus sign	«	Open angle quote
»	Close angle quote	×	Multiplication sign

÷	Division sign	¢	Cent sign
¥	Yen sign	§	Section sign
©	Copyright sign	®	Registered, Registered trademark sign
°	Degree sign	¶	Paragraph sign
...	Ellipsis; Dot dot dot	*f*	Function sign

Controls

The following table shows commands for using Speech Recognition to perform tasks in Windows. Words in italic font indicate that you can say many different things in place of the example word or phrase and get useful results.

To do this	*Say this*
Click any item by saying its name	File; Edit; View; Save; bold
Click any item	Click File; Click bold; Click Save; Click Close
Double-click any item	Double-click Computer; Double-click Recycle Bin; Double-click Folder name
Right-click any item	Right-click Computer; Right-click Recycle Bin; Right-click Folder name
Minimize all windows to show your desktop	Show Desktop
Click something you don't know the name of	Show numbers (Numbers will appear on the screen for every item in the active window)
Click a numbered item	19 OK; 5 OK
Double-click a numbered item	Double-click 19; Double-click 5
Right-click a numbered item	Right-click 19; Right-click 5

Windows

The following table shows commands for using Speech Recognition to work with windows and programs. Words in italic font indicate that you can say many different things in place of the example word or phrase and get useful results.

To do this	*Say this*
Open a program	Open Paint; Open WordPad; Open program name
Switch to an open program	Switch to Paint; Switch to WordPad; Switch to program name; Switch application
Close a program	Close that; Close Paint; Close Documents; Close Internet Explorer (only works with the active window)
Restore	Restore that; Restore Paint; Restore Internet Explorer (only works with the active window)

Minimize	Minimize that; Minimize Paint; Minimize Internet Explorer (only works with the active window)
Maximize	Maximize that; Maximize Paint; Maximize Internet Explorer (only works with the active window)
Cut	Cut that; Cut
Copy	Copy that; Copy
Paste	Paste
Delete	Delete that; Delete
Undo	Undo that; Scratch that; Undo
Scroll direction	Scroll up; Scroll down; Scroll right; Scroll left
Scroll an exact distance in pages	Scroll down 2 pages; Scroll up 10 pages
Scroll an exact distance in other units	Scroll up 5; Scroll down 7
Go to a field in a form or a program	Go to field name; Go to Subject; Go to Address; Go to Cc

Click anywhere on the screen

The following table shows commands for using Speech Recognition to click anywhere on the screen. Words in italic font indicate that you can say many different things in place of the example word or phrase and get useful results.

To do this	***Say this***
Show the mousegrid	Mousegrid
Move the mouse pointer to the center of any mousegrid square	number—or numbers—of the square; 1; 7; 9; 1, 7, 9
Click any mousegrid square	Click number of the square
Select an item to drag with the mousegrid	number—or numbers—of the square where the item appears; 3, 7, 9 (followed by) mark
Select an area where you want to drag the item with the mousegrid	number—or numbers—of the square where you want to drag; 4, 5, 6 (followed by) click

Sync Center

Sync is short for synchronization. In Windows, sync is the process of keeping two or more versions of the same file stored in different locations matched with each other. If you add, change, or delete a file in one location, Windows can add, change, or delete the same file in the other locations that you choose to sync with, whenever you choose to sync.

Sync Center is a feature of Windows that allows you to keep information in sync between your computer and Mobile devices that you plug in to your computer or to which you connect wirelessly (such as portable music players, digital cameras, and mobile phones).

- Files stored in folders on network servers. (These are called offline files because you can access them even when your computer or the server is not connected to the network.)
- Programs that support Sync Center.

System

The system dialog box has the following information.

What edition of Vista is installed on your computer?

As you know, Vista comes in several editions. Not all editions are made equal; if you're failing to find some feature that you could have sworn is supposed to be in Vista, it's good to check here. You might find out that the feature you want is available only on higher-priced versions.

PC's performance in terms of Rating

Ratings are displayed in the Rating column in your library. By default, most items in your library are automatically given an auto rating. The auto rating is controlled by non-Microsoft data providers, such as AMG and some online stores. You can override an auto rating by explicitly choosing a new user rating. You can distinguish between the two types of ratings by the appearance of the stars, which are blue for auto ratings and bright yellow for user ratings.

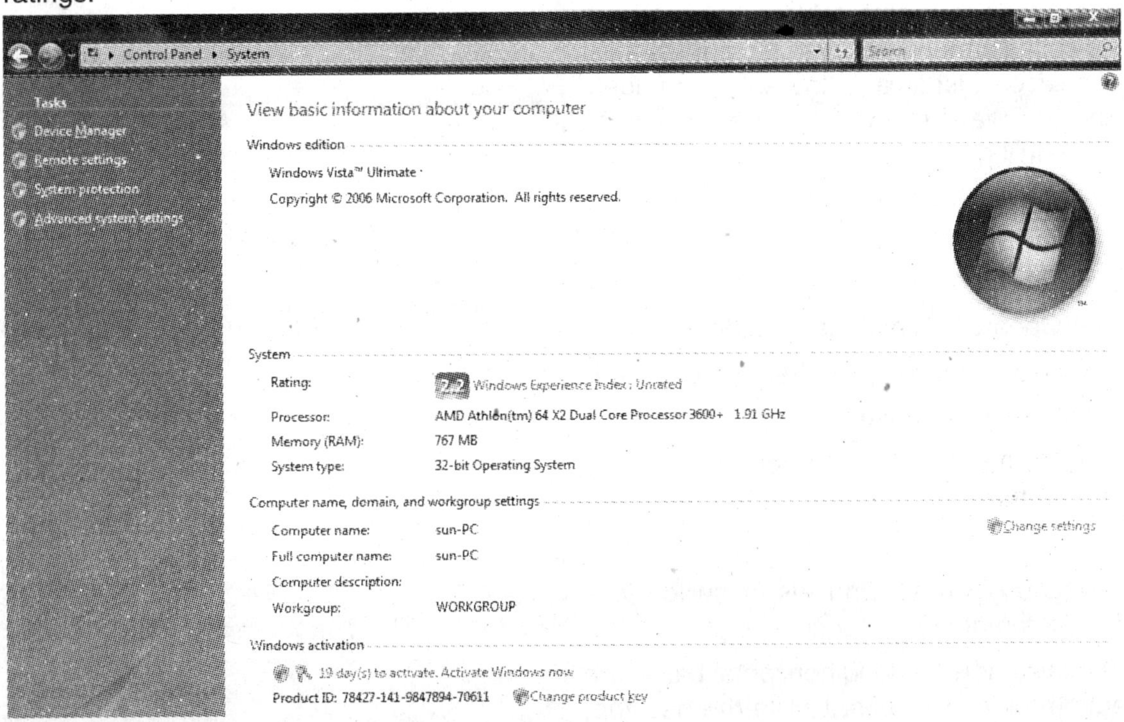

The model name and speed of your PC's processor chip

Such as Pentium 4, 2.6 GHz

How much memory your PC has?

That's a very helpful number to know, particularly if you need to improve your computer's speed.

Your computer's name, domain or workgroup

Remember, your computer name and description are primarily useful on a network, since that's how other people will identify your computer. Unless you tell it otherwise, Vista names your computer after you login name, somtheing like SUN-PC.

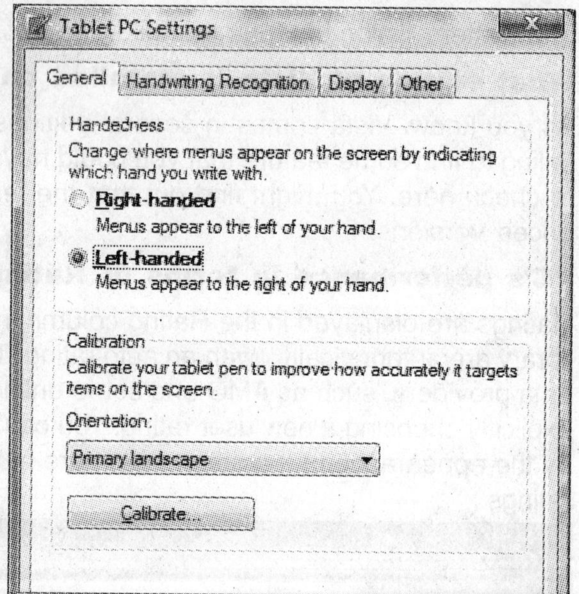

Table PC Settings

This applet is all about managing a Table Pc, one of those touchscreen laptop things. Here, you will find settings that focus on tablet display orientation and calibration, handwriting recognition, and configuring pen input.

Taskbar and Start Menu

The Start menu is the main gateway to your computer's programs, folders, and settings. It's called a menu because it provides a list of choices, just as a restaurant menu does. And as "Start" implies, it's often the place that you'll go to start or open things.

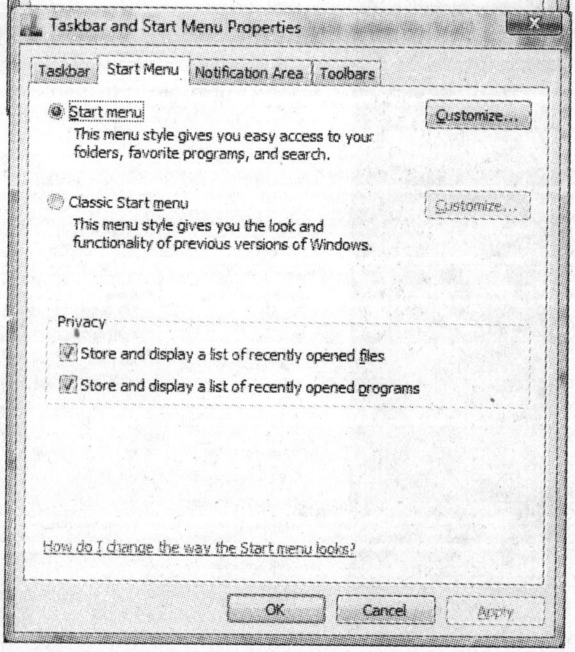

Use the Start menu to do these common activities:

- Start programs
- Open commonly used folders
- Search for files, folders, and programs
- Adjust computer settings
- Get help with the Windows operating system
- Turn off the computer
- Log off from Windows or switch to a different user account

The taskbar is the long horizontal bar at the bottom of your screen. Unlike the desktop, which can get obscured by the windows on top of it, the taskbar is visible almost all the time. It has four main sections:

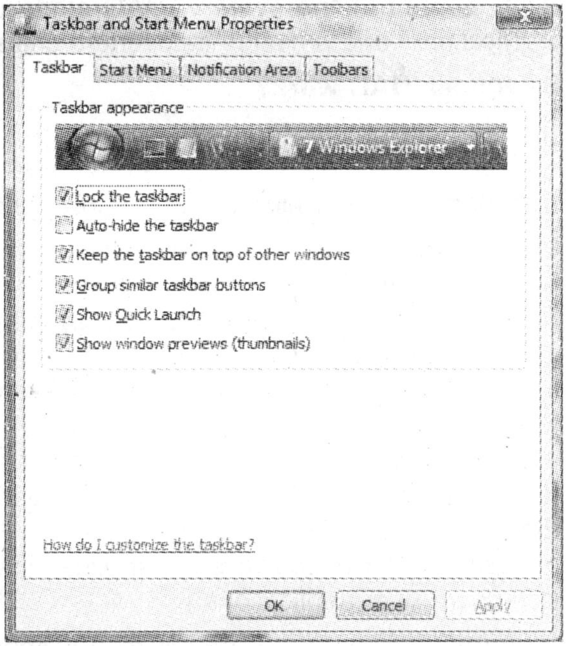

- The Start button , which opens the Start menu.
- The Quick Launch toolbar, which lets you start programs with one click.
- The middle section, which shows you which programs and documents you have open and allows you to quickly switch between them.
- The notification area, which includes a clock and icons (small pictures) that communicate the status of certain programs and computer settings.

Text to Speech

It opens the Speech Properties dialog box. Here is where you configure the voice of Windows—the robotic voice, called Microsoft Anna—that you head any time Windows reads text aloud. Microsoft Word can read text to you, however, and for that reason, you may be happy to know that you can specify Anna's rate of speaking using the dialog box.

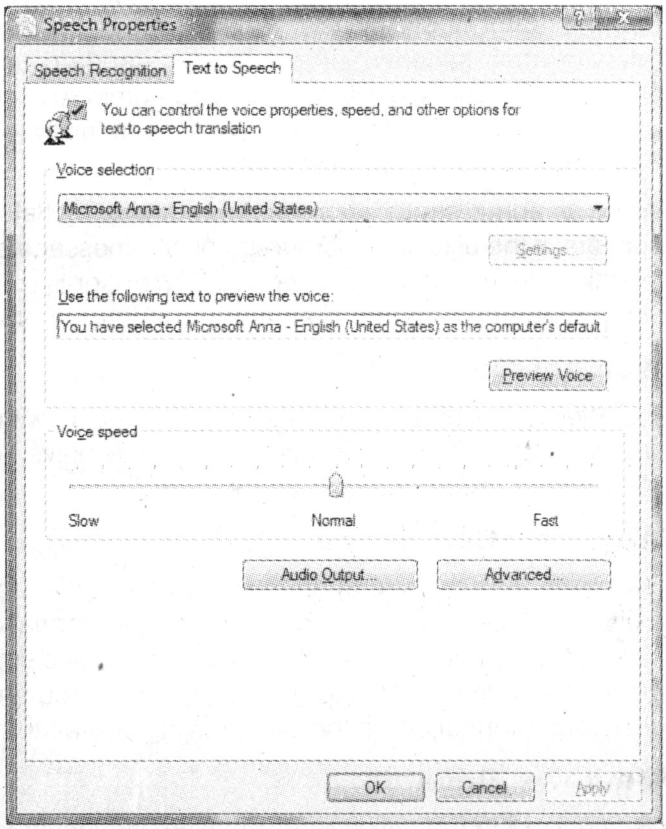

User Accounts

User Account Control (UAC) is a new set of infrastructure technologies in this version of Windows that helps prevent malicious programs, sometimes called "malware," from damaging a system, while also helping organizations to deploy a better-managed desktop.

With UAC, applications and tasks always run in the security context of a non-administrator account, unless an administrator specifically authorizes administrator-level access to the system. UAC stops the automatic installation of unauthorized applications, and prevents inadvertent changes to system settings.

How does UAC work?

In this version of Windows, there are two levels of users: standard users and administrators. Standard users are members of the Users group and administrators are members of the Administrators group on the computer.

Unlike previous versions of Windows, both standard users and administrators access resources and run applications in the security context of standard users by default. When any user logs on to a computer, the system creates an access token for the user. This access token contains information about the level of access that the user is granted, including specific security identifiers (SIDs) and Windows privileges. When an administrator logs on, this version of Windows creates two separate access tokens for the user: a standard user access token and an administrator access token. The standard user access token contains the same user-specific information as the administrator access token, but the administrative Windows privileges and SIDs have been removed. The standard user access token is used to start applications that do not perform administrative tasks ("standard user applications").

When the administrator needs to run applications that perform administrative tasks ("administrator applications"), this version of Windows prompts the users to change or "elevate" their security context from a standard user to an administrator. This default administrator user experience is called Admin Approval Mode. In this mode, applications require specific permission to run as an administrator application (an application that has the same access as an administrator).

When an administrator application is starting, by default a User Account Control message appears. If the user is an administrator, the message gives a choice to allow the application to start or to prevent it from starting. If the user is a standard user, the user can enter the user name and password of an account that is a member of the local Administrators group.

Welcom Center

The Welcome Center, a new Vista feature, is the window that welcomes you every single time you log in. This window conveniently displays how to get started with Vista and pay Microsoft for more products and services.

Windows CardSpace

Ever have to fill out a form on the Internet—name, address, email address—only to go to a differnt site that requests exactly the same information. CardSpace is Microsoft's attempt to solve that duplication-of-effort problem. You are supposed to create a profile containing this kind of information, like a digital ID card. You show your card at a site, and the site gest your information off the card, saving you all that retyping.

Windows Defender

It's important to run antispyware software whenever you're using your computer. Spyware and other potentially unwanted software can try to install itself on your computer any time

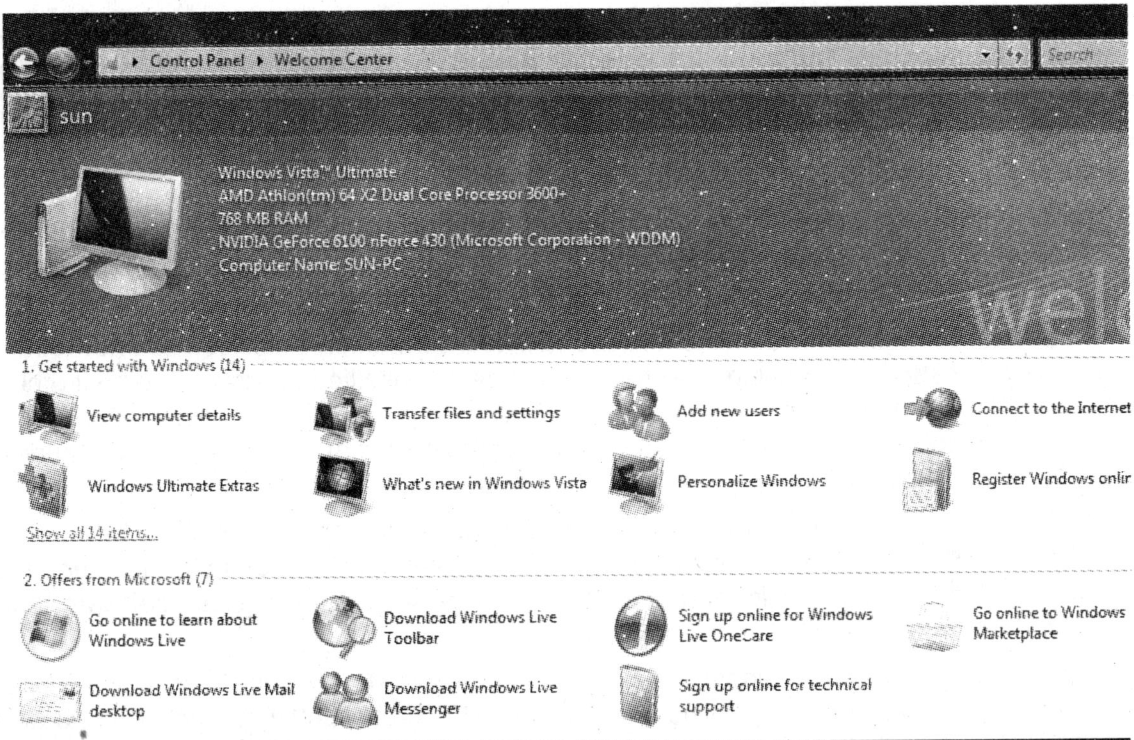
Control Panel ▸ Welcome Center
sun
Windows Vista™ Ultimate
AMD Athlon(tm) 64 X2 Dual Core Processor 3600+
768 MB RAM
NVIDIA GeForce 6100 nForce 430 (Microsoft Corporation - WDDM)
Computer Name: SUN-PC
1. Get started with Windows (14)
View computer details
Transfer files and settings
Add new users
Connect to the Internet
Windows Ultimate Extras
What's new in Windows Vista
Personalize Windows
Show all 14 items...
2. Offers from Microsoft (7)
Go online to learn about Windows Live
Download Windows Live Toolbar
Sign up online for Windows Live OneCare
Go online to Windows Marketplace
Download Windows Live Mail desktop
Download Windows Live Messenger
Sign up online for technical support

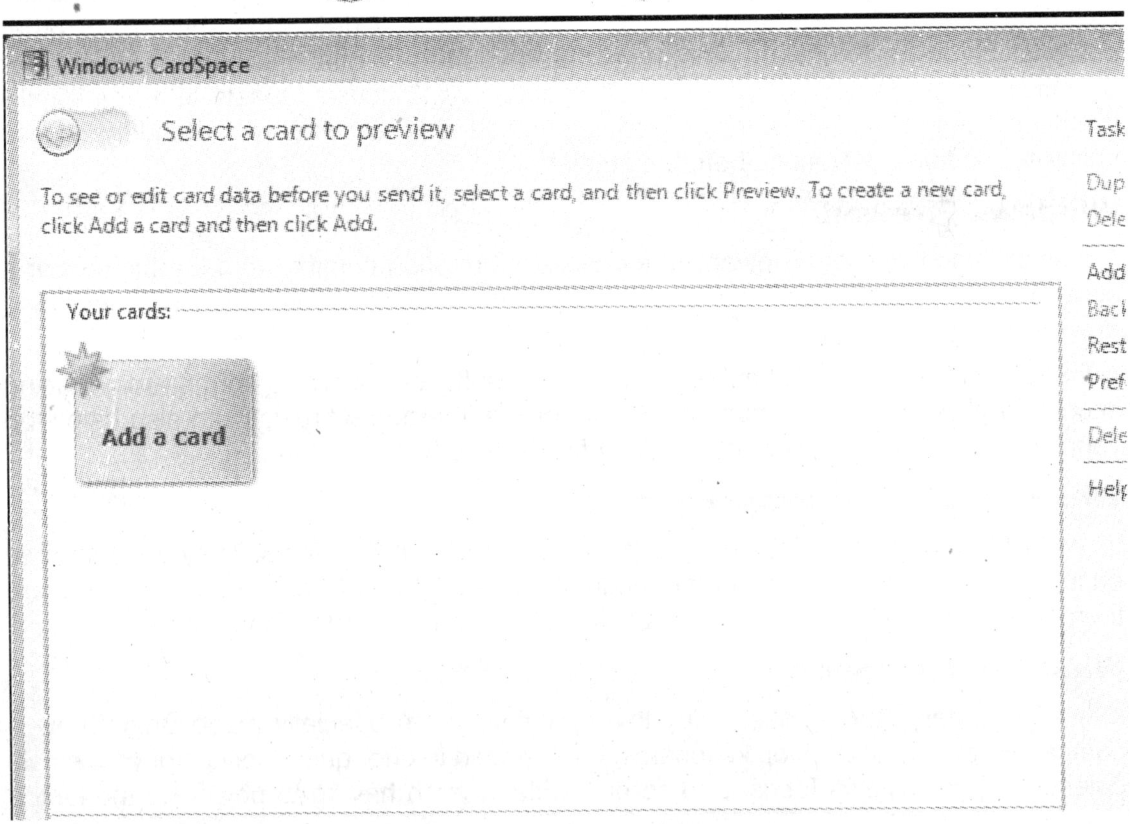
Windows CardSpace
Select a card to preview
To see or edit card data before you send it, select a card, and then click Preview. To create a new card, click Add a card and then click Add.
Your cards:
Add a card

you connect to the Internet. It can also infect your computer when you install some programs using a CD, DVD, or other removable media. Potentially unwanted or malicious software can also be programmed to run at unexpected times, not just when it is installed.

Windows Defender offers three ways to help keep spyware and other potentially unwanted software from infecting your computer:

- Real-time protection.Windows Defender alerts you when spyware or potentially unwanted software attempts to install itself or to run on your computer. It also alerts you when programs attempt to change important Windows settings.
- SpyNet community. The online Microsoft SpyNet community helps you see how other people respond to software that has not yet been classified for risks. Seeing if other members of the community allow software can help you choose whether to allow it on your computer. In turn, if you participate, your choices are added to the community ratings to help other people choose what to do.
- Scanning options. You can use Windows Defender to scan for spyware and other potentially unwanted software that might be installed on your computer, to schedule scans on a regular basis, and to automatically remove any malicious software that is detected during a scan.

When you use Windows Defender, it's important to have up-to-date definitions. Definitions are files that act like an ever-growing encyclopedia of potential software threats. Windows Defender uses definitions to determine if software that it detects is spyware or other potentially unwanted software, and then to alert you to potential risks. To help keep your definitions up to date, Windows Defender works with Windows Update to automatically install new definitions as they are released. You can also set Windows Defender to check online for updated definitions before scanning.

Windows Firewall

A firewall is software or hardware that checks information coming from the Internet or a network, and then either blocks it or allows it to pass through to your computer, depending on your firewall settings.

A firewall can help prevent hackers or malicious software (such as worms) from gaining access to your computer through a network or the Internet. A firewall can also help stop your computer from sending malicious software to other computers.

Windows Sidebar Properties

In Vista, there is a set of hybrid entities that Microsoft calls gadgets. They appear, all at once, floating in fornt of your other windows, at the right side of the screen. They are there when you first fire up Vista, or whenever you press Start + Space bar.

Windows SlideShow

It is a secondary screen, like a tiny text only display on specially made ShideShow—compatible laptops or desktop keyboards. Its designed to offer quick lookups of your email, calendar, Internet news feeds, and so on—without even having to power up the laptop

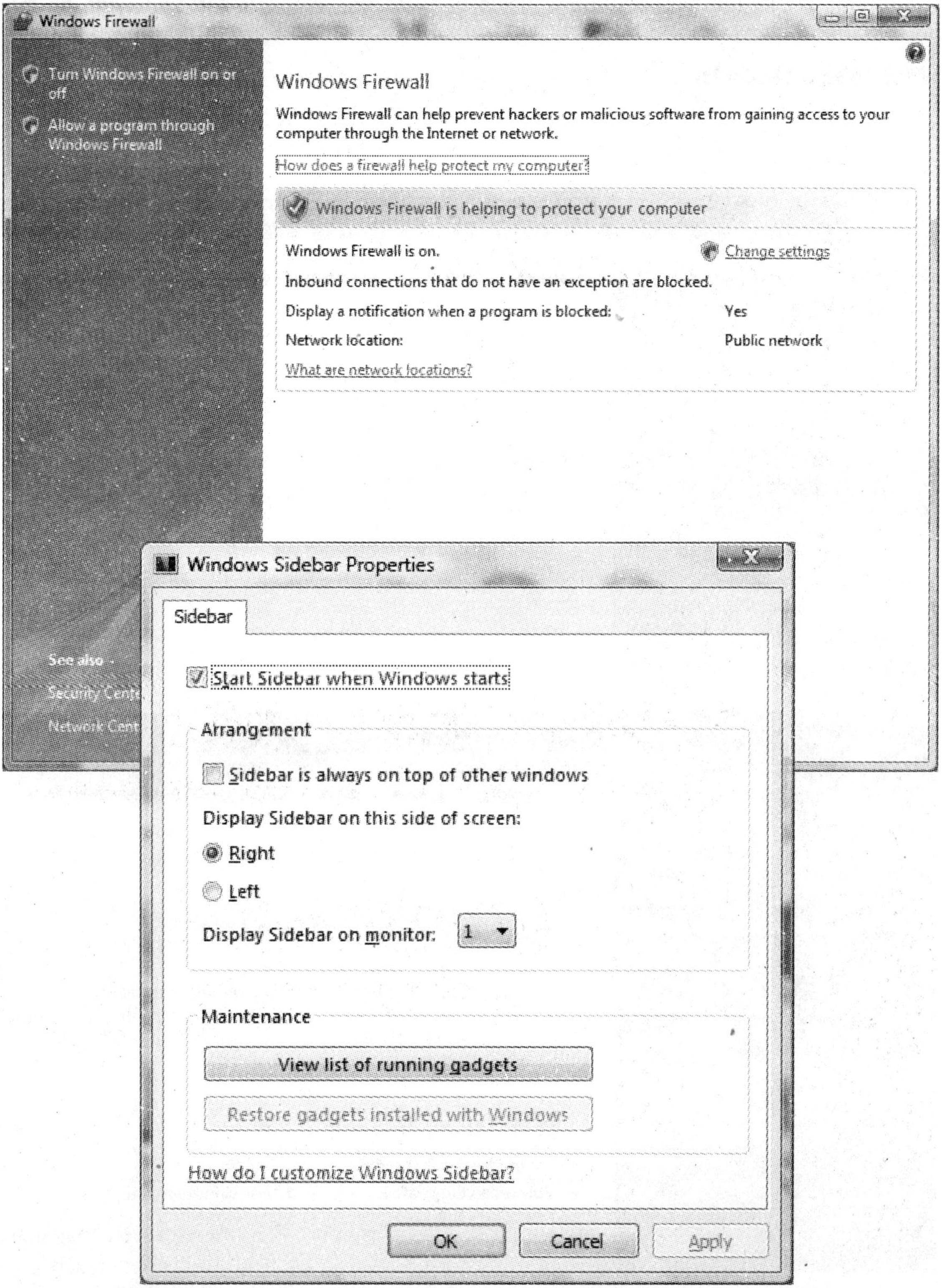
Windows Firewall
Turn Windows Firewall on or off
Allow a program through Windows Firewall
See also
Windows Firewall
Windows Firewall can help prevent hackers or malicious software from gaining access to your computer through the Internet or network.
How does a firewall help protect my computer?
Windows Firewall is helping to protect your computer
Windows Firewall is on.
Change settings
Inbound connections that do not have an exception are blocked.
Display a notification when a program is blocked:
Yes
Network location:
Public network
What are network locations?
Windows Sidebar Properties
Sidebar
Start Sidebar when Windows starts
Arrangement
Sidebar is always on top of other windows
Display Sidebar on this side of screen:
Right
Left
Display Sidebar on monitor:
1
Maintenance
View list of running gadgets
Restore gadgets installed with Windows
How do I customize Windows Sidebar?
OK
Cancel
Apply

itself. This applet lets you configure which gadgets are available for displaying on that little screen.

Windows Update

Because Windows is a constant work in progress, Microsoft frequently releases updates, fixes, patches, and drivers, in hope of constantly improving your computer's speed and security all the time.

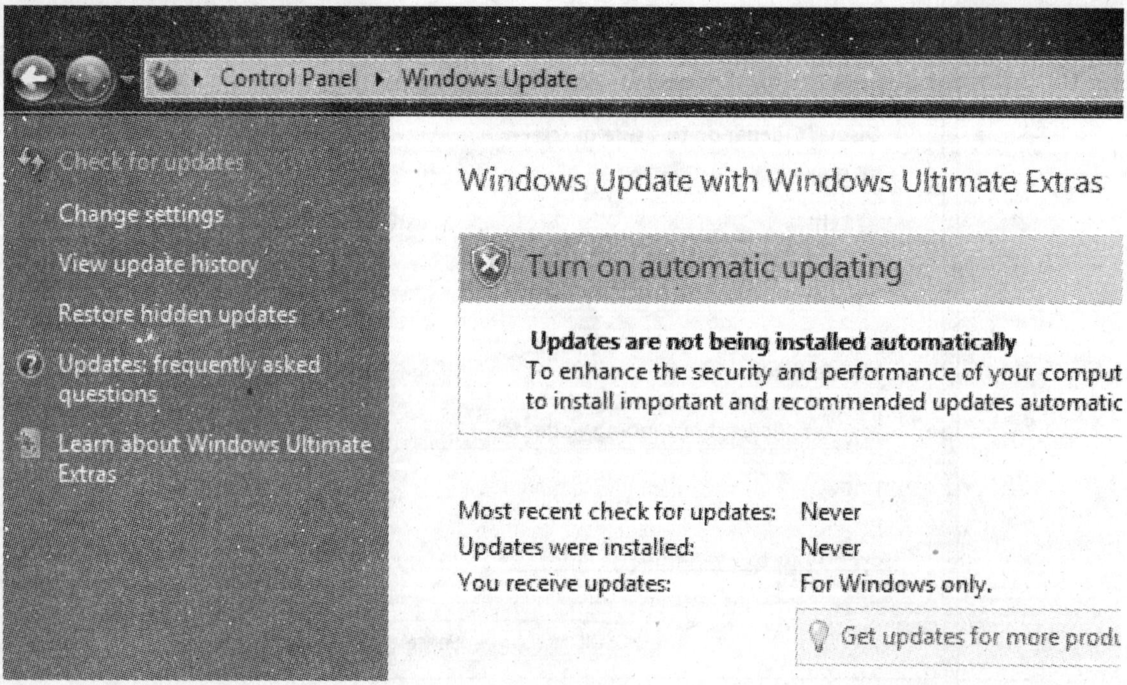

4

Configuring Your System with Windows Vista

Introduction

So far you have studied what all is available in Windows Vista, but what all is for you, you have to find out. Not all changes will be appropriate to your system. Some areas may never apply to how you use Windows Vista, but you may have need of them in future.

Date and Time Settings

Windows Vista keeps track of the date and time based on the information provided at the time of installation. It even makes the correct adjustment for daylight-saving time. If you elect to show the clock on the Taskbar, positioning the pointer over the time will produce a flyover box with the date inside.

Display clock on the Taskbar

1. Right-click on the Taskbar in a blank spot.
2. Select Properties from the pop-menu.
3. Select the Notification Area panel.
4. Make sure that the Clock is clicked in "Select which system icons to always show".

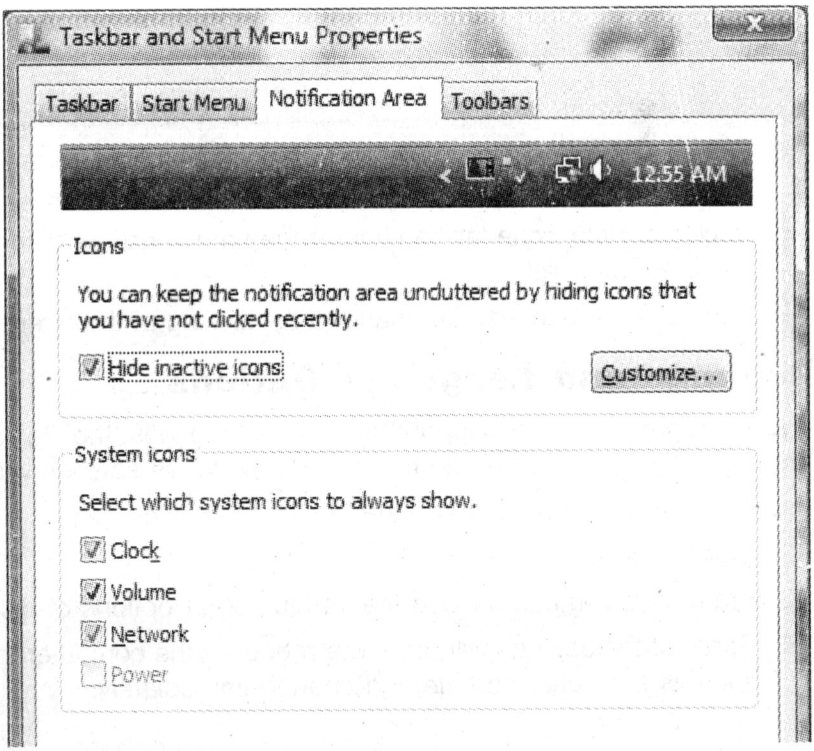

Change the Date or Time Settings

1. Click the Start button and select Control Panel.
2. Click the Date and Time.
3. Date and Time dialog box appear.

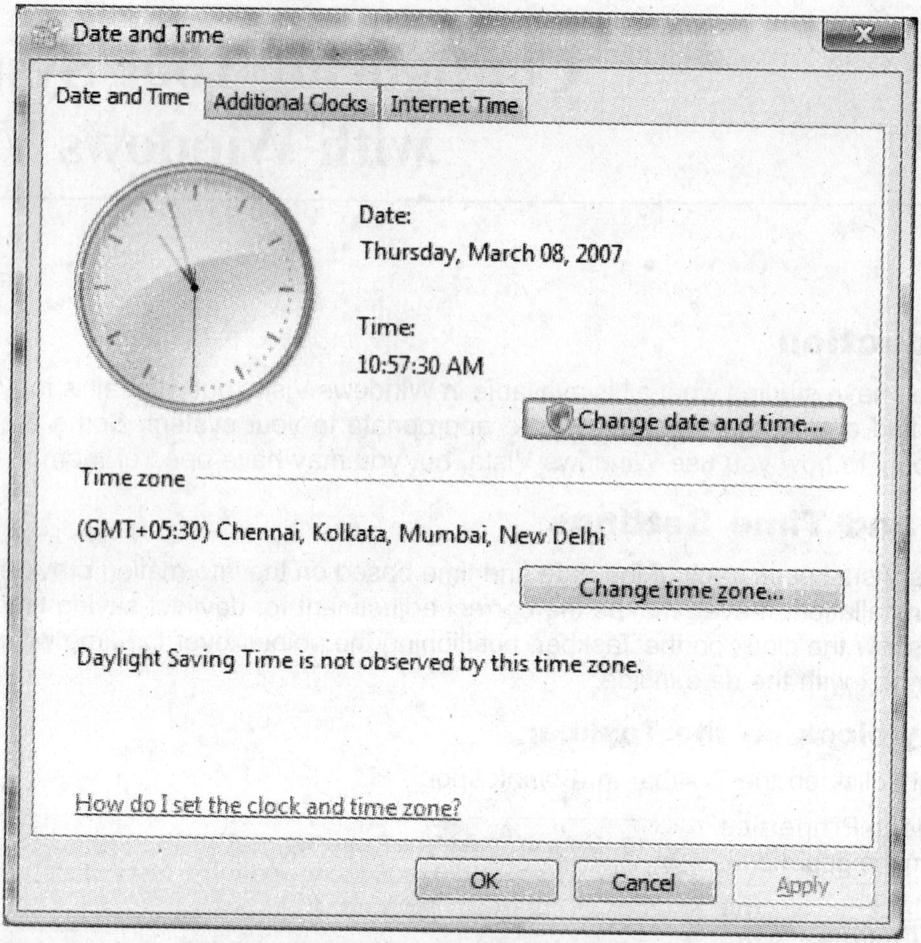

4. To adjust the clock, highlight the portion to be changed in the text box and click the up and down arrows until the time you want is displayed.
6. Click the Time Zone tab to change the time zone, selecting the one you want from the drop-down list.
7. Internet Time can also be changed by clicking at the Internet Time panel.

Regional and Language Options

If you use programs that support international settings, the Regional Settings icon in the Control Panel is where you go to choose how these settings will be displayed.

1. Click the Regional and Languages Options icon.
2. Select Formats.
3. From here you can choose the various other options of display.
4. Some of the settings will require a reboot of the computer to take effect, but others, such as the date and time, will change immediately.

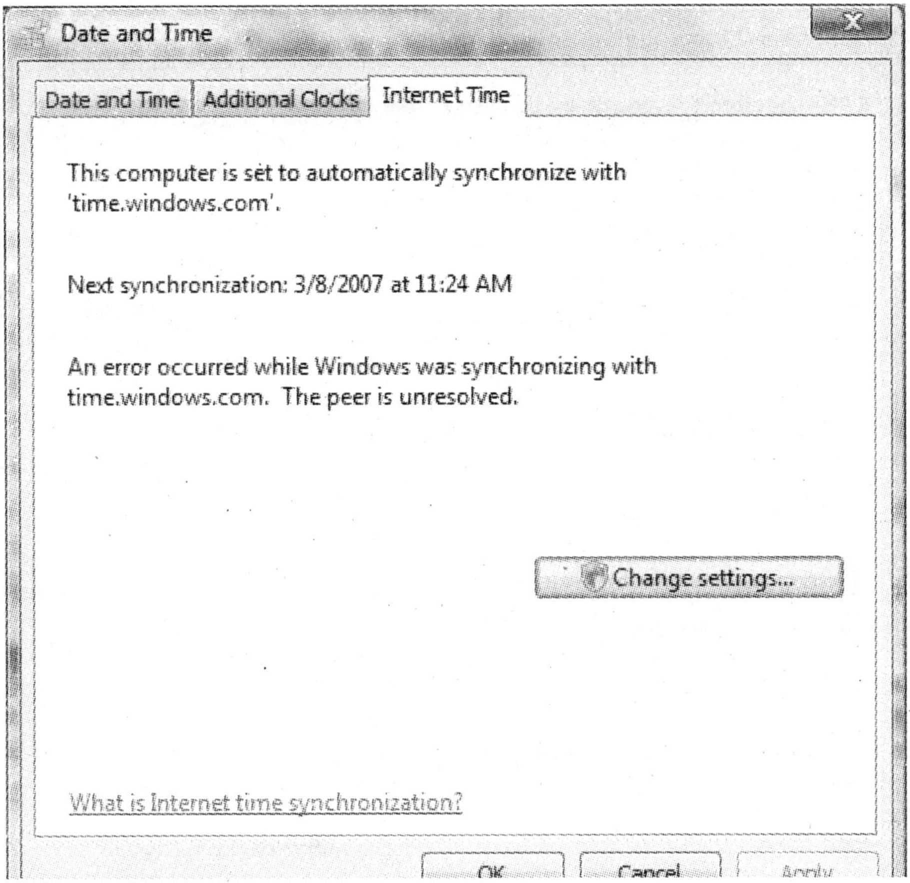

5. Using languages option you can take the support of various other languages which Window supports.
6. Among the other panels which you can change are Location, Keyboards and Languages, and Admistrative.

Keyboard Settings

The installation routine of Windows Vista finds the keyboard plugged into your computer and recognizes it. If you need to change keyboards, adjust the keyboard's speed, or install a keyboard designed for another language, do the following:

1. Click the Start button.
2. Select Control Panel.
3. Click at Keyboard icon to get the keyboard dialog box.
3. One of the feature is Keyboard Speed

Keyboard Speed

In the Keyboard Properties dialog box, click the Speed tab to adjust keyboard rates. Here are the available settings:

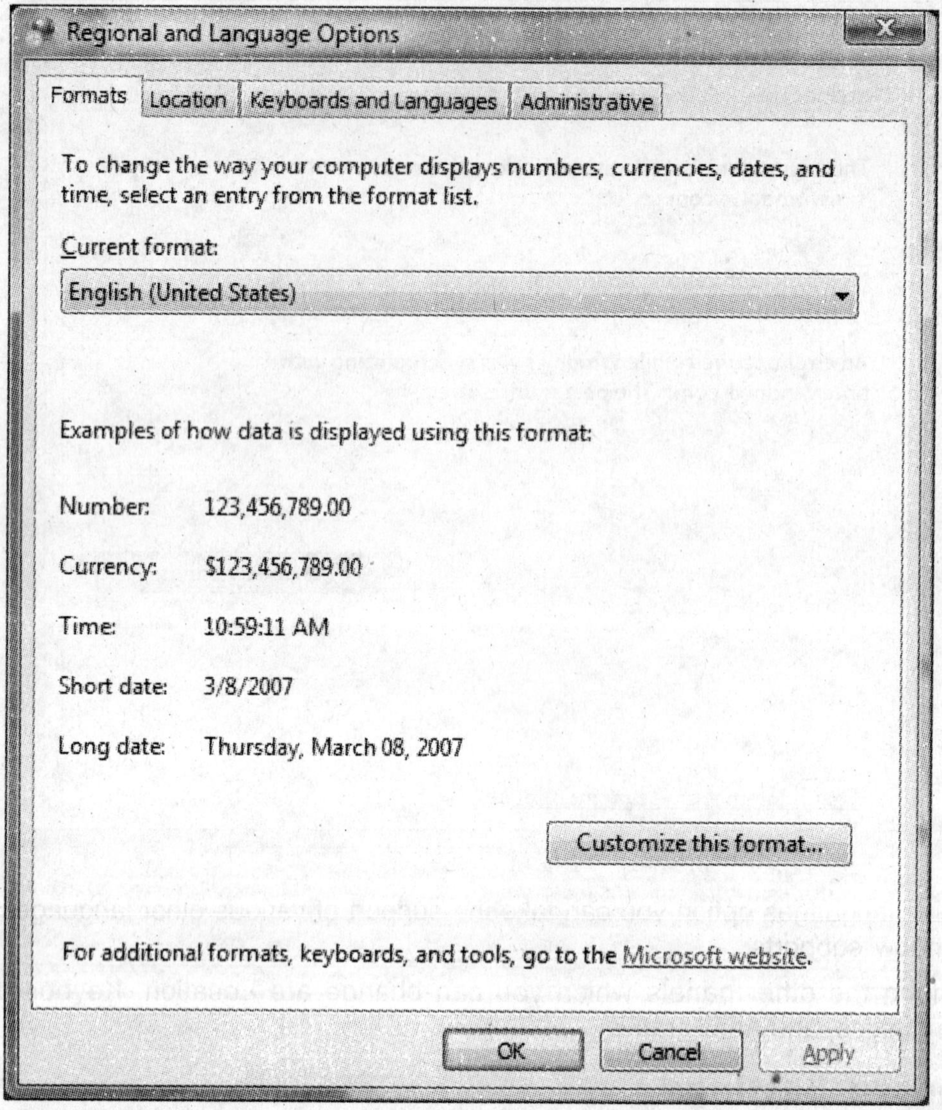
Regional and Language Options
Formats
Location
Keyboards and Languages
Administrative
To change the way your computer displays numbers, currencies, dates, and time, select an entry from the format list.
Current format:
English (United States)
Examples of how data is displayed using this format:
Number: 123,456,789.00
Currency: $123,456,789.00
Time: 10:59:11 AM
Short date: 3/8/2007
Long date: Thursday, March 08, 2007
Customize this format...
For additional formats, keyboards, and tools, go to the Microsoft website.
OK
Cancel
Apply

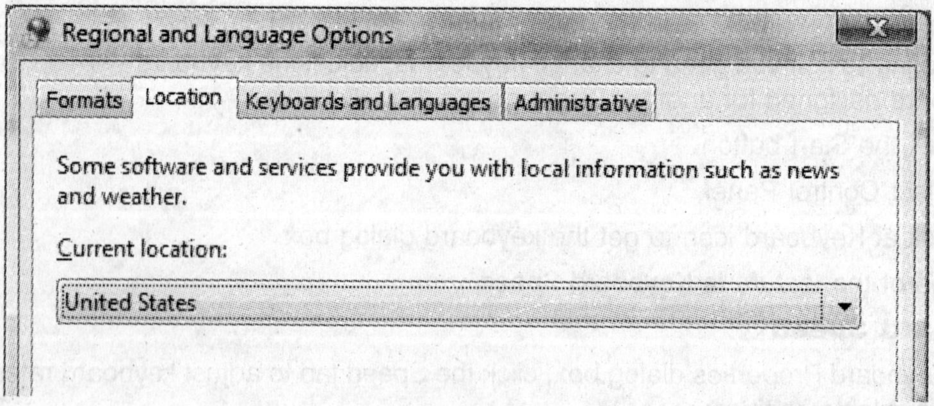
Regional and Language Options
Formats
Location
Keyboards and Languages
Administrative
Some software and services provide you with local information such as news and weather.
Current location:
United States

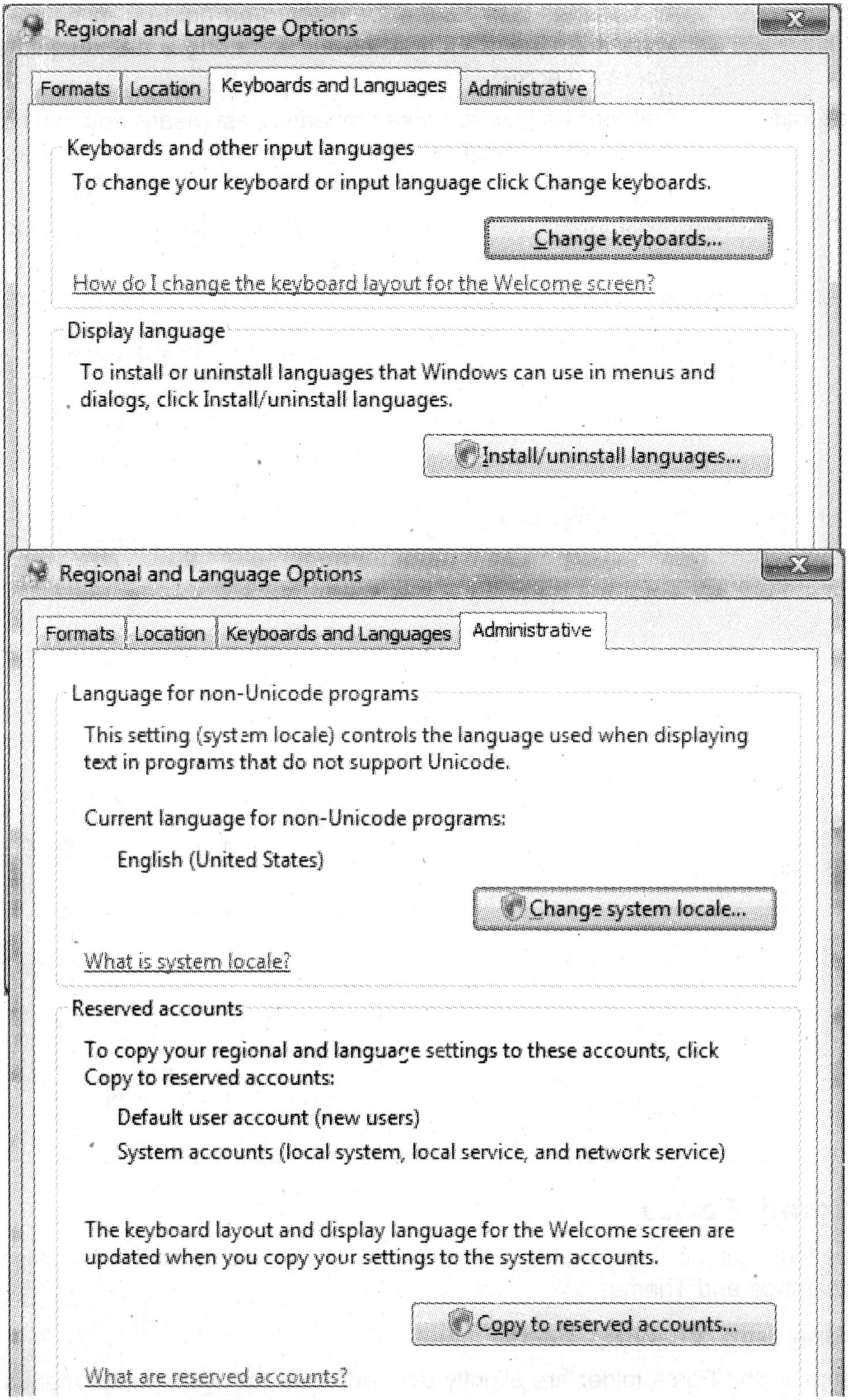
Regional and Language Options
Formats
Location
Keyboards and Languages
Administrative
Keyboards and other input languages
To change your keyboard or input language click Change keyboards.
Change keyboards...
How do I change the keyboard layout for the Welcome screen?
Display language
To install or uninstall languages that Windows can use in menus and dialogs, click Install/uninstall languages.
Install/uninstall languages...
Regional and Language Options
Formats
Location
Keyboards and Languages
Administrative
Language for non-Unicode programs
This setting (system locale) controls the language used when displaying text in programs that do not support Unicode.
Current language for non-Unicode programs:
English (United States)
Change system locale...
What is system locale?
Reserved accounts
To copy your regional and language settings to these accounts, click Copy to reserved accounts:
Default user account (new users)
System accounts (local system, local service, and network service)
The keyboard layout and display language for the Welcome screen are updated when you copy your settings to the system accounts.
Copy to reserved accounts...
What are reserved accounts?

Repeat delay Determines how long a key has to be held down before it starts repeating. The difference between the Long and Short setting is only about a second.

Repeat rate Determines how fast a key repeats. Fast means you can hold down a key and almost instantly get a stream of letters. Click in the practice area to test this setting.

Cursor blink rate Makes the cursor blink faster or slower. The blinking cursor on the left demonstrates the setting.

The other one is Hardware, which shows the hardware features of the keyboard.

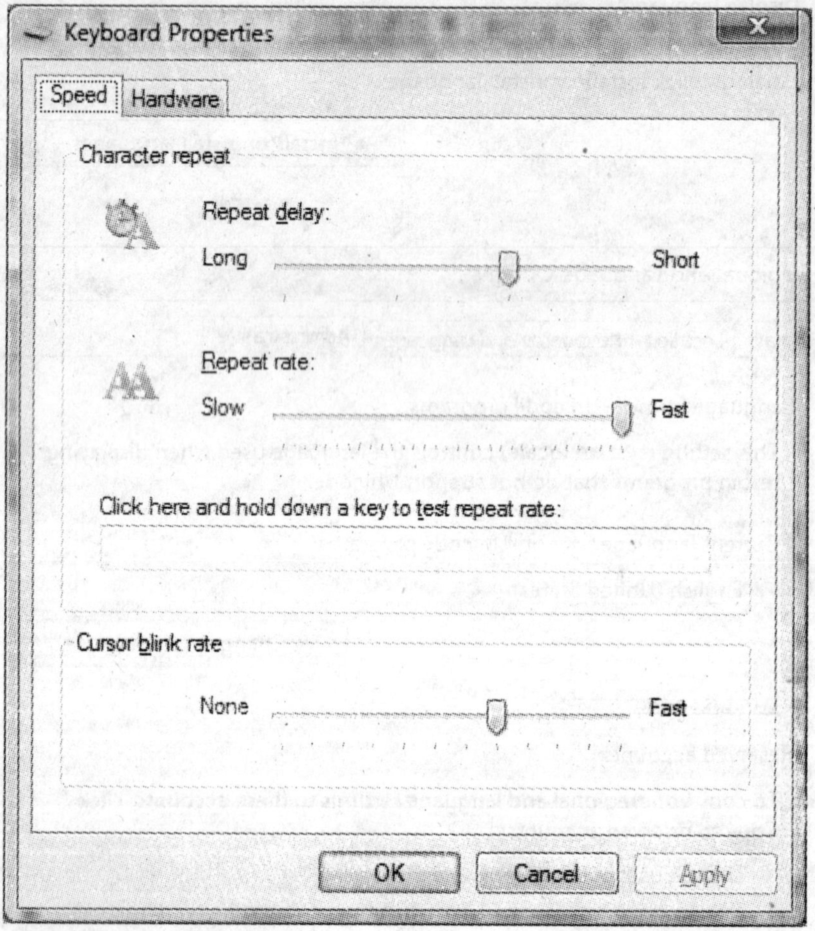

Managing Fonts

TrueType fonts can be easily managed in Windows. Fonts are located in See Also part of the Appearance and Themes.

Selecting and Viewing Fonts

The menus in the Fonts folder are slightly different from the usual folder menus. In the

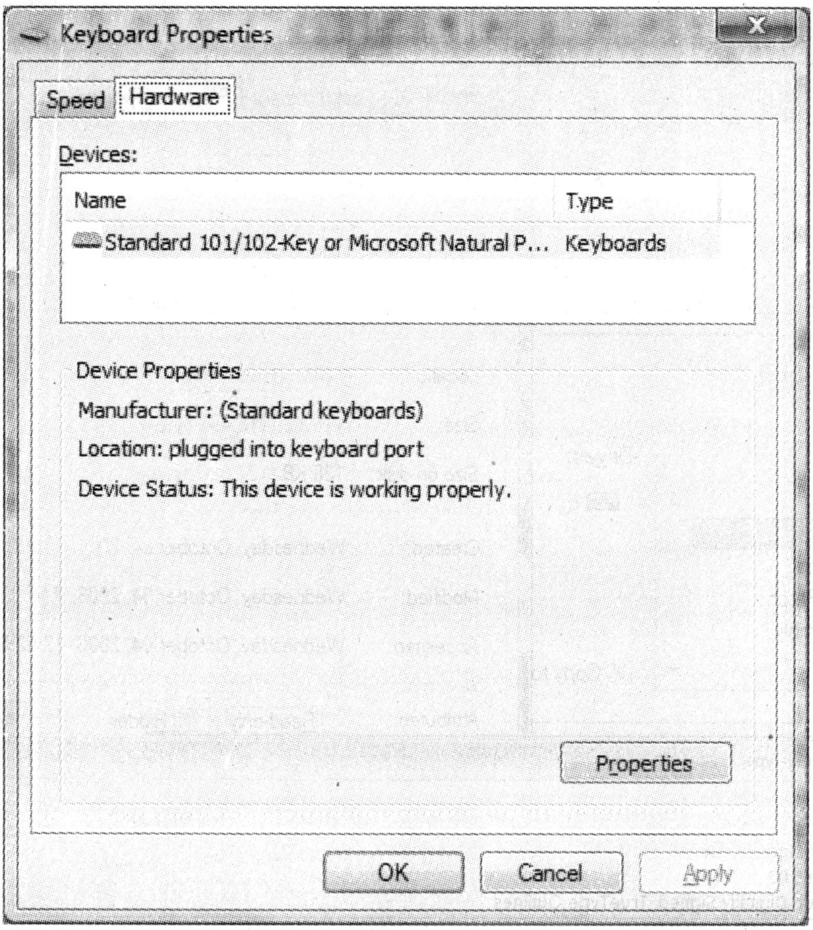

view menu, you will find, in addition to the choices of viewing icons and lists, an option called List Fonts by Similarity. Choose that option to see a view like that is shown below. Select a font in the drop-down box at the top, and the other fonts will line up in terms of their degree of similarity. To see how similar, you can right-click any of the font names and select Open from the pop-menu menu. Windows will open with a complete view of the font in question. TrueType fonts located elsewhere can be moved into this folder.

Fonts don't have to be physically located in the Windows/Fonts folder to be recognized by Windows Vista. You can make a shortcut to a font in another folder and put the shortcut in the Fonts folder. The shortcut is all you need for the font to be installed.

Installing New Fonts

It is quite easy. Select Install New Font from the File Menu in the font dialog box. Once selected you can tell the system where the fonts which you want to add are lying. Highlight the font or fonts which you want to install and click Ok button to install the fonts.

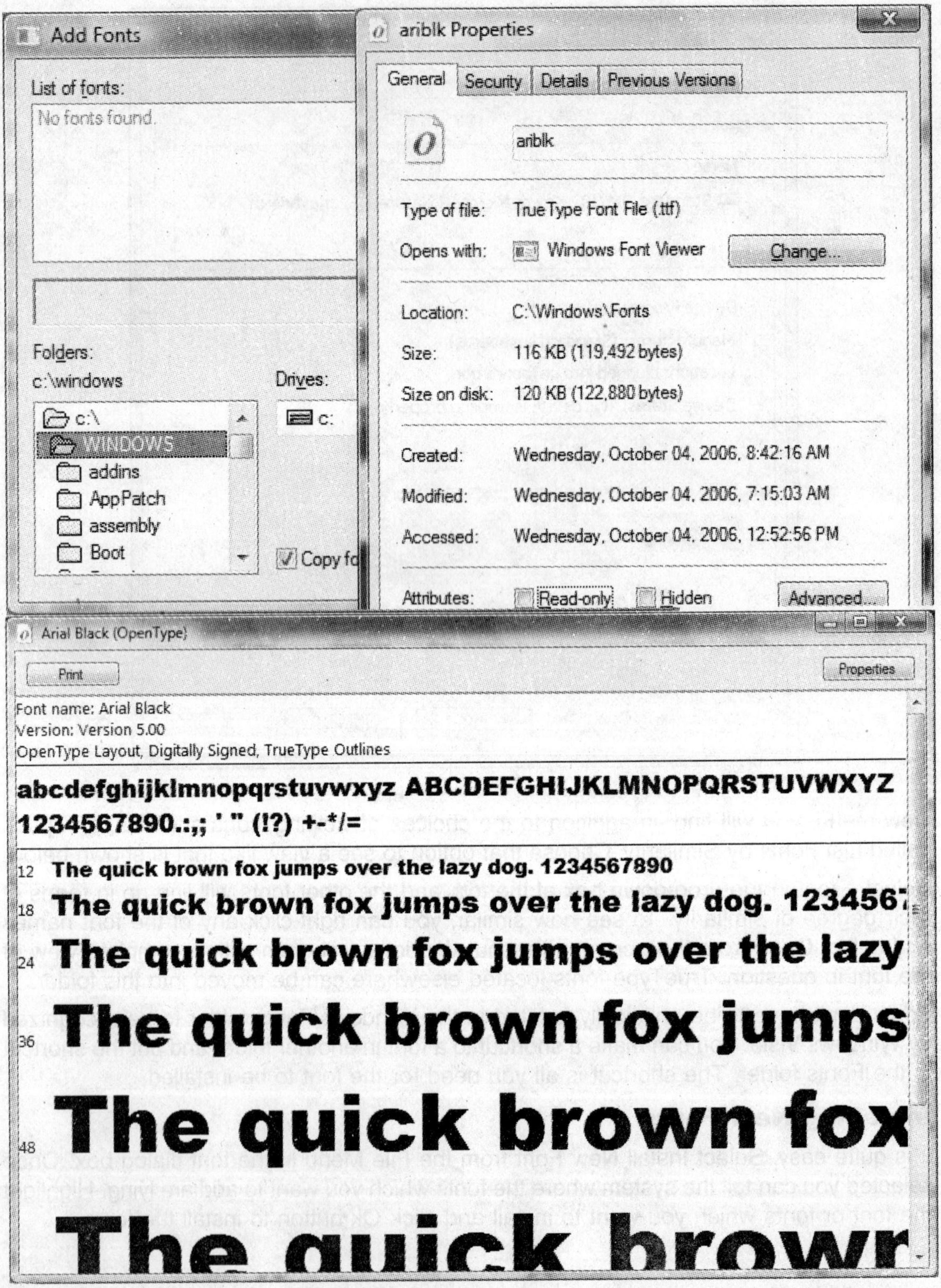
Add Fonts
List of fonts:
No fonts found.
Folders:
c:\windows
Drives:
c:\
WINDOWS
addins
AppPatch
assembly
Boot
c:
aribIk Properties
General
Security
Details
Previous Versions
aribIk
Type of file: TrueType Font File (.ttf)
Opens with: Windows Font Viewer
Change...
Location: C:\Windows\Fonts
Size: 116 KB (119,492 bytes)
Size on disk: 120 KB (122,880 bytes)
Created: Wednesday, October 04, 2006, 8:42:16 AM
Modified: Wednesday, October 04, 2006, 7:15:03 AM
Accessed: Wednesday, October 04, 2006, 12:52:56 PM
Attributes: Read-only Hidden
Advanced...
Arial Black (OpenType)
Print
Properties
Font name: Arial Black
Version: Version 5.00
OpenType Layout, Digitally Signed, TrueType Outlines
abcdefghijklmnopqrstuvwxyz ABCDEFGHIJKLMNOPQRSTUVWXYZ
1234567890.:,; ' " (!?) +-*/=
12 The quick brown fox jumps over the lazy dog. 1234567890
18 The quick brown fox jumps over the lazy dog.
24 The quick brown fox jumps over the lazy
36 The quick brown fox jumps
48 The quick brown fox

Passwords

When you sign on to Windows Vista for the first time, you are asked to provide a name and password. If you are the only one using a computer and you don't want to deal with a password everytime your turn the machine on, leave the password blank.

On the other hand, if you later want to start using a password or change the one you have, click User Accounts icon in the Control Panel. Here among the other options you have the option of changing user name, password, picture, etc.

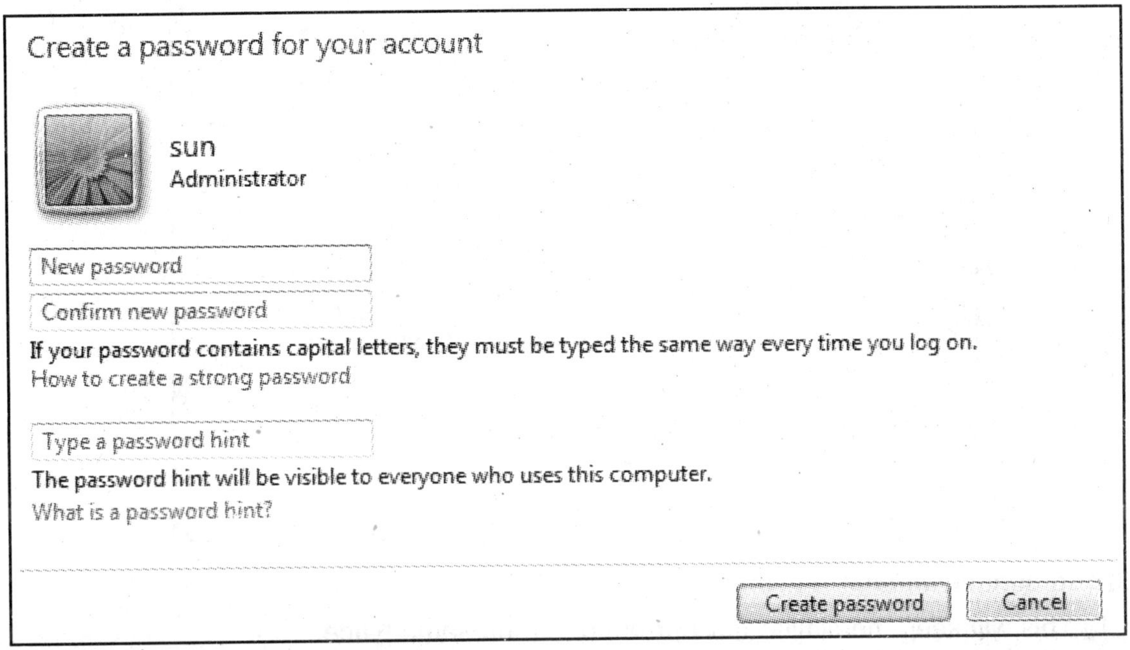

Setting Taskbar Properties

To set the taskbar properties do the following:

1. Right-click on the Taskbar in a blank spot.
2. Click Properties.

Locking taskbar

1. Select or deselect Lock the taskbar.
2. Put a checkmark in the box next to Show Clock.

Autohiding the taskbar

1. Select or deselect Auto-hide the taskbar.
2. Put a checkmark in the box next to Show Clock.

Keep the taskbar on top of other windows

1. This will make sure that taskbar is above all the windows.

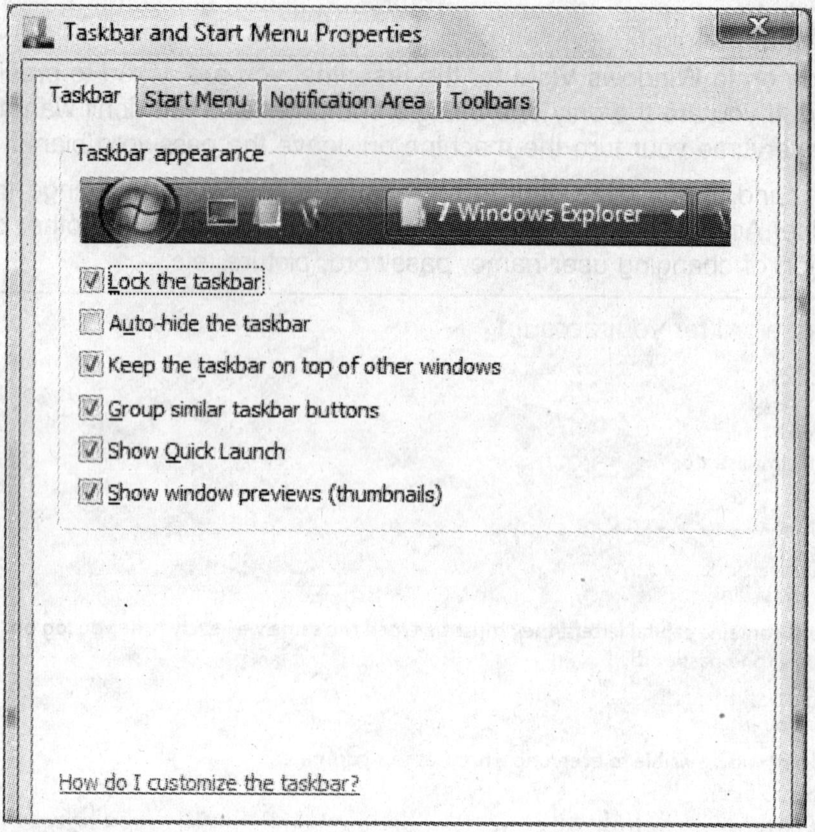

Group similar taskbar button

1. This will keep the similar taskbar button at the same place.

Show Quick Launch

1. You can choose to show/hide the Quick Launch.

Show window previews (thumbnails)

1. You can show or hide window previews.

Setting Monitor Display Properties

Options here will depend on monitor and adapter type being used.

1. Right-click empty area on desktop.
2. Click Personalize.

Select a colour quality

1. Select the desired palette in Colour palette list.

Set desktop

1. Drag a picture to make it the desktop background.

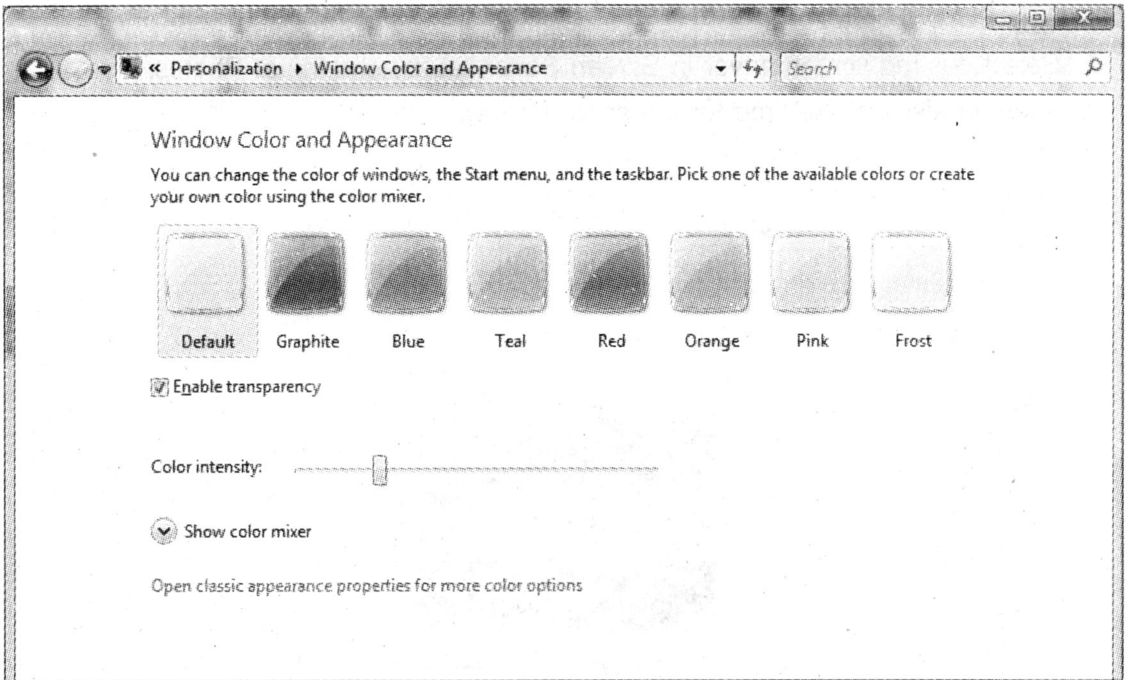

« Personalization ▸ Window Color and Appearance
Search
Window Color and Appearance
You can change the color of windows, the Start menu, and the taskbar. Pick one of the available colors or create your own color using the color mixer.
Default
Graphite
Blue
Teal
Red
Orange
Pink
Frost
Enable transparency
Color intensity:
Show color mixer
Open classic appearance properties for more color options

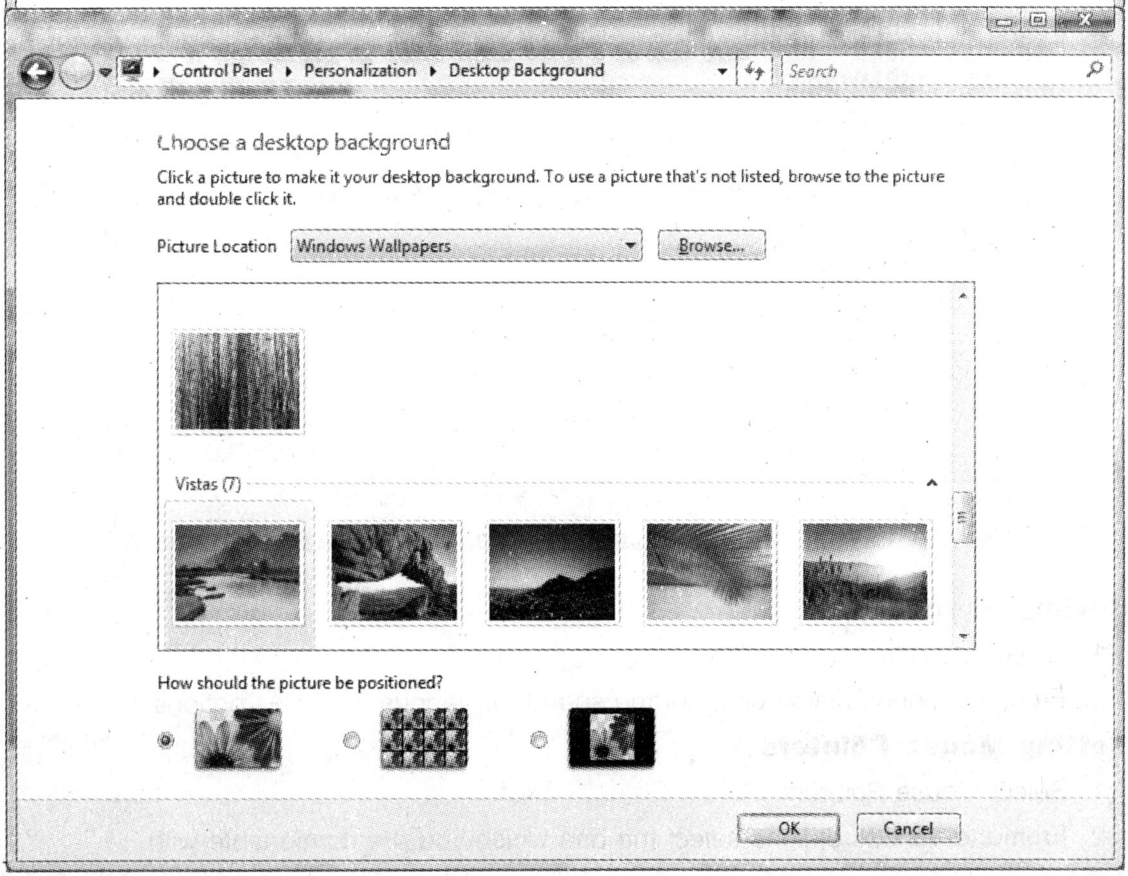

▸ Control Panel ▸ Personalization ▸ Desktop Background
Search
Choose a desktop background
Click a picture to make it your desktop background. To use a picture that's not listed, browse to the picture and double click it.
Picture Location
Windows Wallpapers
Browse...
Vistas (7)
How should the picture be positioned?
OK
Cancel

Setting Screen Saver

1. Select desired screen saver in Screen Saver list, by clicking at Photos.
2. You can also set the time for the screen saver.
3. See the preview of the screen saver.

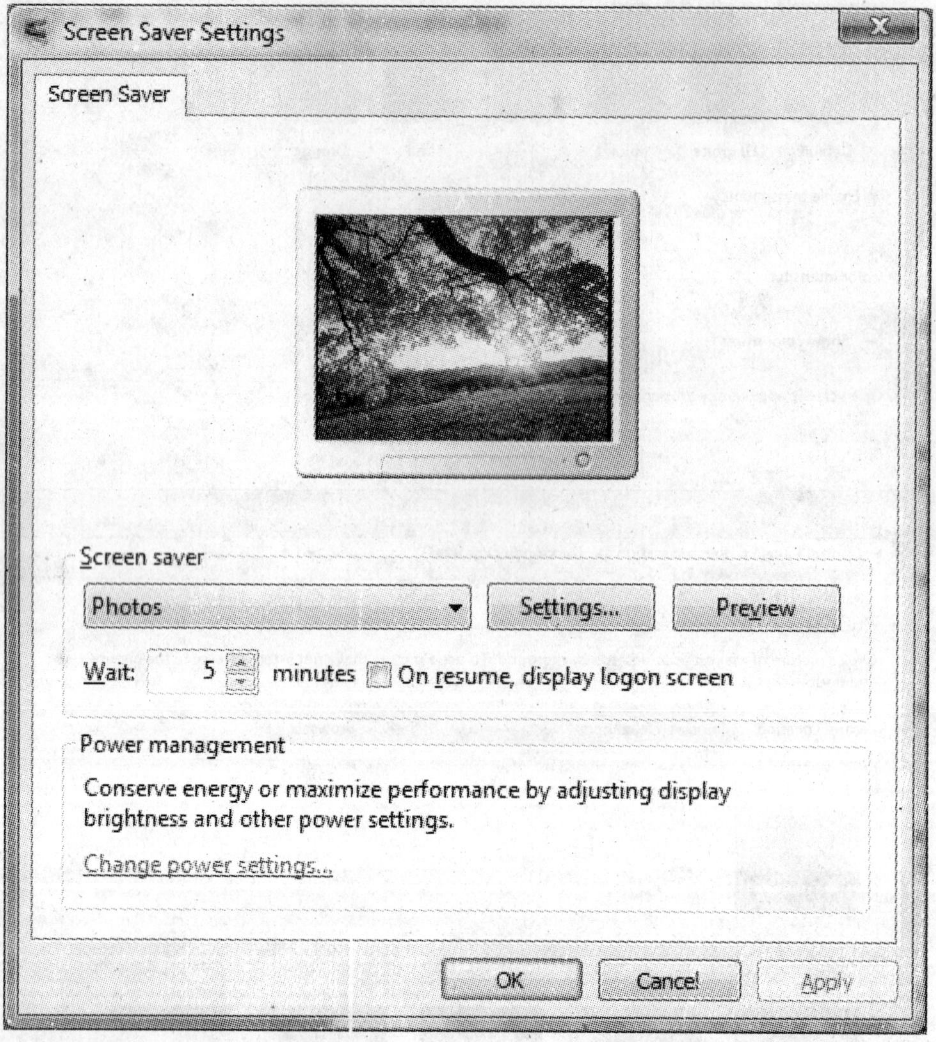

Setting Sounds

1. Select Sounds.
2. From the Sound dialog box, set the sound for various Windows options.

Setting Mouse Pointers

1. Select Mouse Pointers.
2. From the various options select the one which you are comfortable with.

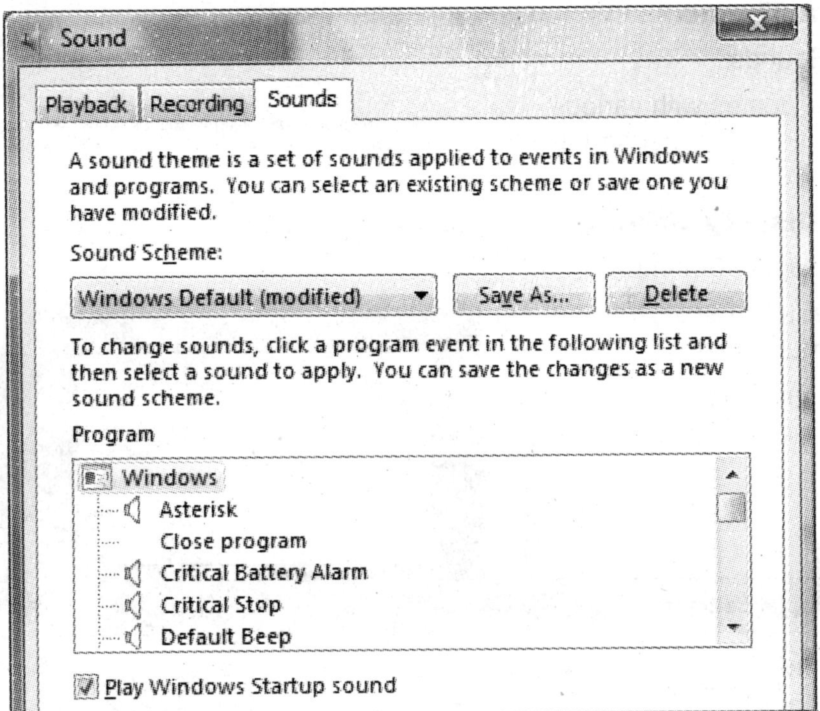
Sound
Playback
Recording
Sounds
A sound theme is a set of sounds applied to events in Windows and programs. You can select an existing scheme or save one you have modified.
Sound Scheme:
Windows Default (modified)
Save As...
Delete
To change sounds, click a program event in the following list and then select a sound to apply. You can save the changes as a new sound scheme.
Program
Windows
Asterisk
Close program
Critical Battery Alarm
Critical Stop
Default Beep
Play Windows Startup sound

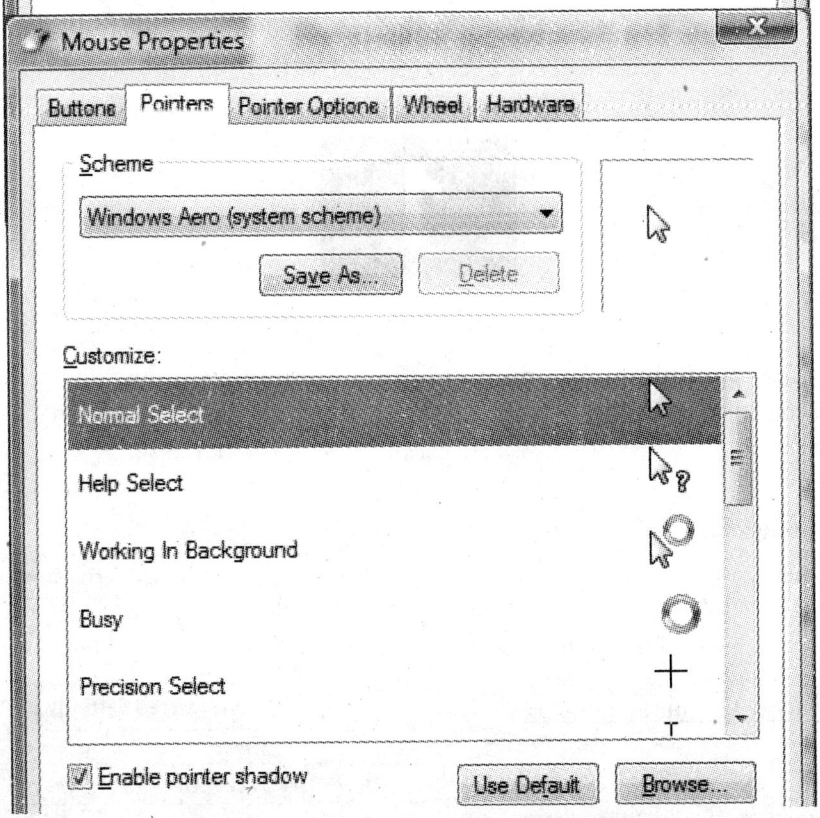
Mouse Properties
Buttons
Pointers
Pointer Options
Wheel
Hardware
Scheme
Windows Aero (system scheme)
Save As...
Delete
Customize:
Normal Select
Help Select
Working In Background
Busy
Precision Select
Enable pointer shadow
Use Default
Browse...

Selecting a Theme

1. Select Sounds.
2. Windows comes with various themes, you can choose the one wanted by you.

Selecting Display Settings

1. Select Display Settings.
2. Choose the resolution to match your monitor.
3. Choose the colors.

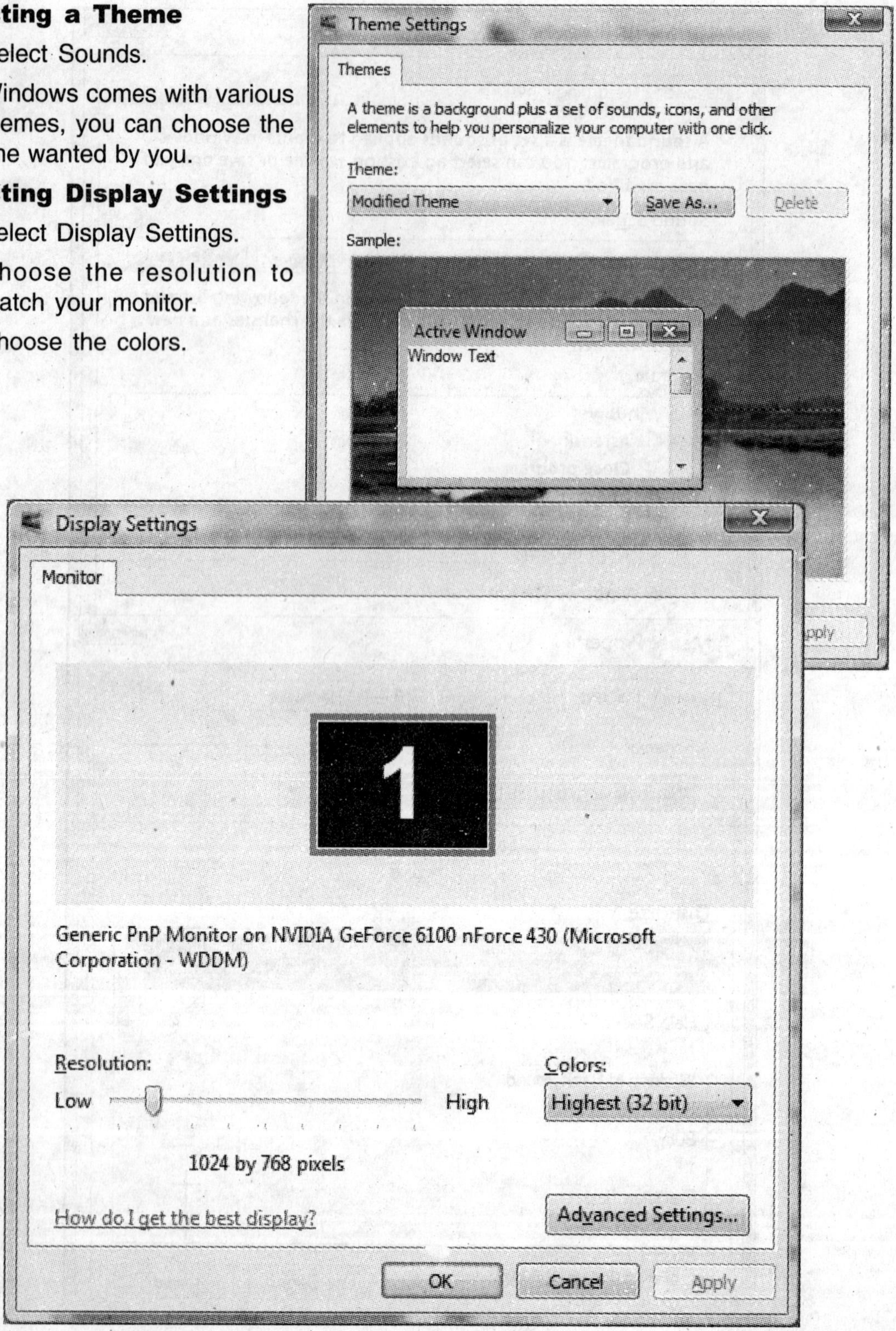

Setting up Networking and Internet

Now I will introduce you to Windows Vista's ability to perform in a multitude of network configurations. In addition to working well with major network operating systems, Windows Vista has sophisticated 32-bit network components built-in, allowing Windows Vista to fulfil many network demands that you may want to place on it.

With built-in sharing, printer sharing and access control, Windows Vista can operate as a high-performance **peer-to-peer network** operating system. Additionally Windows Vista can operate well as a client on a **client-server network**.

Peer-To-Peer Networking

The term peer-to-peer networking refers to a type of network where every computer connected to the network can share its resources with the rest of the network. In other words, every computer on the network can act like a file server and share its files and printers with other computers.

Setting up Network and Internet

Windows Vista allow you to set up Networking in a flash. It takes you through a set of wizards and once you have given all the answers correctly, your network is installed.

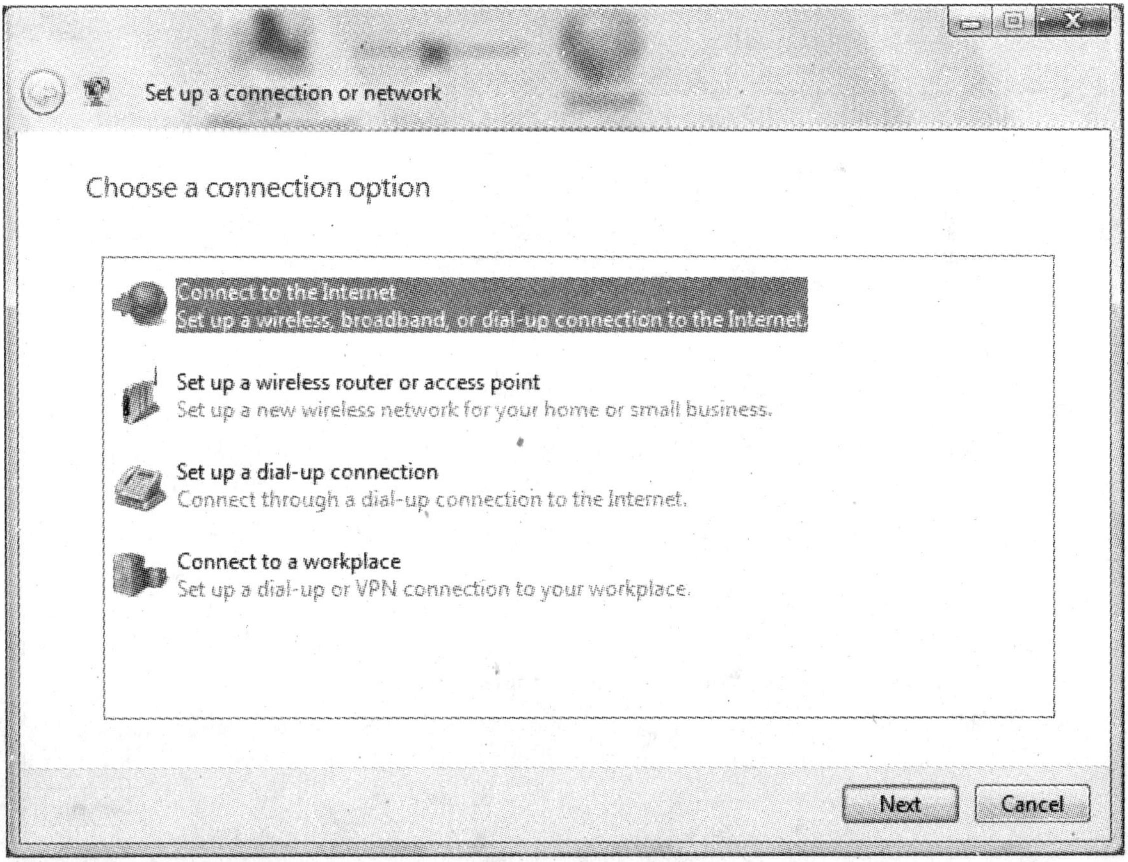

To set up networking do the following,

1. Click the **Start** button.
2. Select **Control Panel**.
3. Select **Network and Internet Connections**.
4. Click on the **Network Connections** icon.
5. From the Network Tasks click at **Connect to the Internet** task button.
6. The first wizard screen as shown below comes on screen.
7. Click Next to reach next screen.
8. Select among the options which you want to use. In our case, we would select Set up home or small office network.
9. Click at the option and press Next.
10. Another wizard screen would come on screen. Press Next to move further.
11. The next screen tells you that a network can be used for sharing files, printers, etc.

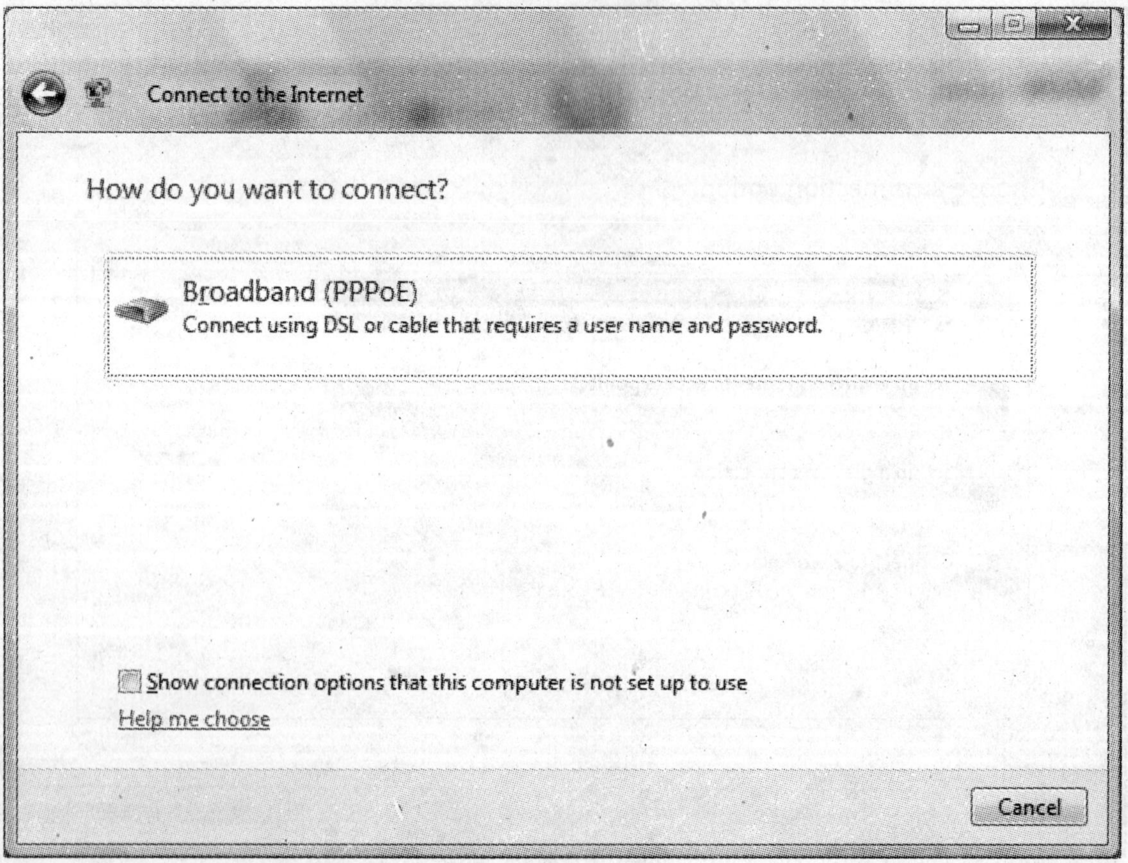

12. Next it tells you what all you would need for networking.
13. Press Next.
14. The next screen tells you about connection methods.
15. Next it asks you to provide a name to the computer.
16. Next it asks you name the network.
17. The next screen asks you to confirm the information given by you so far.
18. The connection takes some time to take place.
19. Well it says that it is alomost done.
20. Next you can provide one of the information required by the system.
21. If you provide the system with Windows Vista CD, it will take the required files from there and ask you to restart the computer.
22. Once done, your computer will have the networking installed in it.

After these options have been set, your computer is ready to share its resources with the other computers on the network. Now let's see how to share files on the network.

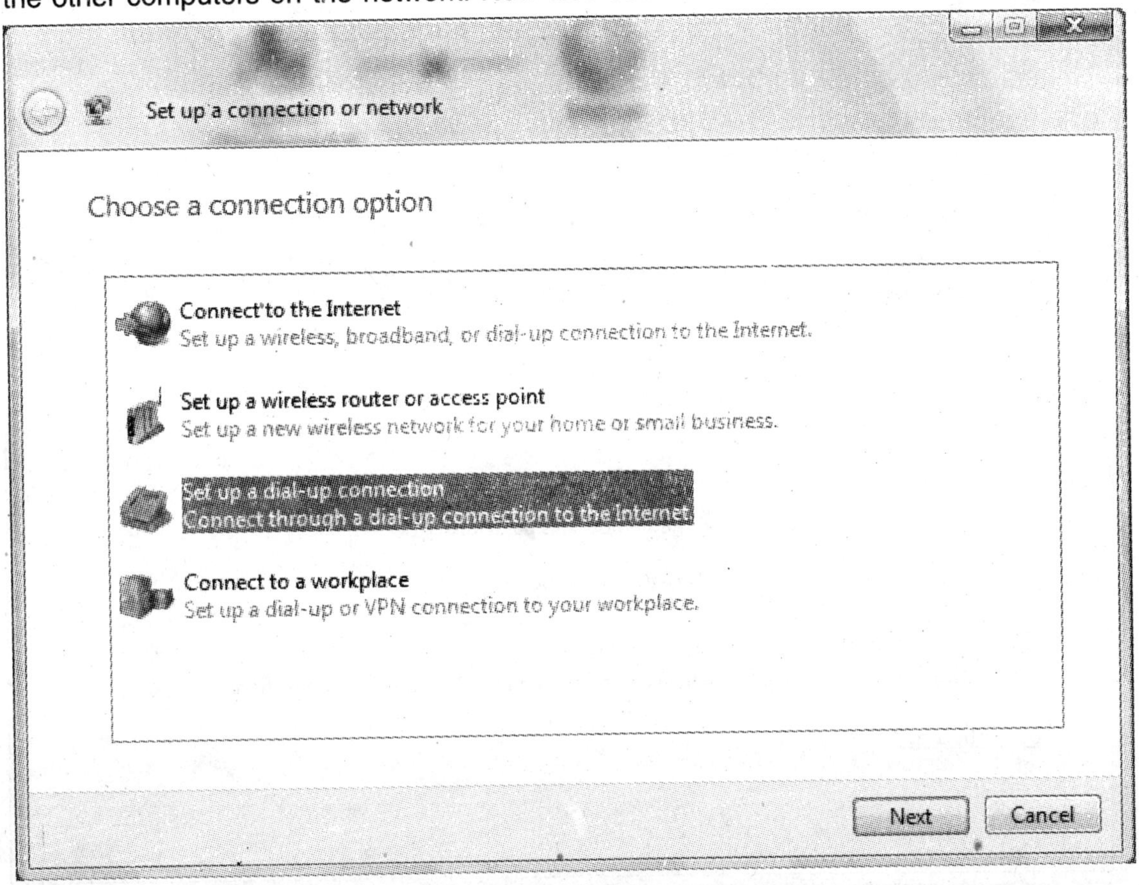

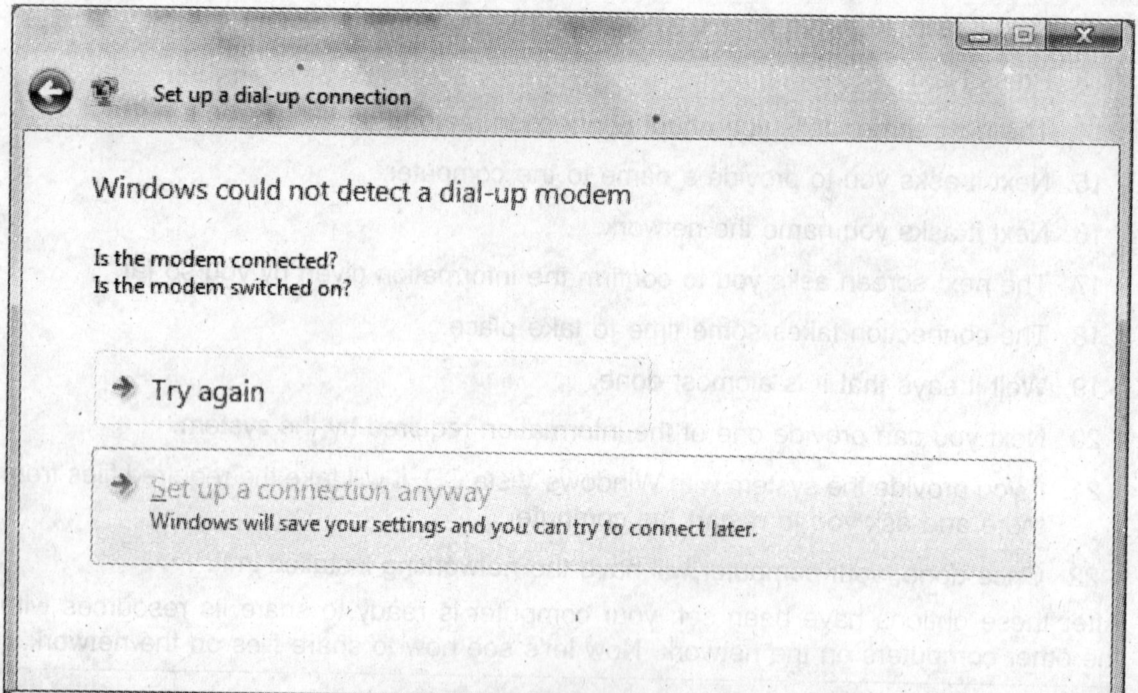
Set up a dial-up connection
Windows could not detect a dial-up modem
Is the modem connected?
Is the modem switched on?
Try again
Set up a connection anyway
Windows will save your settings and you can try to connect later.

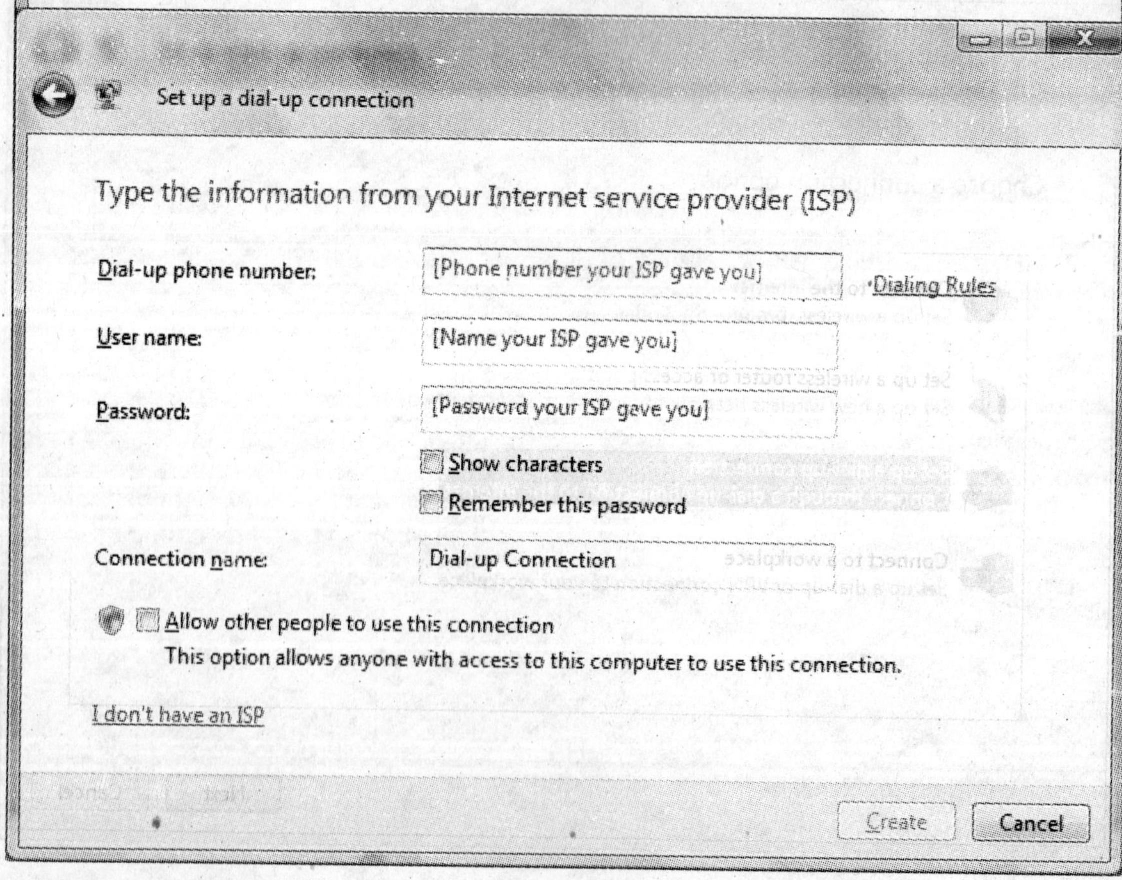
Set up a dial-up connection
Type the information from your Internet service provider (ISP)
Dial-up phone number:
[Phone number your ISP gave you]
Dialing Rules
User name:
[Name your ISP gave you]
Password:
[Password your ISP gave you]
Show characters
Remember this password
Connection name:
Dial-up Connection
Allow other people to use this connection
This option allows anyone with access to this computer to use this connection.
I don't have an ISP
Create
Cancel

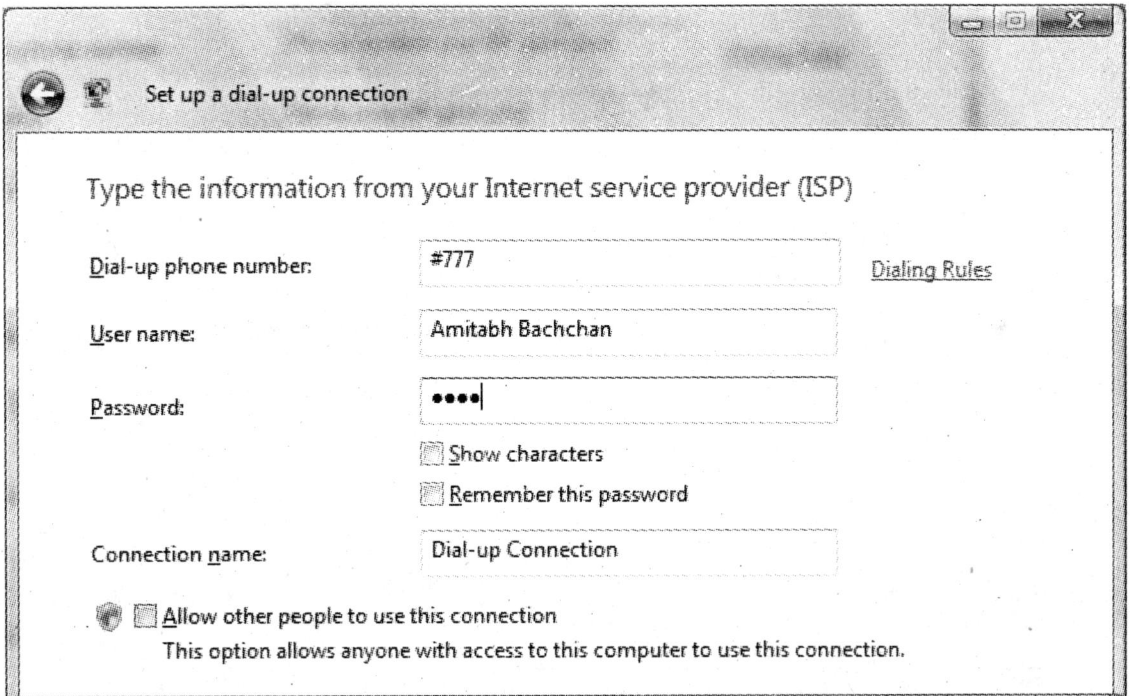
Set up a dial-up connection
Type the information from your Internet service provider (ISP)
Dial-up phone number:
#777
Dialing Rules
User name:
Amitabh Bachchan
Password:
Show characters
Remember this password
Connection name:
Dial-up Connection
Allow other people to use this connection
This option allows anyone with access to this computer to use this connection.

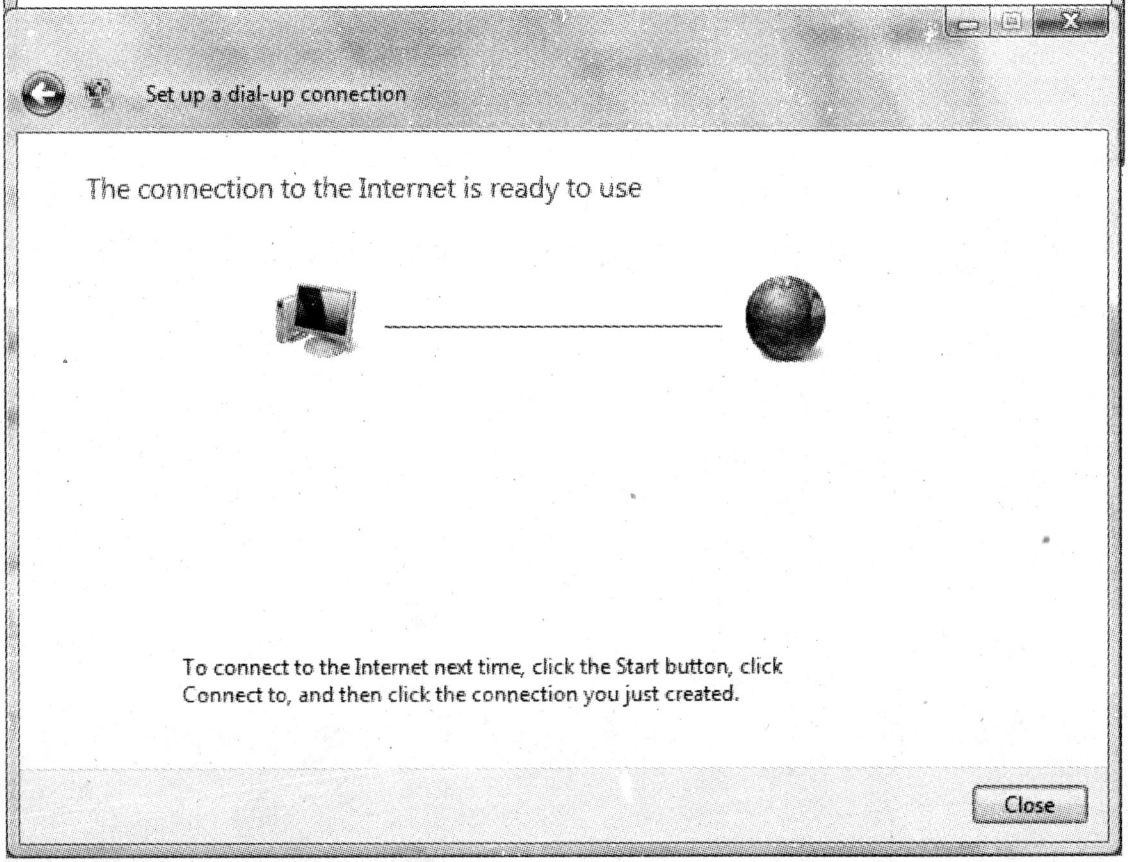
Set up a dial-up connection
The connection to the Internet is ready to use
To connect to the Internet next time, click the Start button, click
Connect to, and then click the connection you just created.
Close

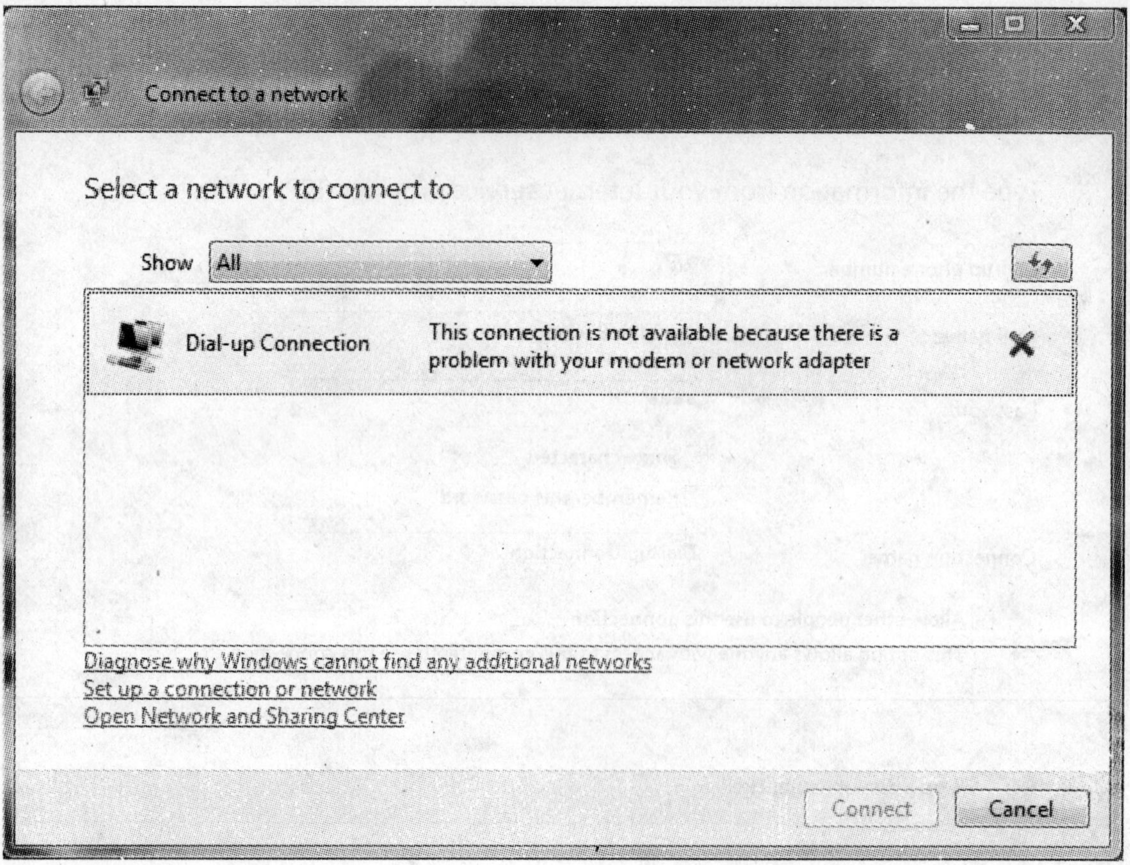
Connect to a network
Select a network to connect to
Show All
Dial-up Connection
This connection is not available because there is a problem with your modem or network adapter
Diagnose why Windows cannot find any additional networks
Set up a connection or network
Open Network and Sharing Center
Connect
Cancel

5 Maintain and Protect Your System with Windows Vista

Introduction

Computers are capable of producing definite results only when they are properly maintained. It is likely to give some errors if not maintained at regular intervals. For this there are different commands available under Windows Vista. I will discuss here few of them.

Disk Fragmentation

As you might know that when you write to a hard disk, it writes at a place where it finds free space and stores its location in the FAT. This way when you keep on working with deleting and adding files at random, there is bound to be filled up and blank space in hard disk at random. What disk fragmentation does is to put all the blank space at one side and the filled files on the other. This makes the working much faster than before.

So to run your hard disk more efficiently, you must run Disk Defragmentation at least once a month.

Running Disk Defragmentation

1. Click Start, Programs, Accessories, System Tools and then Disk Defragmenter.
2. The Disk Defragmentation dialog box, as shown next, will open.

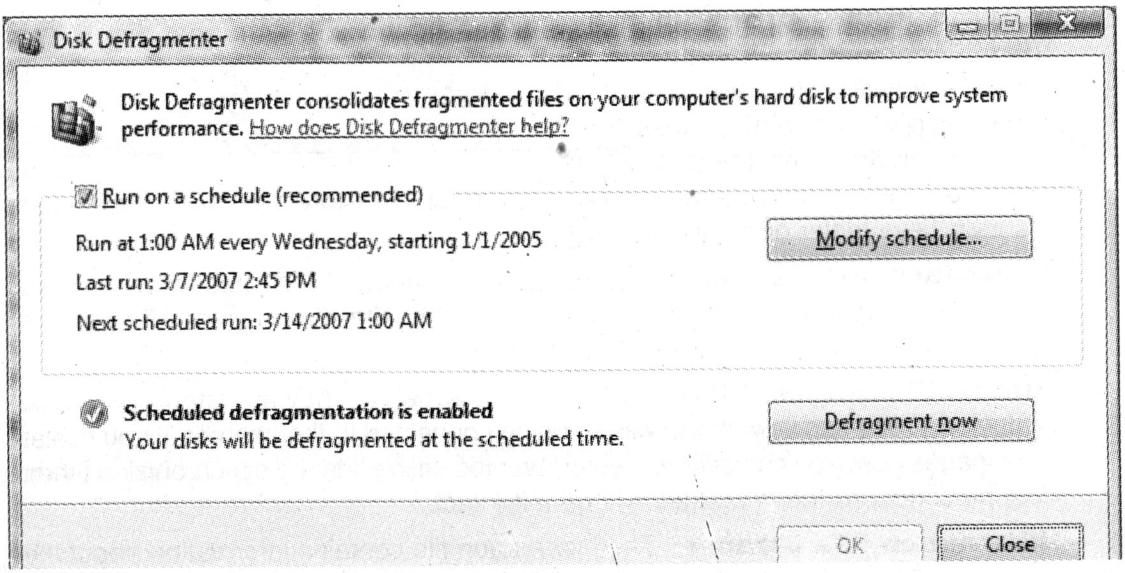

3. Click at Modify Schedule to change the time of running.
4. Start Defragmentation by clicking at Defragment now.

Disk Cleanup

While running Windows operating system does create a lot of temporary files to speed up the working of the software. When you run **Disk Cleanup** it checks for files that can be safely deleted and then presents a listing of such files.

Running Disk Cleanup

1. Click Start, Programs, Accessories, System Tools and then Disk Cleanup.
2. The Disk Cleanup dialog box, as shown here, will open.

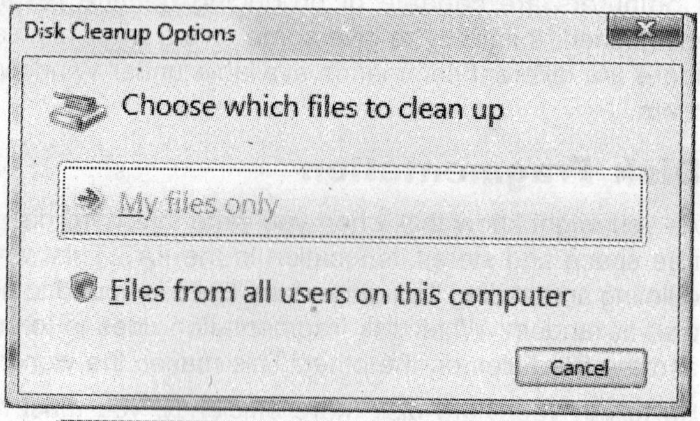

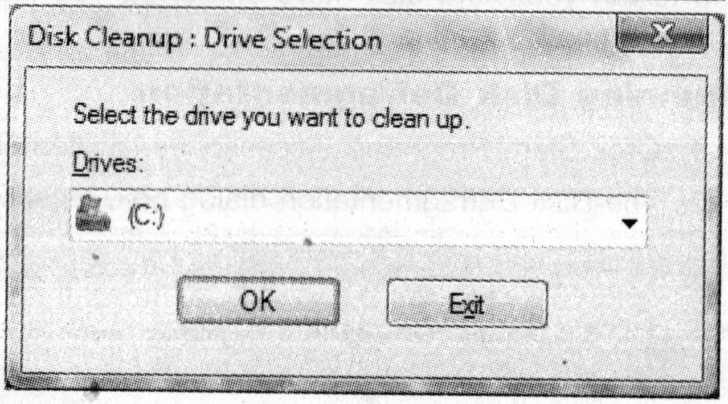

3. You have the choice to select "My files only" or "Files from all users on this computer".
4. Click at the drive which you want to clean up, in the next dialog box.
4. Once clicked Ok, it will show you the files which can be deleted, as shown in the dialog box.
5. Put a checkmark next to the categories you want to delete. Various type of files listed here are:

Downloaded program files Downloaded Program Files are ActiveX controls and Java applets downloaded automatically from the Internet when you view certain pages. They are temporarily stored in the Downloaded Program Files folder on your hard disk.

Temporary Internet files These are from various Web sites that you have visited, and they can make reconnecting to a Web site much faster. But there is no point in keeping them around forever.

Offline Webpages Offline pages are webpages that are stored on your computer so you can view them without being connected to the Internet. If you delete these pages now, you can still view your favorites offline later by synchronizing them. Your personalized for webpages will be left intact.

Hibernation File Cleaner The hibernation file contains information about the state of your computer as it enters hibernation. If you do not use the hibernation power setting, you can remove this file to free up disk space. Removing this file disable hibernation. If you use hibernation on this computer, do not remove this file. To adjust power settings or to enable hibernation, click Power Options.

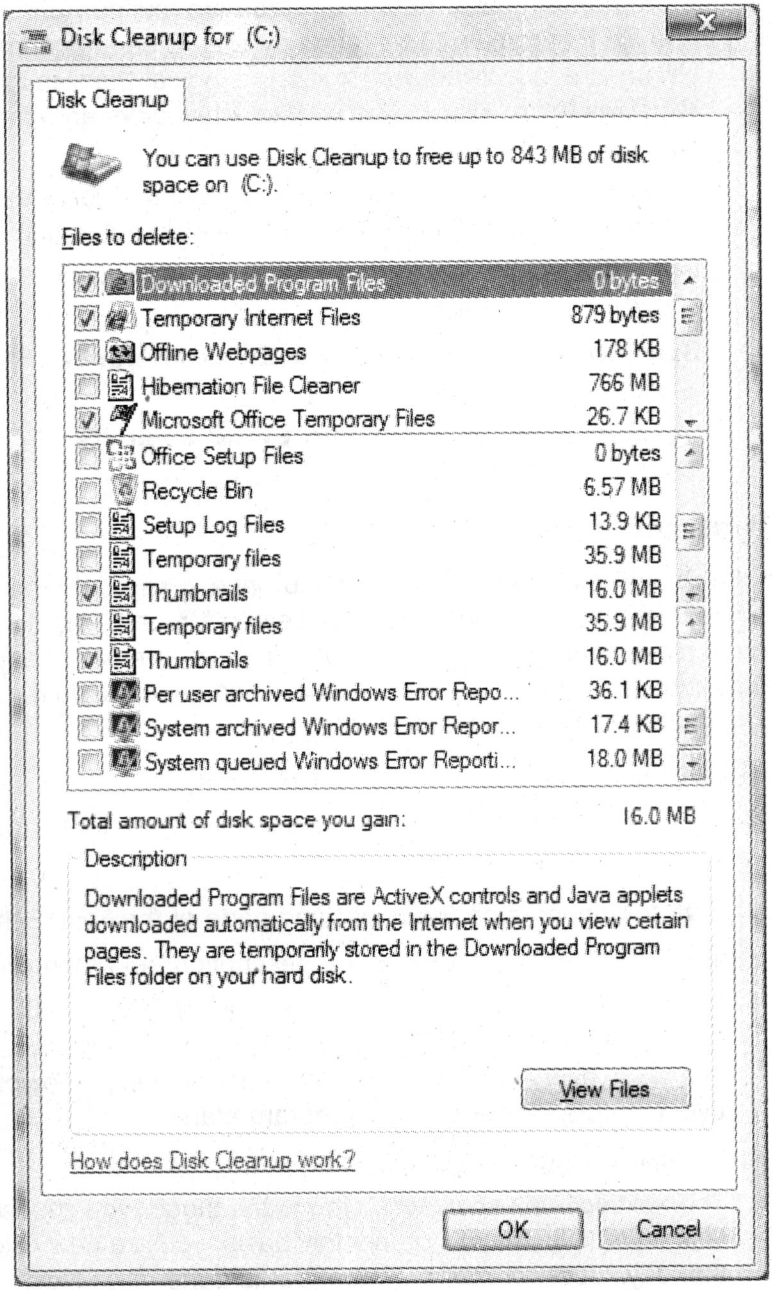

Microsoft Office Temporary Files Microsoft Office maintains log files for diagnostic purposes as well as other temporary data files. These files are left over from a previous Office session and can be deleted.

Office Setup Files Installation files used by Office. If these files are removed from your computer, you may be prompted for your original installation media or source during any Reinstall, Repair, or Patch operation.

Recycle Bin If the Recycle Bin settings are correctly configured, you should not need to empty the bin to clear space on your hard drive. If the Recycle Bin is too large, reset it to some smaller size.

Setup Log Files Files created by Windows.

Temporary files These are files created by Windows and Windows programs.

In the normal course of events, these are routinely deleted by the operating system. Any file that remain to be found by Disk Cleanup can be safely deleted. If you are still unsure, use Windows Explorer to look at the files in the Temp folder inside your Windows folder. Any file older than a few days are strays and should be deleted.

Thumbnails Windows keeps a copy of all of your picture, video, and document thumbnails so they can be displayed quickly when you open a folder. If you delete these thumbnails, they will be automatically recreated as needed.

Per user archived Windows Error Reports Files used for error reporting and solution checking.

System archived Windows Error Reports Files used for error reporting and solution checking.

System queued Windows Error Reports Files used for error reporting and solution checking.

System Tune-up

In the above few cases, I said do thing once a week, do this once a month but when it comes to actual doing, you are very likely to forget it. Thanks to Windows Vista it allows you to remember all this. For this we have the command called **Task Scheduler** that takes cares of all the above commands. All you need to do is to set up **Task Scheduler** to run automatically on a schedule you specify.

Adding a Task

1. Click Start, All Programs, Accessories, System Tools and Task Scheduler.
2. Click Create Basic Task.

   This link appears on the right hand pane of the Task Scheduler. A wizard appears.
3. Type a name for the task and a description, and then click Next.

   Now you are supposed to choose what Windows Vista calls a "trigger"—in plain English, when to run the task. You can specify that it runs dialy, weekly, monthly, or just once; every time the computer starts or every time you log in; or when a specific event occurs — like when a program starts.
4. Choose a trigger and then click Next.

   The next screen varies according to the trigger you choose. If you choose to run the task on a daily, weekly, or monthly basis, you are now asked to specify when during that day, week, or month. Once that is done, click Next.
5. Choose an action; click Next.

   Now you are supposed to say what program, email, or message you want the PC to fire up.

   If you chose the email option, you now fill out a form with the recipient's name, address, subject line, message body, and so on; you can even specify an attachment.

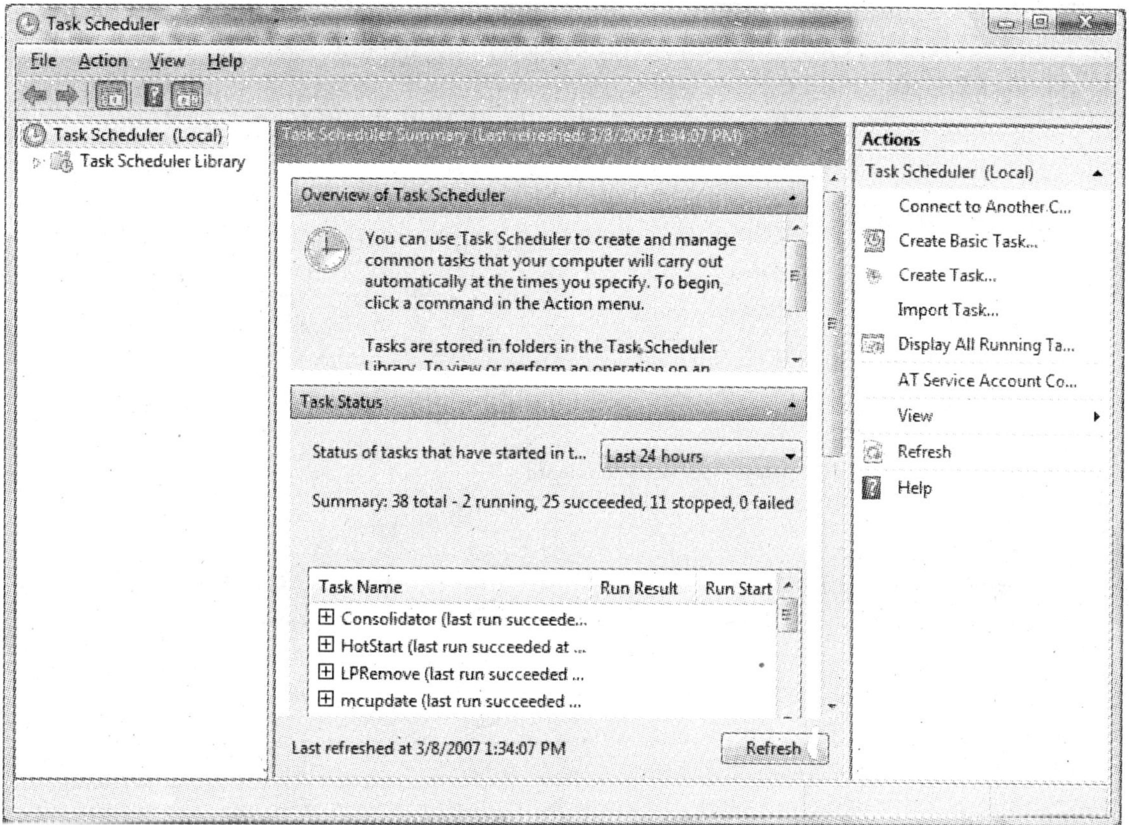
Task Scheduler
File Action View Help
Task Scheduler (Local)
Task Scheduler Library
Task Scheduler Summary (Last refreshed: 3/8/2007 1:34:07 PM)
Overview of Task Scheduler
You can use Task Scheduler to create and manage common tasks that your computer will carry out automatically at the times you specify. To begin, click a command in the Action menu.
Tasks are stored in folders in the Task Scheduler
Task Status
Status of tasks that have started in t...
Last 24 hours
Summary: 38 total - 2 running, 25 succeeded, 11 stopped, 0 failed
Task Name
Run Result
Run Start
Consolidator (last run succeede...
HotStart (last run succeeded at ...
LPRemove (last run succeeded ...
mcupdate (last run succeeded ...
Last refreshed at 3/8/2007 1:34:07 PM
Refresh
Actions
Task Scheduler (Local)
Connect to Another C...
Create Basic Task...
Create Task...
Import Task...
Display All Running Ta...
AT Service Account Co...
View
Refresh
Help

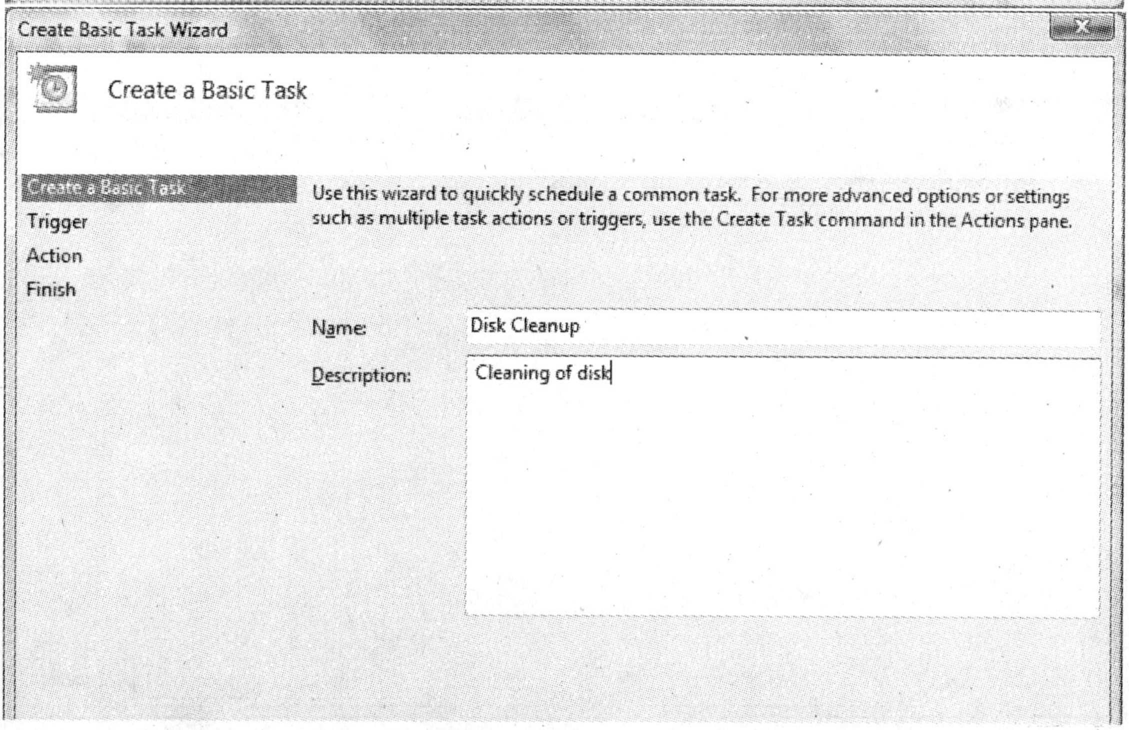
Create Basic Task Wizard
Create a Basic Task
Create a Basic Task
Trigger
Action
Finish
Use this wizard to quickly schedule a common task. For more advanced options or settings such as multiple task actions or triggers, use the Create Task command in the Actions pane.
Name:
Disk Cleanup
Description:
Cleaning of disk

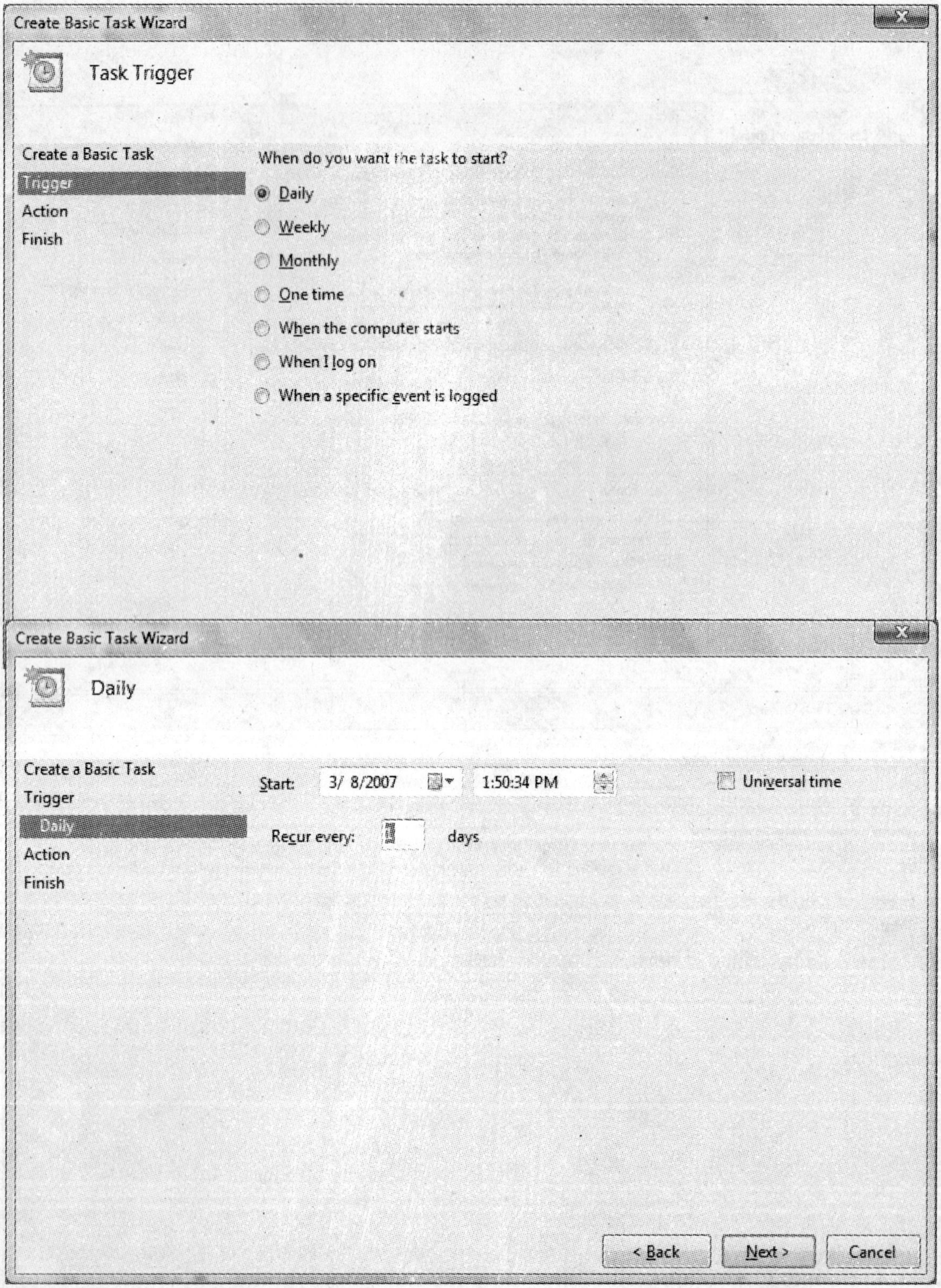
Create Basic Task Wizard
Task Trigger
Create a Basic Task
Trigger
Action
Finish
When do you want the task to start?
Daily
Weekly
Monthly
One time
When the computer starts
When I log on
When a specific event is logged
Create Basic Task Wizard
Daily
Create a Basic Task
Trigger
Daily
Action
Finish
Start:
3/ 8/2007
1:50:34 PM
Universal time
Recur every:
1
days
< Back
Next >
Cancel

If you chose to run a program, you now browse to select the program. At this point, programmers can also add arguments, which are codes that customize how the program starts.

And if you opted to display a message, you get to type a name and text for the message. At the appointed time, an actual Window dialog box will appear on the screen—except that it will contain text that you wrote.

6. Complete the details about the email, program, or phony dialog box, and then click Next.

   Finally, a screen appears, summarizing the task, when it will run, and so on. To edit it, click the Back button.

7. To confirm the automated task, click Finish.

   You return to the Task Scheduler window. Although you may have to scroll down to see it, your new task appears in the Active Tasks list at the bottom of the window. If all goes well, Vista will fire it up at the moment you specified.

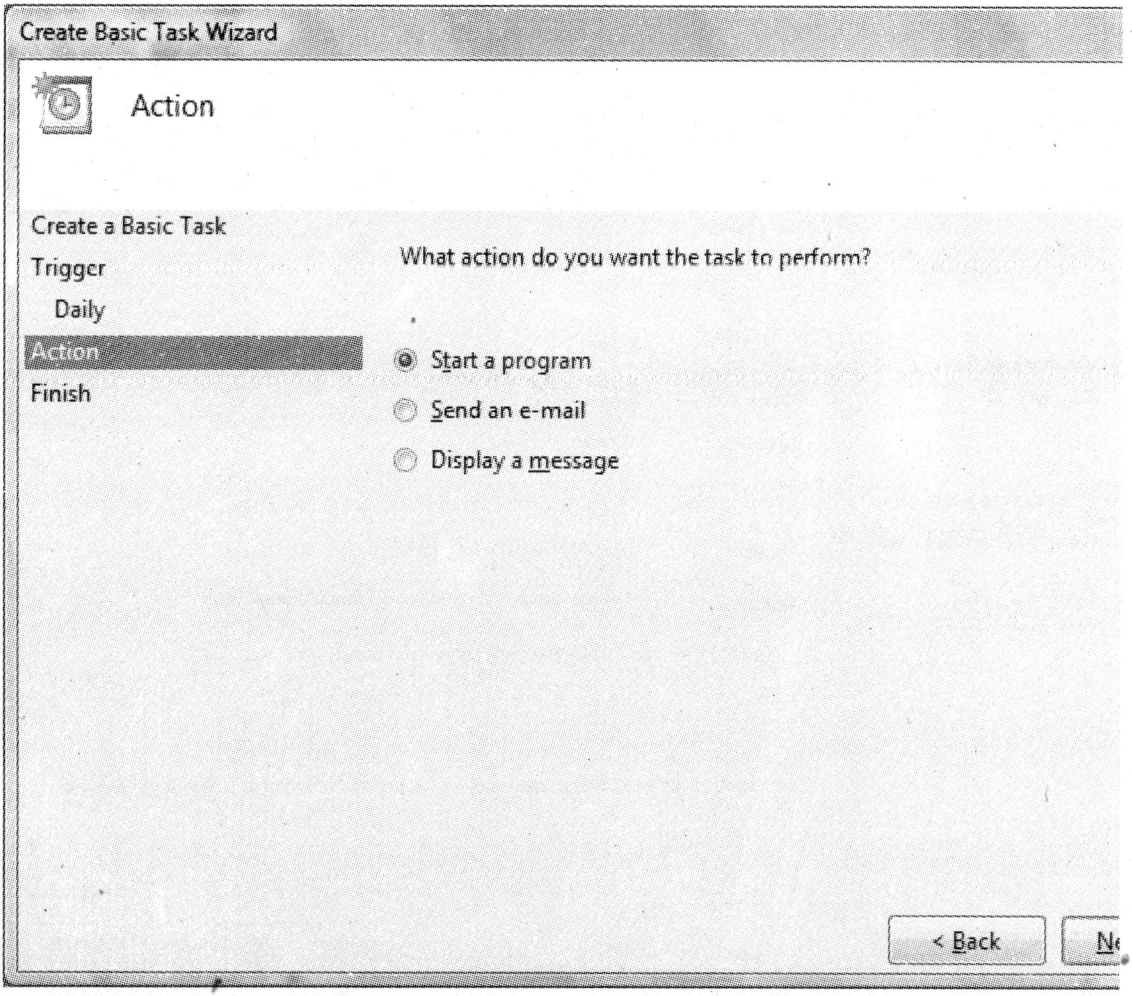

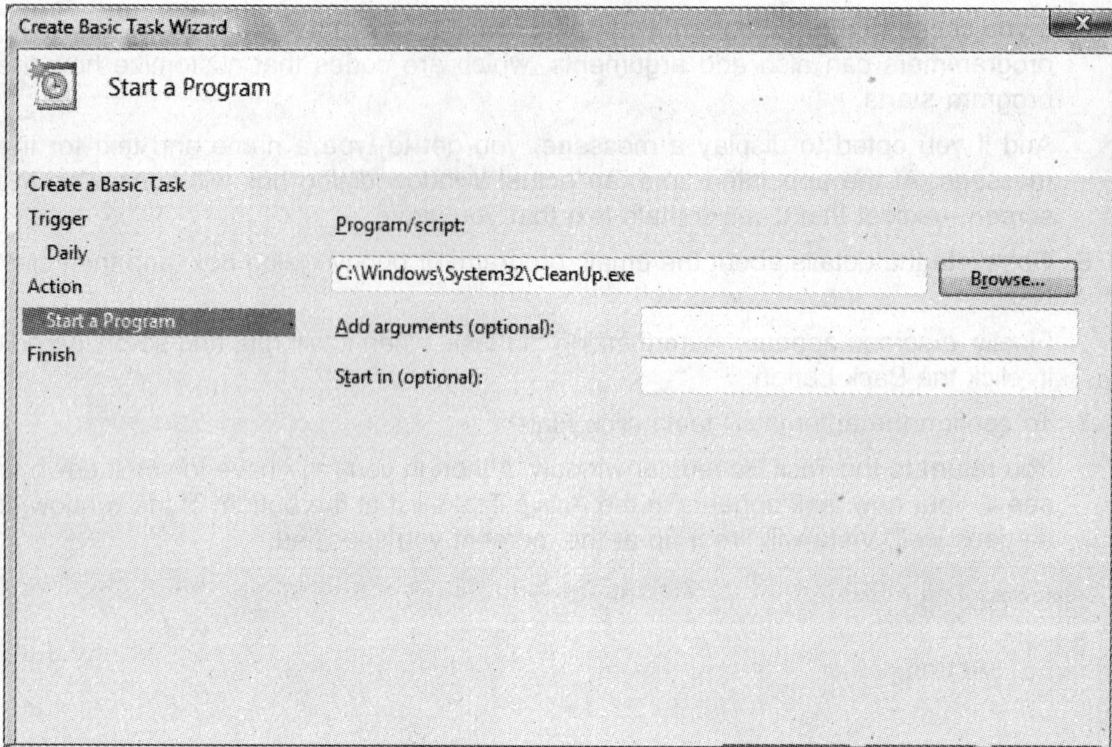
Create Basic Task Wizard
Start a Program
Create a Basic Task
Trigger
Daily
Action
Start a Program
Finish
Program/script:
C:\Windows\System32\CleanUp.exe
Browse...
Add arguments (optional):
Start in (optional):

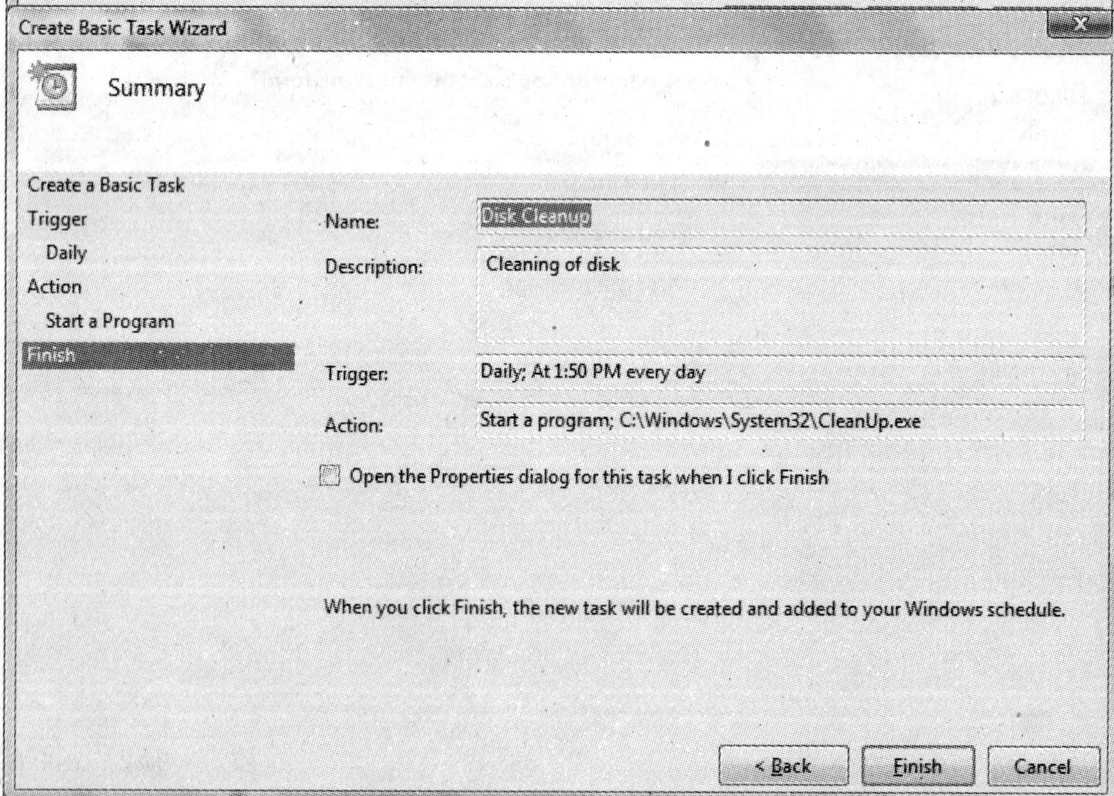
Create Basic Task Wizard
Summary
Create a Basic Task
Trigger
Daily
Action
Start a Program
Finish
Name:
Disk Cleanup
Description:
Cleaning of disk
Trigger:
Daily; At 1:50 PM every day
Action:
Start a program; C:\Windows\System32\CleanUp.exe
Open the Properties dialog for this task when I click Finish
When you click Finish, the new task will be created and added to your Windows schedule.
< Back
Finish
Cancel

Checking Disk

In the earlier versions of Windows, you had ScanDisk, which is missing here in Vista. Now you can perform the same operation from the Hard disk checkup.

You can check your hard disk or scan it for errors and correct them in case needed, you can do the following:

1. Open My Computer, and then select the local disk you want to check.
2. Right click the mouse, click Properties.
3. On the Tools tab, under Error-checking, click Check Now.
4. Under Check disk options, select the Scan for and attempt recovery of bad sectors check box.

Your disk will be checked in 2 phases and errors if any will be pointed out.

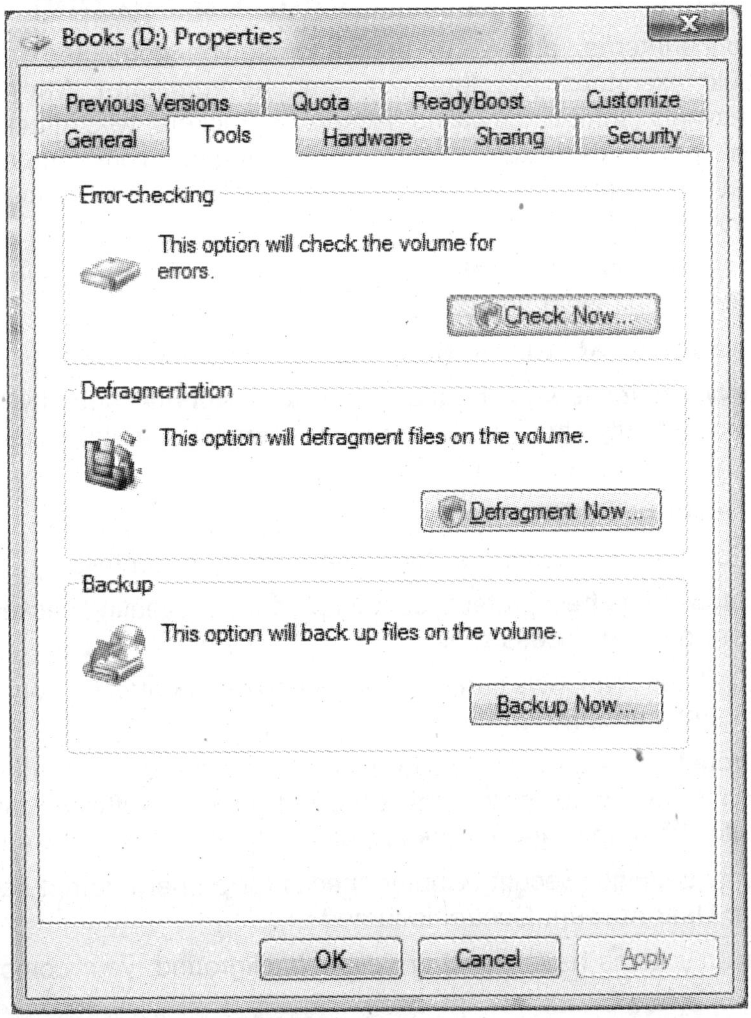

Automatically fix file system errors

Clearly, you want this option turned on, so that any problems Windows finds are taken care of automatically.

Scan for and attempt recovery of bad sectors

If you turn on this option, whenever the scan finds a damaged section of a drive, it moves any files located there elsewhere on the drive. Then the program surrounds that hard-disk area with the imaginary tape, so that Windows won't use the damaged area for storing files in the future.

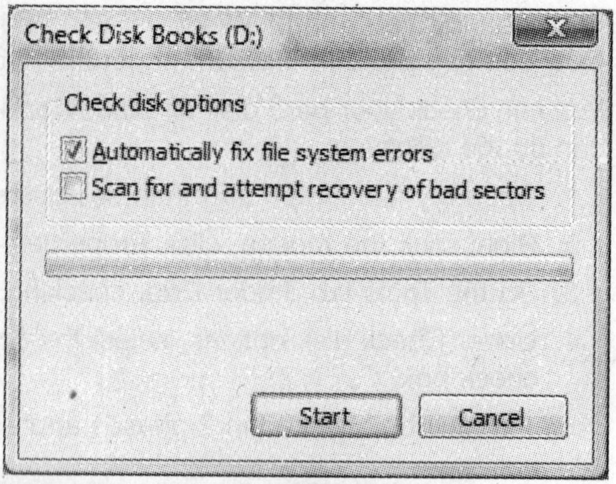

Understanding Security and Safe Computing

If you connect to the Internet, allow other people to use your computer, or share files with others, you should take steps to protect your computer from harm. Why? Because there are computer criminals (sometimes called hackers or crackers) who attack other people's computers. These people can attack directly, by breaking into your computer through the Internet and stealing your personal information, or indirectly, by creating malicious software (or malware) designed to harm your computer.

Fortunately, you can protect yourself by taking a few simple precautions. This article describes the threats and what you can do to defend against them.

Check your security status with Windows Security Center

Windows Security Center is your headquarters for computer security. It shows your computer's current security status and recommends anything that you should do to help make your computer more secure. To open it:

Click to open Security Center.

Security Center checks your computer for these security essentials:

- Firewall. A firewall can help protect your computer by preventing hackers or malicious software from gaining access to it.
- Automatic updates. Windows can routinely check for updates for your computer and install them automatically.
- Malware protection. Antivirus software can help protect your computer against viruses, worms, and other security threats. Antispyware software can help protect your computer from spyware and other potentially unwanted software.
- Other security settings. Security Center checks for proper Internet security settings and whether User Account Control is turned on.

If any of the security items have a red or yellow background, your computer might be

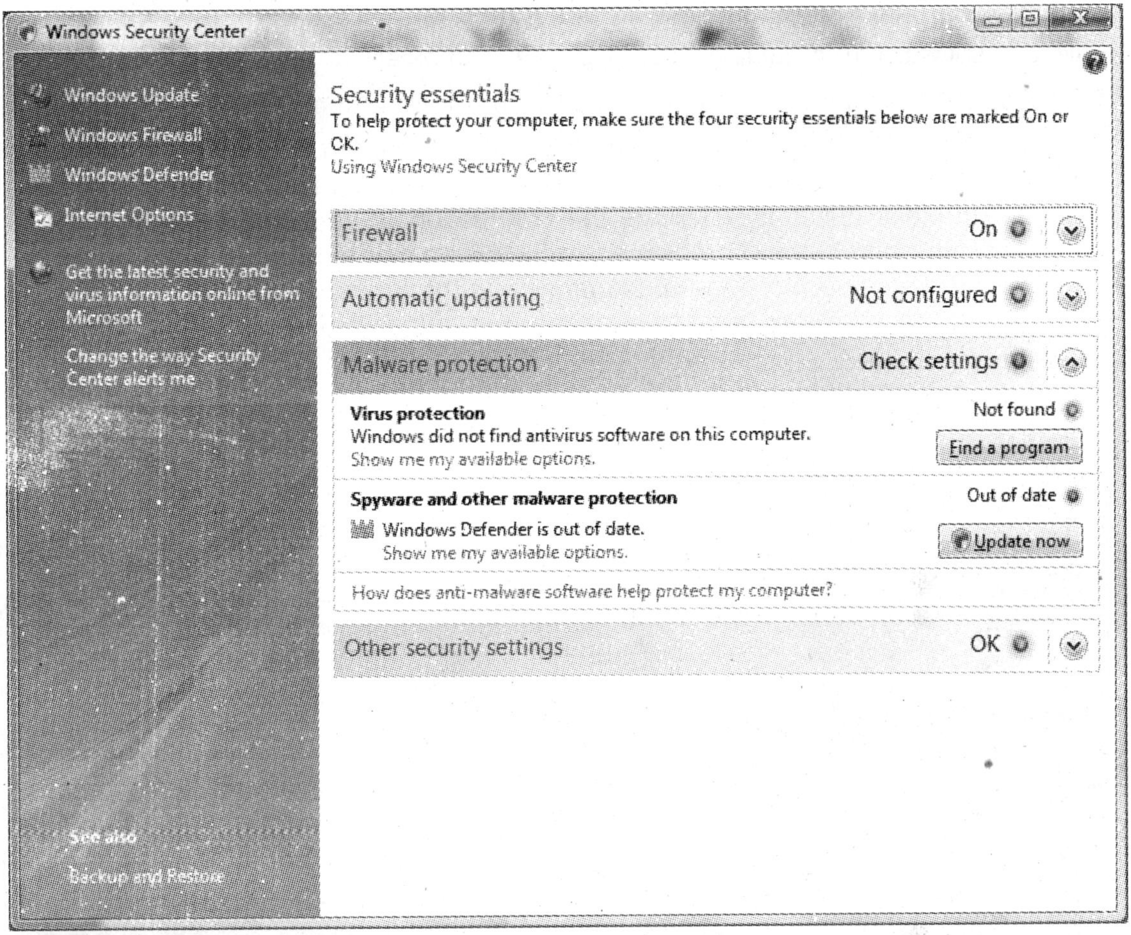

vulnerable to security threats. To fix the problem, click an item to expand it, and then follow the instructions.

What are security alerts?

If Windows detects that your computer might need enhanced security in any one of the security areas—firewall, automatic updating, malware protection, or other security settings—you will see a notification every time you log on until the problem is fixed. Notifications are displayed in the notification area of the taskbar.

Click the notification to open Security Center, where you can learn how to fix the problem.

- To turn off security notifications or hide the Security Center icon in the notification area, open Security Center, click Change the way Security Center alerts me, and then choose an option. Even if you turn off notifications, Security Center will continue to check and display security status.

Use a firewall

A firewall is software or hardware that checks information coming from the Internet or a network and then either turns it away or allows it to pass through to your computer, depending on your firewall settings. In this way, a firewall helps prevent hackers and malicious software from gaining access to your computer.

Windows Firewall is built into Windows and is turned on automatically.

If you run a program such as an instant messaging program or a multiplayer network game that needs to receive information from the Internet or a network, the firewall asks if you want to block or unblock (allow) the connection. If you choose to unblock the connection, Windows Firewall creates an exception so that the firewall won't bother you when that program needs to receive information in the future.

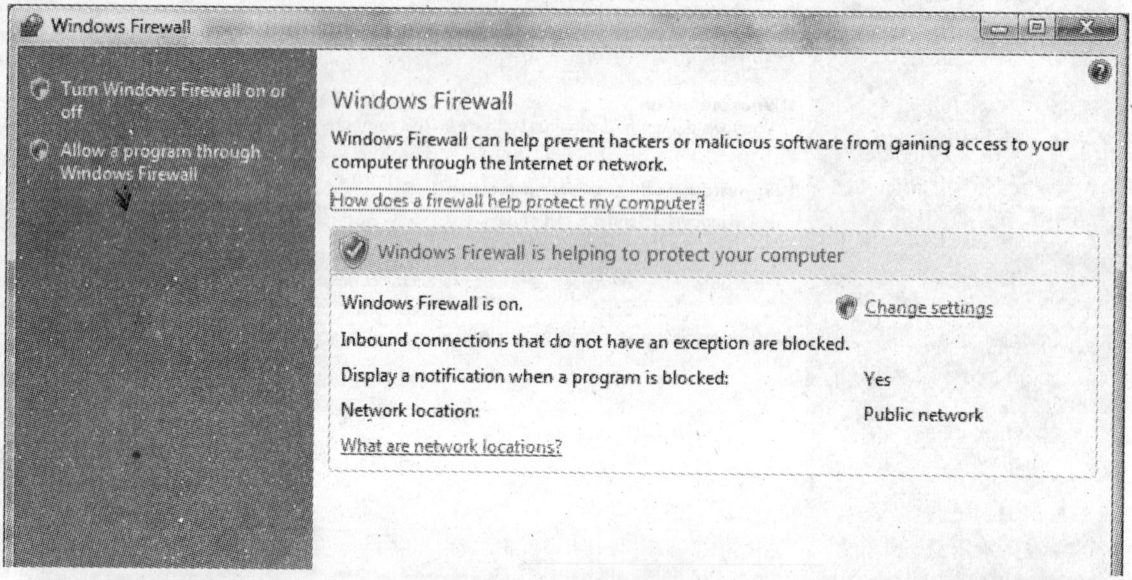

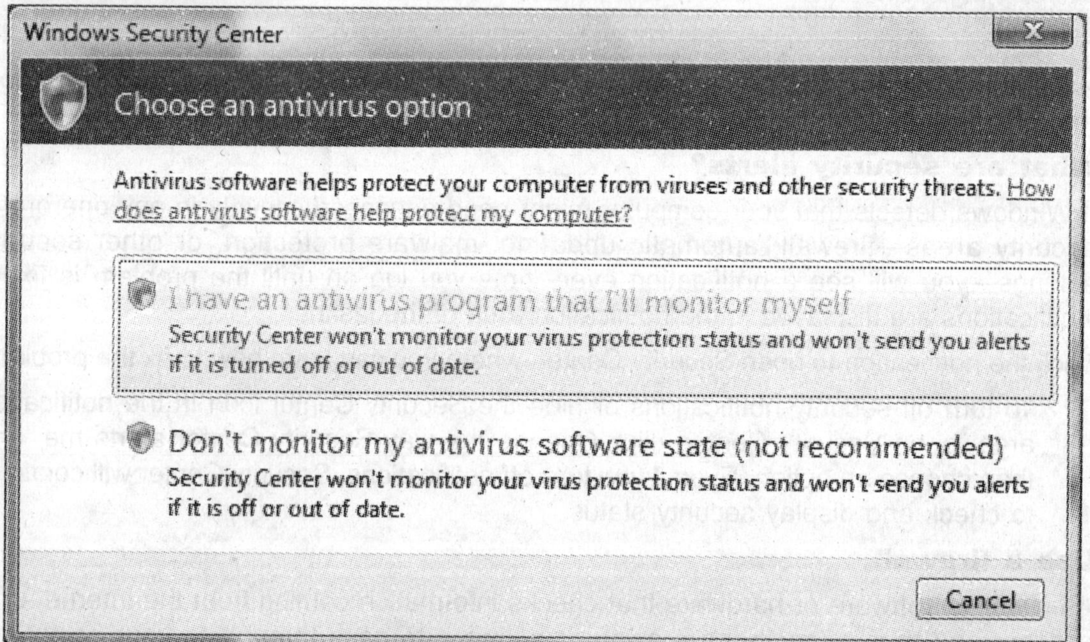

Use virus protection

Viruses, worms, and Trojan horses are programs created by hackers that use the Internet to infect vulnerable computers. Viruses and worms can replicate themselves from computer to computer, while Trojan horses enter a computer by hiding inside an apparently legitimate program, such as a screen saver. Destructive viruses, worms, and Trojan horses can erase information from your hard disk or completely disable your computer. Others don't cause direct damage, but worsen your computer's performance and stability.

Antivirus programs scan e mail and other files on your computer for viruses, worms, and Trojan horses. If one is found, the antivirus program either quarantines (isolates) it or deletes it entirely before it damages your computer and files.

Windows does not have a built-in antivirus program, but your computer manufacturer might have installed one. Check Security Center to find out if your computer has antivirus protection. If not, go to the Microsoft Antivirus Partners webpage to find an antivirus program.

Because new viruses are identified every day, it's important to select an antivirus program with an automatic update capability. When the antivirus software is updated, it adds new viruses to its list of viruses to check for, helping to protect your computer from new attacks. If the list of viruses is out of date, your computer is vulnerable to new threats. Updates usually require an annual subscription fee. Keep the subscription current to receive regular updates.

- If you do not use antivirus software, you expose your computer to damage from malicious software. You also run the risk of spreading viruses to other computers.

Use spyware protection

Spyware is software that can display advertisements, collect information about you, or

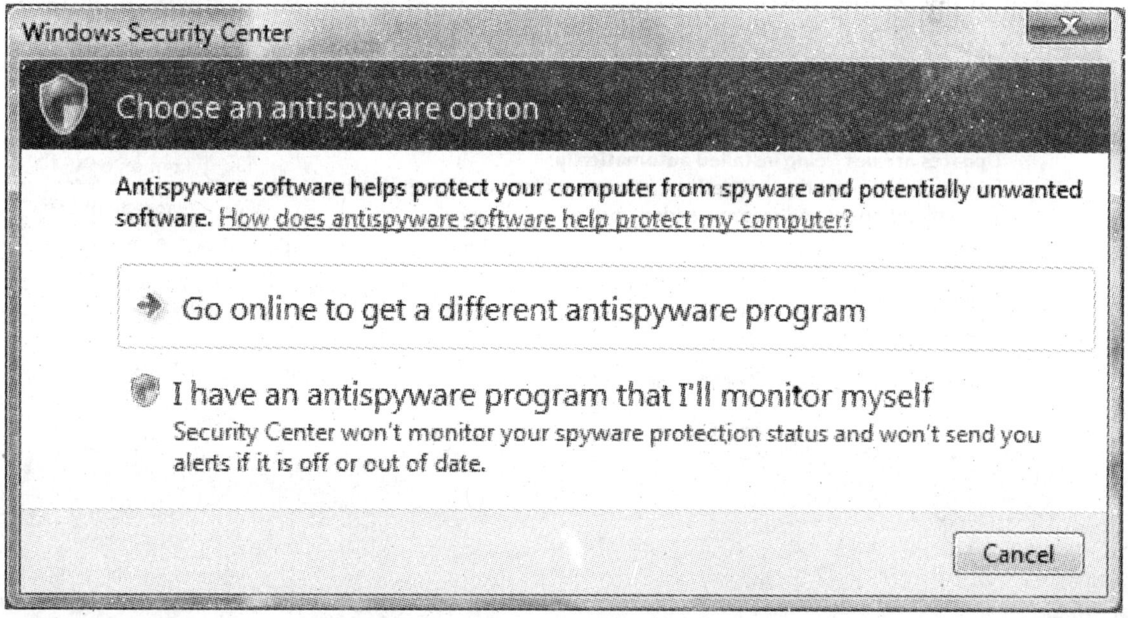

change settings on your computer, generally without appropriately obtaining your consent. For example, spyware can install unwanted toolbars, links, or favorites in your web browser, change your default home page, or display pop-up ads frequently. Some spyware displays no symptoms that you can detect, but it secretly collects sensitive information, such as which websites you visit or text that you type. Most spyware is installed through free software that you download, but in some cases simply visiting a website results in a spyware infection.

To help protect your computer from spyware, use an antispyware program. This version of Windows has a built-in antispyware program called Windows Defender, which is turned on by default. Windows Defender alerts you when spyware tries to install itself on your computer. It also can scan your computer for existing spyware and then remove it.

Because new spyware appears every day, Windows Defender must be regularly updated to detect and guard against the latest spyware threats. Windows Defender is updated as needed whenever you update Windows. For the highest level of protection, set Windows to install updates automatically.

Update Windows automatically

Microsoft regularly offers important updates to Windows that can help protect your computer against new viruses and other security threats. To ensure that you receive these updates as quickly as possible, turn on automatic updating. That way, you don't have to worry that critical fixes for Windows might be missing from your computer.

Updates are downloaded behind the scenes when you're connected to the Internet. The updates are installed at 3:00 A.M. unless you specify a different time. If you turn off your

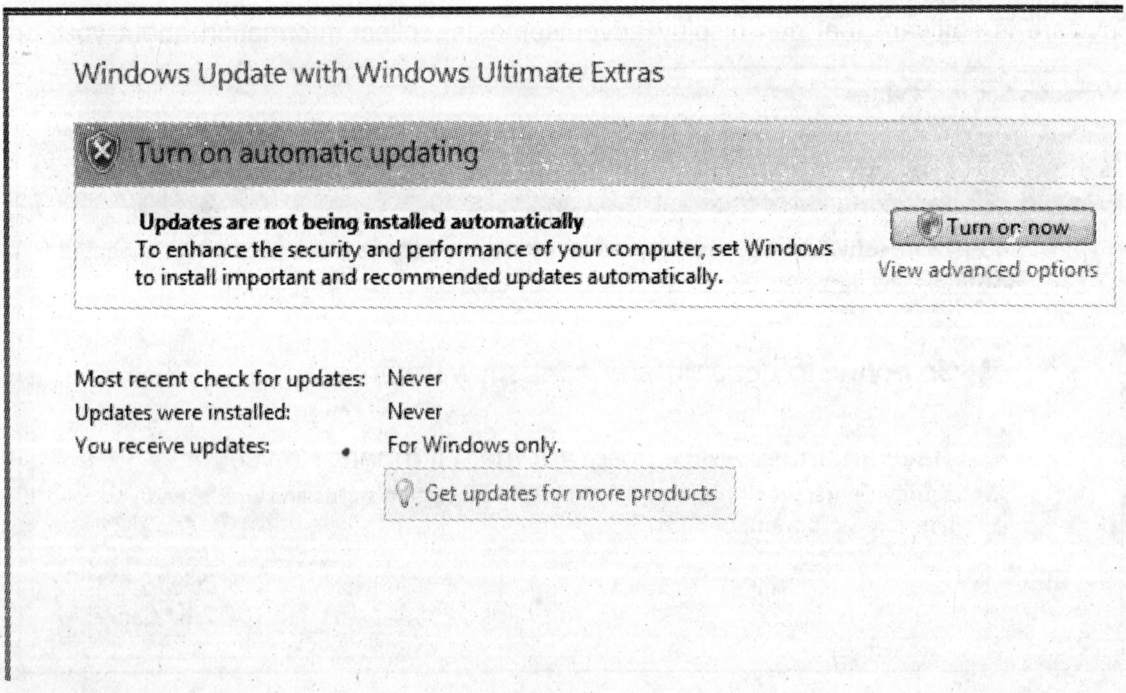

computer before then, you can install updates before shutting down. Otherwise, Windows will install them the next time you start your computer.

To turn on automatic updating

1. Click to open Windows Update.
2. Click Change settings.
3. Make sure Install updates automatically (recommended) is selected.
4. Under Recommended updates, make sure the Include recommended updates when downloading, installing, or notifying me about updates check box is selected, and then click OK. If you are prompted for an administrator password or confirmation, type the password or provide confirmation.

Use a standard user account

When you log on to your computer, Windows grants you a certain level of rights and privileges depending on what kind of user account you have. There are three different types of user accounts: standard, administrator, and guest.

Although an administrator account provides complete control over a computer, using a standard account can help make your computer more secure. That way, if other people (or hackers) gain access to your computer while you are logged on, they can't tamper with the computer's security settings or change other user accounts.

To determine your account type

Click to open User Accounts.

The account type appears under your name.

If you are currently using an administrator account, see Change a user's account type to learn how to change it to a standard account.

Tips for using e mail and the web safely

- Use caution when opening e mail attachments. e mail attachments (files attached to e mail messages) are a primary source of virus infection. Never open an attachment from someone you don't know. If you know the sender but were not expecting an attachment, verify that the sender actually sent the attachment before you open it.
- Guard your personal information carefully. If a website asks for a credit card number, bank information, or other personal information, make sure that you trust the website and verify that its transaction system is secure.
- Use the Phishing Filter in Internet Explorer. Phishing is the practice of creating fraudulent e mail messages and websites in order to trick computer users into revealing personal or financial information. The fraudulent e mail message or website appears to be from a trusted source, such as a bank, credit card company, or reputable online merchant. The Phishing Filter helps detect phishing websites to protect you from scams.

- Be careful when clicking hyperlinks in e mail messages. Hyperlinks (links that open websites when you click them) are often used as part of phishing and spyware scams, but they can also transmit viruses. Only click links in e mail messages that you trust.
- Only install add-ons from websites that you trust. Web browser add-ons, including ActiveX controls, allow webpages to display things like toolbars, stock tickers, video, and animation. However, add-ons can also install spyware or other malicious software. If a website asks you to install an add-on, make sure that you trust it before doing so.

Windows security information for IT Pros

This topic provides information about three new security features available in Windows Vista: User Account Control (UAC), BitLocker Drive Encryption, and Trusted Platform Module (TPM) Services. There are links to additional information about the common administration and troubleshooting tasks and tools associated with implementing a Windows security strategy.

User Account Control (UAC)

BitLocker Drive Encryption

User Account Control

User Account Control (UAC) is a new set of infrastructure technologies in this version of Windows that helps organizations deploy a better-managed desktop and mitigate the impact of malware. UAC requires all users to run applications and tasks with a standard user account, limiting administrator-level access to authorized processes. It also allows desktops to be locked down, which stops unauthorized applications from installing and stops standard users from making inadvertent changes to system settings.

Common tasks

These links will take you to additional information on the Microsoft Web site.

Useful tools

This section describes the Microsoft Web site downloads and tools associated with this version of Windows that help you configure and manage UAC

Management Console

UAC is controlled through the Local Security Settings Microsoft Management Console (MMC) snap-in. You can find this MMC snap-in the following location: %windir%\System32\secpol.msc.

Downloads

No UAC-related downloads were available when this documentation was last updated.

Deployment

For information about deploying UAC, go to the following resources on the Microsoft Web site:

Operations

For operational information about UAC, go to the following resources on the Microsoft Web site:

BitLocker Drive Encryption

BitLocker Drive Encryption is an integral new security feature that provides considerable off-line data and operating system protection for your computer. BitLocker ensures that data stored on the computer is not revealed to anyone who tampers with the machine while the installed operating system is offline.

BitLocker Drive Encryption works with Trusted Platform Module (TPM) by encrypting the entire Windows volume, which assures early boot component integrity and data protection. BitLocker Drive Encryption is designed to provide a seamless end-user experience at startup with systems that have a compatible TPM microchip and BIOS.

TPM version 1.2 TPM with the appropriate BIOS modifications (to support the Static Root of Trust Measurement as defined by the Trusted Computing Group) is required to store the encryption keys on the computer. However, BitLocker Drive Encryption can be used on computers without a compatible version of TPM. Encryption keys are stored on an USB flash drive to validate the user's identity at startup.

Useful tools

This section describes the Microsoft Web site downloads and tools associated with this version of Windows that help you configure and manage BitLocker Drive Encryption.

Management Console

No Microsoft Management Console (MMC) snap-ins related to BitLocker Drive Encryption were available when this documentation was last updated.

Downloads

No BitLocker Drive Encryption-related downloads were available when this documentation was last updated.

Deployment

For information about deploying BitLocker Drive Encryption, go to the following resources on the Microsoft Web site:

Operations

For operational information about BitLocker Drive Encryption, go to the following resources on the Microsoft Web site:

Trusted Platform Module Services

Trusted Platform Module (TPM) Services is a new set of features in this version of Windows that is used to administer the TPM Security Hardware in your computer. TPM Services architecture provides the infrastructure for hardware-based security by providing access to and assuring application-level sharing of the TPM. This means that application-level sharing can be built in through software development and that the services can be administered through a graphical user interface.

Useful tools

This section describes the Microsoft Web site downloads and tools associated with this version of Windows that help you configure and manage TPM Services.

Management Console

You can find the Microsoft Management Console (MMC) snap-in for TPM Services in the following location: %windir%\System32\tpm.msc.

To open MMC with elevated privileges, click Start, click All Programs, and then click Accessories. Right-click Command Prompt and then click Run as administrator. If Windows displays a security message asking your permission to run this program, click Allow. In the command prompt that opens, type tpm.msc.

Downloads

No TMP Services-related downloads were available when this documentation was last updated.

Windows CardSpace

Microsoft Windows CardSpace™ is a system for creating relationships with websites and online services. Windows CardSpace manages the user names and passwords that you use to register with and log on to websites and online services with Information Cards.

Management Console

You can find Microsoft Management Console (MMC) snap-ins for Windows security in the following location: %windir%\System32*.msc.

To open MMC with elevated privileges, click Start, click All Programs, and then click Accessories. Right-click Command Prompt and then click Run as administrator. If Windows displays a security message asking your permission to run this program, click Allow. In the command prompt that opens, type mmc.exe to start MMC. In the console tree of MMC, click File, click Add/Remove Snap-in, and then select the appropriate snap-ins and click Add.

The following security snap-ins are available:

- Authorization Manager
- Certificate Templates
- Certificates
- Certification Authority
- IP Security Monitor
- IP Security Policy Management
- Security Configuration and Analysis
- Group Policy Management

- Group Policy Object Editor
- Network Access Protection
- Shared Folders
- Security Templates

Tips for creating a strong password

Passwords provide the first line of defense against unauthorized access to your computer. The stronger your password, the more protected your computer will be from hackers and malicious software. You should make sure you have strong passwords for all accounts on your computer.

What makes a password strong (or weak)?

A strong password:

- Is at least eight characters long.
- Does not contain your user name, real name, or company name.
- Does not contain a complete word.
- Is significantly different from previous passwords.
- Contains characters from each of the following four categories:

<table>
<tr><th>Character category</th><th>Examples</th></tr>
<tr><td>Uppercase letters</td><td>A, B, C</td></tr>
<tr><td>Lowercase letters</td><td>a, b, c</td></tr>
<tr><td>Numbers</td><td>0, 1, 2, 3, 4, 5, 6, 7, 8, 9</td></tr>
<tr><td>Symbols found on the keyboard (all keyboard characters not defined as letters or numerals) and spaces</td><td>‘ ~ ! @ # $ % ^ & * ( ) _ - + = { } [ ] \ | : ; “ ‘ < > , . ? /</td></tr>
</table>

A password might meet all the criteria above and still be a weak password. For example, Hello2U! meets all the criteria for a strong password listed above, but is still weak because it contains a complete word. H3ll0 2 U! is a stronger alternative because it replaces some of the letters in the complete word with numbers and also includes spaces.

Help yourself remember your strong password by following these tips:

- Create an acronym from an easy-to-remember piece of information. For example, pick a phrase that is meaningful to you, such as My son's birthday is 12 December, 2004. Using that phrase as your guide, you might use Msbi12/Dec,4 for your password.
- Substitute numbers, symbols, and misspellings for letters or words in an easy-to-remember phrase. For example, My son's birthday is 12 December, 2004 could become Mi$un's Brthd8iz 12124 (it's OK to use spaces in your password).

- Relate your password to a favorite hobby or sport. For example, I love to play badminton could become ILuv2PlayB@dm1nt()n.

If you feel you must write down your password in order to remember it, make sure you don't label it as your password, and keep it in a safe place.

6 Additional Commands of Windows Vista

Windows Mail

Don't be shocked by this new term. It is the new name for Outlook Express.

Getting started with e mail

E mail (short for electronic mail) is a fast and convenient way to communicate with others. You can use e mail to:

- Send and receive text messages. You can send an e mail message to any person with an e mail address. The message arrives in the recipient's e mail inbox within seconds or minutes—whether he or she is your next-door neighbor or lives halfway around the world.

E mail is two-way. You can receive messages from anyone who knows your e mail address, and then read and reply to those messages.

- Send and receive files. Besides text, you can send almost any type of file in an e mail message, including documents, pictures, and music. A file sent in an e mail message is called an attachment.
- Send messages to groups of people. You can send an e mail message to many people simultaneously. Recipients can reply to the whole group, allowing for group discussions.
- Forward messages. When you receive an e mail message, you can forward it to others without retyping it.

One advantage of e mail over the telephone or regular mail is its convenience: You can send a message at any time of day or night. If the recipients aren't in front of their computers and online (connected to the Internet) when you send the message, they'll find it waiting for them the next time they check their e mail. If they are online, you might get a reply within minutes.

E mail is also free. Unlike sending a regular letter, no stamp or fee is required, no matter where the recipient lives. The only charges that apply are those that you pay for an Internet connection.

What do I need before I can use e mail?

To use e mail, you need three things:

- An Internet connection. To connect your computer to the Internet, you must first sign up with an Internet service provider (ISP). An ISP provides you with access to the Internet, usually for a monthly fee. You also need a modem.

- An e mail program or web-based service. You can use Windows Mail, an e mail program included with Windows. You can also use any other e mail program, once you install it on your computer.

  If you prefer, you can sign up instead with a free web-based e mail service, such as Gmail, MSN Hotmail, or Yahoo! Mail. These services allow you to check your e mail with a web browser from any computer connected to the Internet.
- An e mail address. You get an e mail address from your ISP or web-based e mail service when you sign up. An e mail address consists of a user name (a nickname you choose, not necessarily your real name), the @ sign, and the name of your ISP or web-based e mail provider—for example, someone@example.com.

Setting up Windows Mail

Once you have an e mail address and an Internet connection, you're ready to send and receive e mail. To use e mail in Windows Mail, you must first set up an e mail account. Before you add an account, you'll need to get some information from your ISP: your e mail address, password, the names of your incoming and outgoing e mail servers, and certain other details. See Where to find your e mail account information.

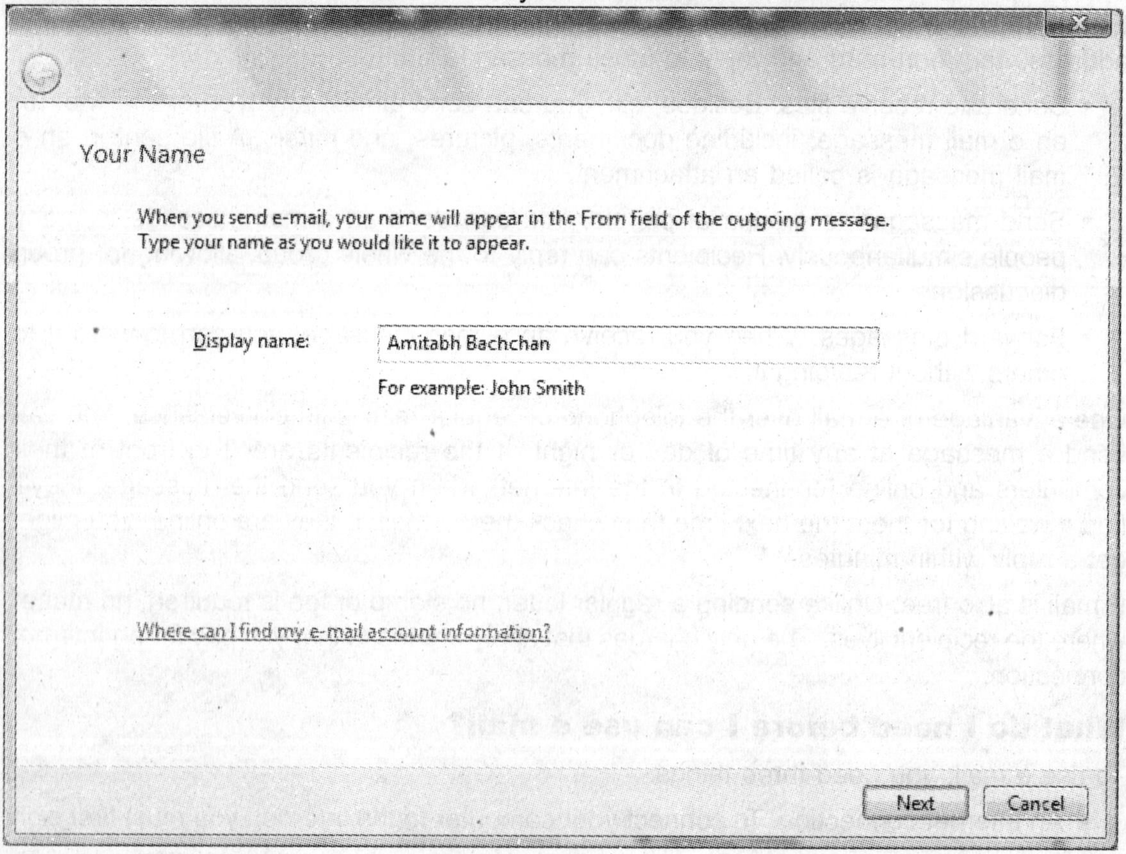

To add an e mail account in Windows Mail

1. Click to open Windows Mail.
2. On the Tools menu, click Accounts.
3. Click Add, click e mail Account, click Next, and then follow the instructions.

During setup, you'll be asked to pick a display name. This is the name that recipients will see when you send them an e mail message.

Reading e mail messages

Windows Mail checks to see if you've received e mail whenever you start the program and every 30 minutes after that. E-mail you receive appears in your Inbox. The Inbox is one of several folders that hold e mail.

To see a list of e mail you've received, click Inbox in the Folders list. Your e mail messages appear in the message list. The list shows who sent the mail, the subject, and when it was received.

To read a message, click it in the message list. The contents of the message appear below the message list in the Preview pane. To read the message in a separate window, double-click it in the message list.

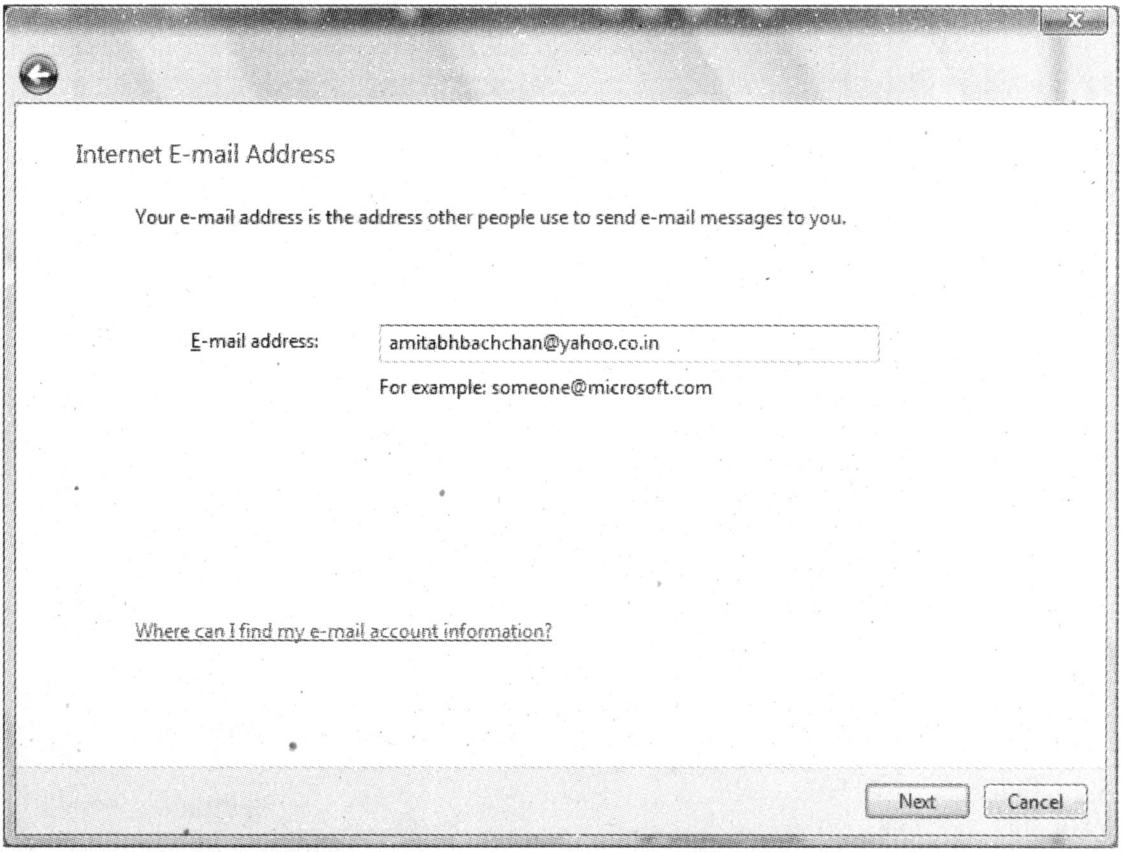

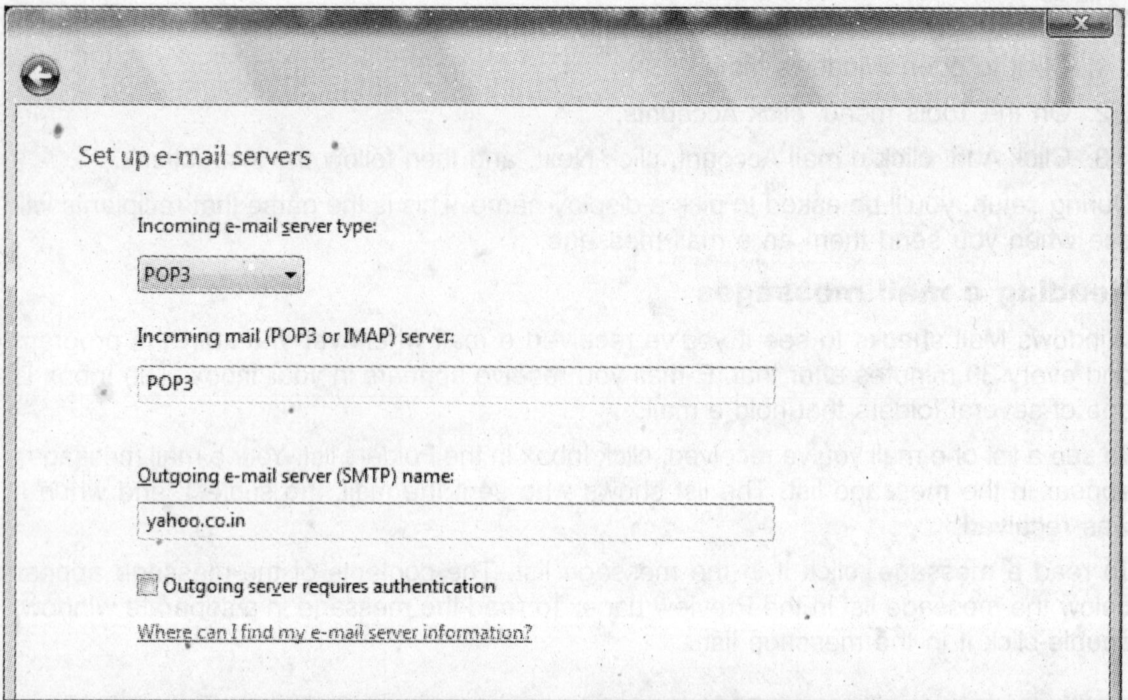
Set up e-mail servers
Incoming e-mail server type:
POP3
Incoming mail (POP3 or IMAP) server:
POP3
Outgoing e-mail server (SMTP) name:
yahoo.co.in
Outgoing server requires authentication
Where can I find my e-mail server information?

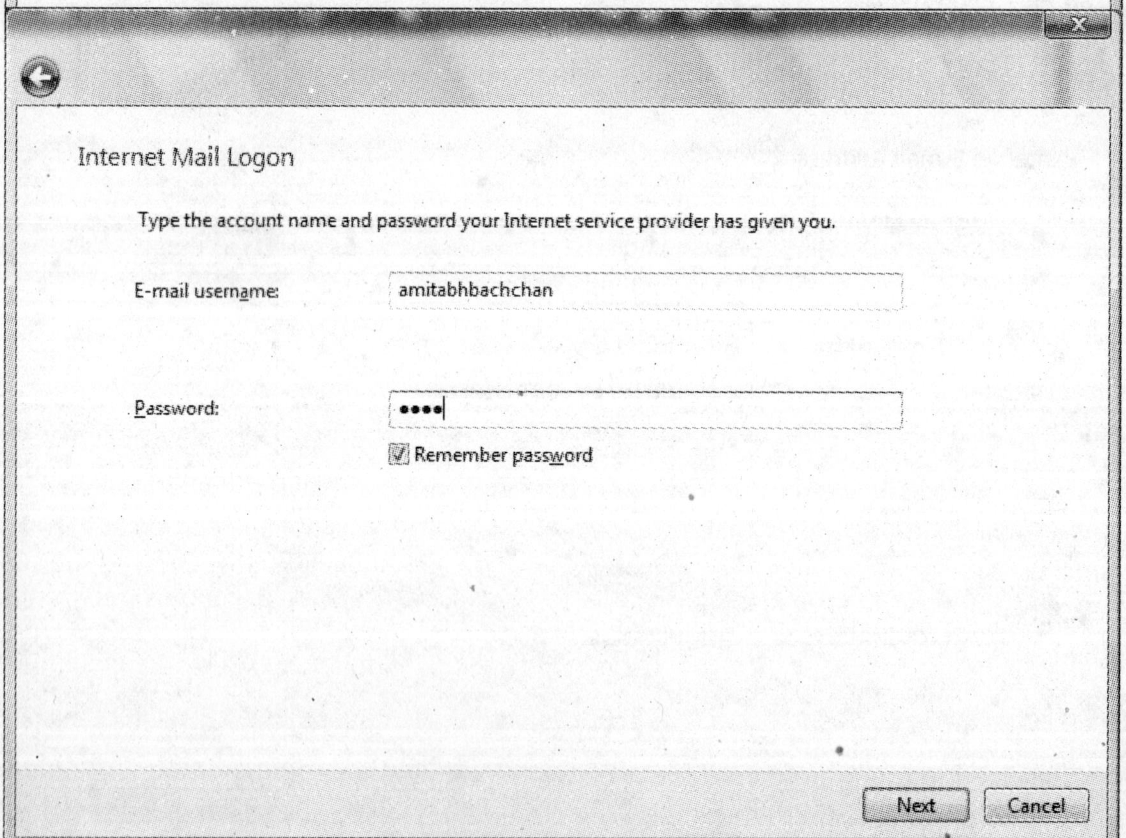
Internet Mail Logon
Type the account name and password your Internet service provider has given you.
E-mail username:
amitabhbachchan
Password:
Remember password
Next
Cancel

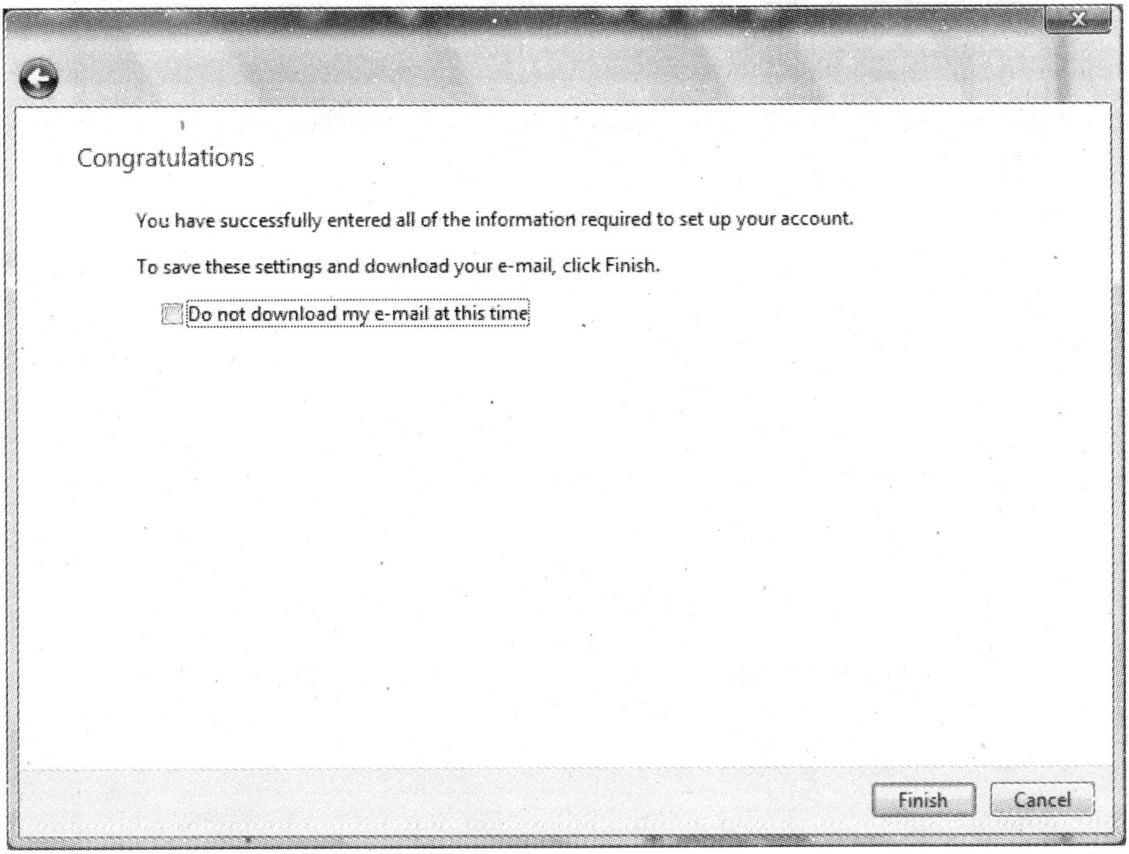

To reply to a message, click the Reply button.

Creating and sending e mail messages

To create a new e mail message in Windows Mail, click the Create Mail button. A new message window opens.

Here's how to fill out the message window in Windows Mail and most other e mail programs:

1. In the To box, type the e mail address of at least one recipient. If you're sending the message to multiple recipients, type a semicolon (;) between e mail addresses.
2. In the Cc box, you can type the e mail addresses of any secondary recipients—people who should know about the message but don't need to act on it. They'll receive the same message as the people in the To box. If there are no secondary recipients, leave this box blank.
3. In the Subject box, type a title for your message.
4. In the large blank area, type your message.

To attach a file to the message, click the Attach File to Message button on the toolbar (located just below the menu bar). Locate the file, select it, and then click Open. The file now appears in the Attach box in the message header.

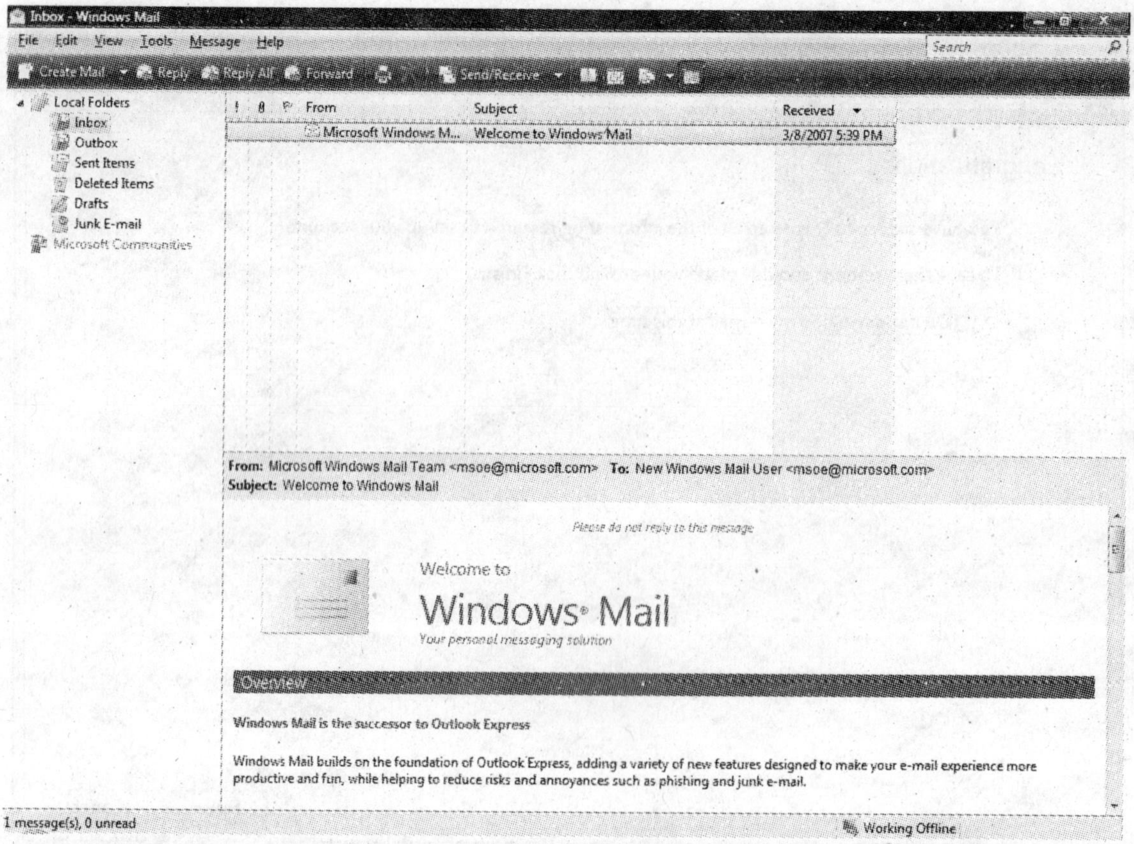

- To change the style, font, size, or color of the text, select the text, and then click one of the buttons on the formatting bar (located just above the message area).

E mail etiquette

Like telephone conversations and face-to-face communication, e mail communication has certain implied rules of behavior. These rules are referred to as e mail etiquette or netiquette (a combination of "Internet" and "etiquette"). For effective communication, follow these guidelines:

- Be careful with humor and emotion. E mail does not convey emotion well, so the recipient might not understand your intended tone. Sarcastic humor is particularly risky because the recipient might interpret it literally and take offense. To convey emotion, consider using emoticons (see "Using emoticons" in this article).
- Think before you send. Writing and sending an e mail message is fast and easy—sometimes too easy. Make sure you've thought out your message first, and avoid writing when you're angry. Once you send the message, you can't get it back.
- Use a clear and concise subject line. Summarize the contents of the message in a few words. People who receive a large amount of e mail can use the subject to prioritize the message.

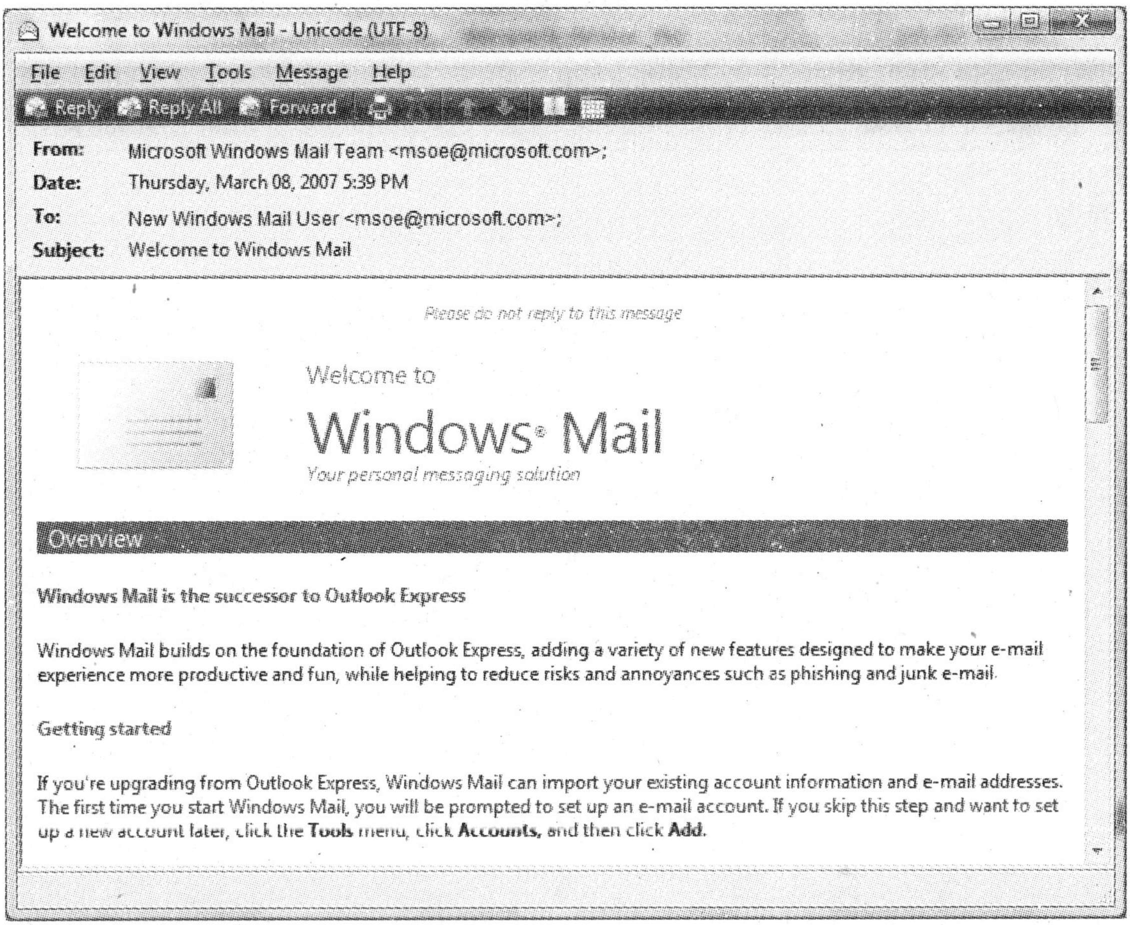

- Keep messages short. Although an e mail message can be of any length, e mail is designed for quick communication. Many people don't have the time or patience to read more than a few paragraphs.
- Avoid using ALL CAPITAL LETTERS. Many people perceive sentences written in all uppercase letters as "yelling" and find it annoying or offensive.
- Be careful with sensitive or confidential information. Any recipient can forward your message to others—either intentionally or accidentally.

Additionally, in formal or business communication, avoid spelling and grammatical errors. Sloppy e mail conveys an unprofessional image. Proofread your messages before you send them, and if your e mail program has a spelling checker, use it. See Check spelling in a Windows Mail message.

Dealing with junk e mail

Just as you might receive unsolicited advertisements, flyers, and catalogs in your regular mail, you'll probably receive junk e mail (often called spam) in your Inbox. Junk e mail might include advertisements, fraudulent schemes, pornography, or legitimate offers.

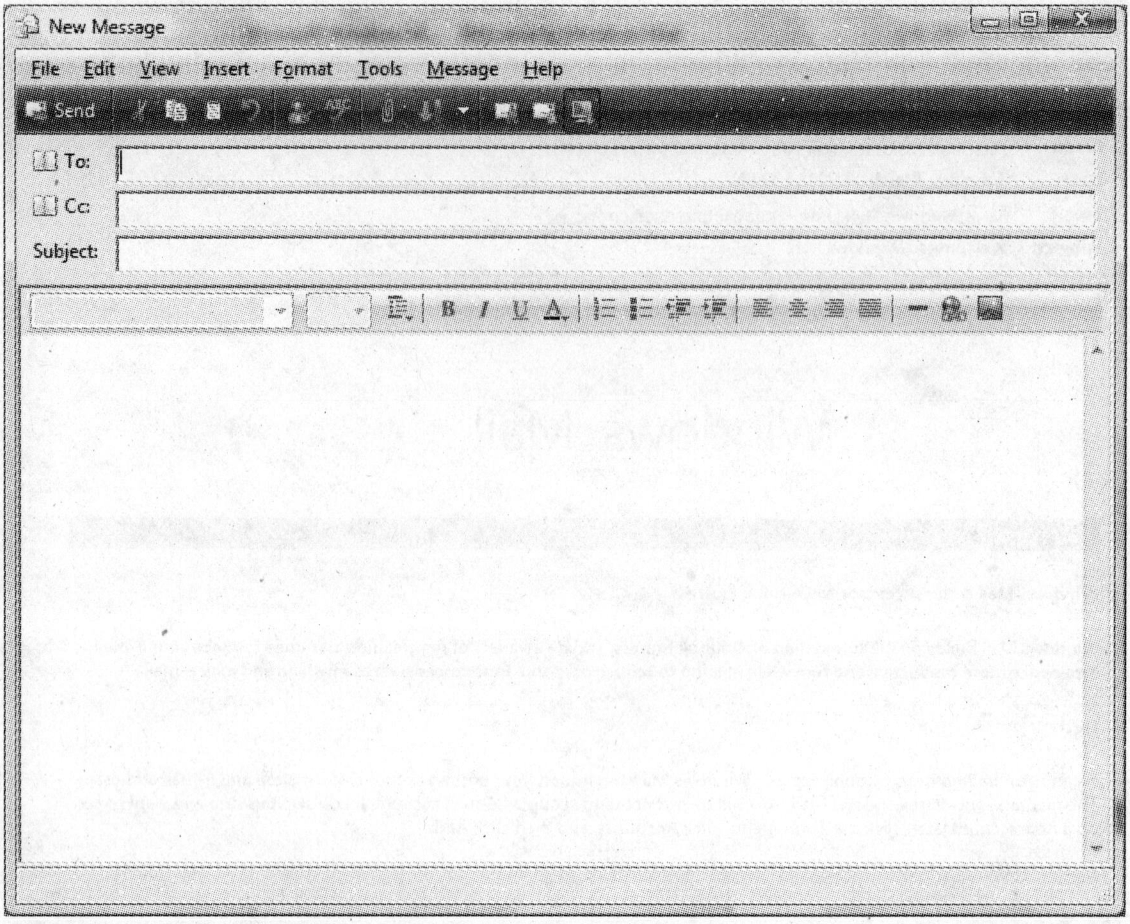

Because it's very inexpensive for marketers to send junk e mail, it's not uncommon for people to receive a large amount of it.

Windows Mail includes a junk e mail filter that analyzes the content of messages sent to you and moves suspicious messages to a special junk e mail folder, where you can view or delete them at any time. And if a junk e mail message slips past the filter into your Inbox, you can specify that any future messages from the sender be automatically moved to the junk e mail folder. See Block spam and other unwanted e mail.

To help prevent junk e mail:

- Use caution in giving out your e mail address. Avoid publishing your real e mail address in newsgroups, on websites, or in other public areas of the Internet.
- Before you give your e mail address to a website, check the site's privacy statement to be sure it does not permit the disclosure of your e mail address to other companies.
- Never reply to a junk e mail message. The sender will know that your e mail address is valid and might sell it to other companies. You're then likely to receive even more junk e mail.

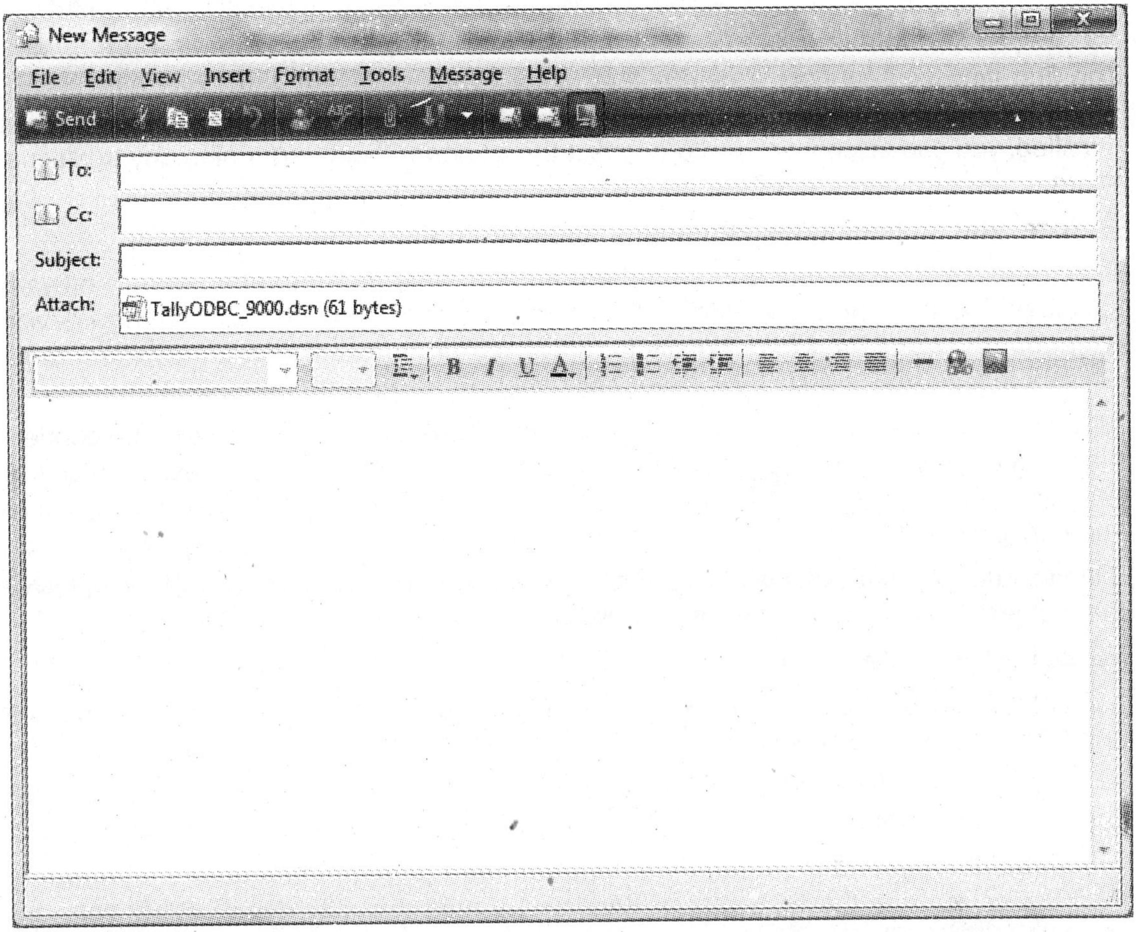

Using emoticons

Because it's often difficult to convey emotion, intent, or tone through text alone, early Internet users invented emoticons (a combination of "emotion" and "icons")—sequences of keyboard characters that symbolize facial expressions. For example, :) looks like a smiling face when you look at it sideways. Below are some examples of emoticons.

Emoticon	***Meaning***
:) or :-)	Smiling, happy, or joking
:(or :-(	Frowning or unhappy
;-)	Winking
:-l	Indifferent or ambivalent
:-o	Surprised or concerned
:-x	Not saying anything
:-p	Sticking out your tongue (usually in fun)
:-D	Laughing

Install a USB device

The first time you connect a device that plugs into a universal serial bus (USB) port, Windows automatically installs driver software for that device. After driver software is installed, you can disconnect and reconnect the device without performing any additional steps.

Before you install your device

Check the instructions included with the device to determine whether driver software should be installed before you connect the device. Typically, Windows detects a new device after you connect it, and then installs the driver software automatically. However, some devices require you to install the driver software before plugging the device in.

Also, while most devices that have power switches should be turned on before you connect them, others require that you turn them on during the installation process. Because of issues like this, it's a good idea to read the instructions included with a new device before you connect it.

If the instructions that came with your device contradict the information in this topic, follow the instructions that came with the device.

Plugging your device in

If your USB device uses a power cord, you should connect the device to a power source and turn it on before connecting it.

Next, determine which USB port you want to connect your device to. If your computer has USB ports on the front, consider using one of those if you plan to frequently connect and disconnect the device.

Plug the device into the USB port. If Windows is able to install device driver software automatically, you'll be notified that the device is ready to use. Otherwise, Windows will prompt you to insert a disc containing driver software for the device.

After installation is complete, check the information for your device to see if any additional software that might have been included with the device should be installed.

Notes

- When connecting a device to a USB port on a USB hub, monitor, or other device that's plugged into your computer, ensure that the USB port has enough power to support your device. Smaller devices, such as USB flash drives and mice, and devices with their own power cords, such as printers, typically work properly when connected to an unpowered USB hub. Some devices that use more power, such as USB-powered scanners and web cameras, require a hub that has its own power cord to function properly. If a device doesn't work properly when connected to a hub, try connecting it directly to one of your computer's USB ports.
- Devices that transfer large amounts of information, such as external hard disks, scanners, and video cameras, function best when connected to high-speed USB 2.0 ports. Some older computers may include only USB 1.x ports, or a mix of USB

1.x and 2.0 ports. If your device requires a high-speed port to function properly, check information provided by the manufacturer for your computer to ensure that the port you're using supports USB 2.0. If your computer includes only USB 1.x ports, you can add USB 2.0 ports by installing a USB 2.0 card inside your computer.

Connecting and disconnecting devices

Most USB devices can be removed and unplugged at will. When unplugging storage devices, such as USB flash drives, you should be sure that the computer has finished saving any information to the device before removing it. If the device has an activity light, wait for a few seconds after the light has finished flashing before unplugging it.

If you see the Safely Remove Hardware icon in the notification area at the far right of the taskbar, you can use this to ensure that devices have finished all operations in progress and are ready to remove. Click the icon and you'll see a list of devices. Click the device you want to remove.

You can use any USB port when plugging in a device that you've previously installed. However, the first time you plug a device into a particular port, Windows will install the driver software for that device again.

Windows Contacts

It is a new feature in Windows Vista; a central directory for phone numbers, email addresses, and mailing addresses. It is not so much a program as a specialized Explorer window, complete with individual icons that represent the people in your social circle.

Managing your contacts

You can use Windows to keep track of people and organizations by creating contacts for them in Windows Contacts. Each contact contains the information for one person or organization.

When you need to look up a friend's e mail address or phone number, you can open your Contacts folder and find it there. When you want to take notes about a business contact, you can store them in the Contacts folder. No matter what type of contact information you want to remember about someone, you can put it in the Contacts folder—even a picture.

The Contacts folder also functions as the address book for Windows Mail. When you create an e mail message in Windows Mail, you select the recipient from your Contacts folder. Even if you don't use Windows Mail as your e mail program, you can still use Windows Contacts to store information about people and organizations. Use Windows Contacts to keep track of all the people and organizations you communicate with

What's in a contact?

You can store as much or as little information as you like about each contact, including any of the following:

- E mail addresses. Store as many e mail addresses as you want for a contact, and set one as the preferred address. (The preferred e mail address is what Windows

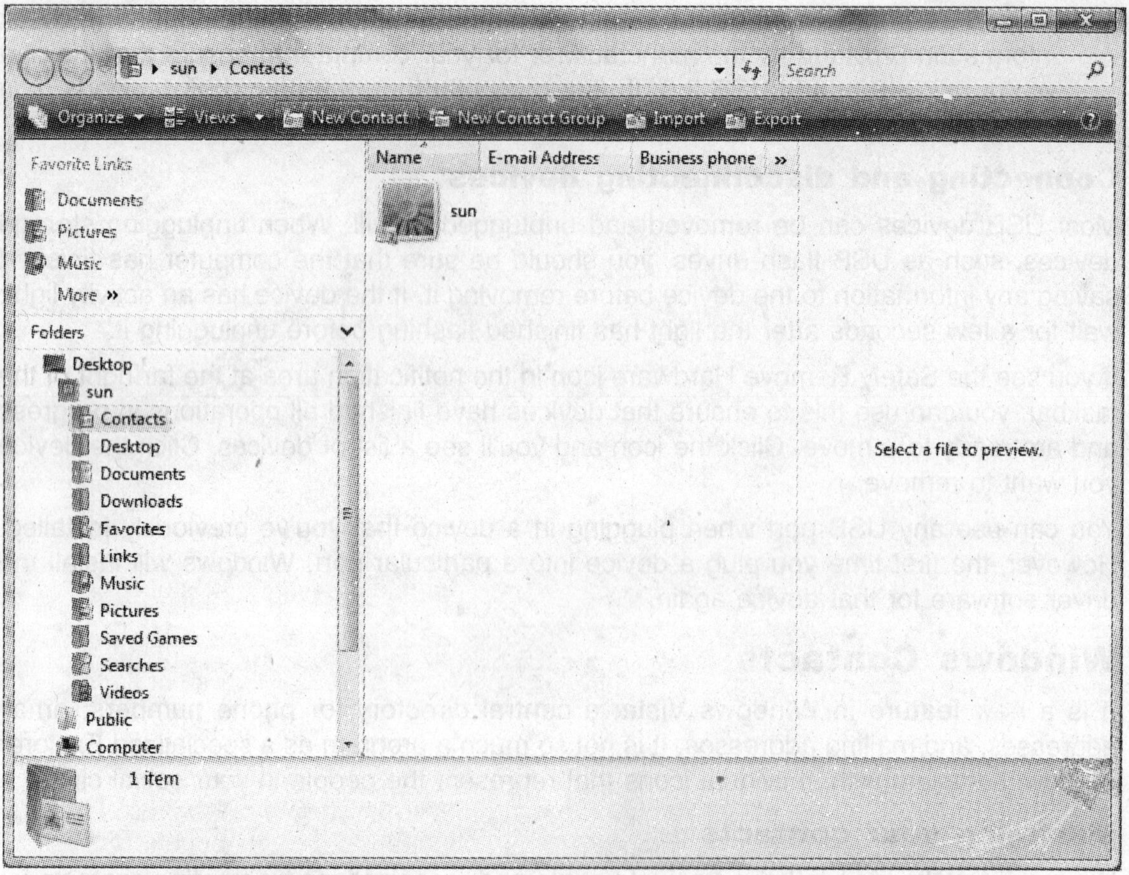

Mail will use if you want to send someone e mail quickly without selecting from a list of all their addresses.)

- A picture. Adding a picture of a contact can help you remember the person.
- Phone numbers. You can store home, work, cell, and fax phone numbers for a contact.
- Street addresses. You can store both home and work street addresses for a contact.
- Family information. You can enter information here about a contact's spouse or partner, children, gender, birthday, and anniversary.
- Website addresses. You can store both home and work website addresses for a contact.
- Notes. Type any other information about a contact.

Finding the Contacts folder

Click to open Windows Contacts.

- You can find the Contacts folder yourself by clicking the Start button , clicking All Programs, and then clicking Windows Contacts.

Adding a contact

1. Click to open Windows Contacts.
2. Click New Contact, and then type the information you want for the contact in any of the boxes on the available tabs. You don't have to fill in all the boxes; just enter as much information as you want about the contact.

Adding information to a contact

1. Click to open Windows Contacts.
2. Double-click the contact you want to change.
3. Click the tab where you want to add information, and then type in any of the available boxes.

Adding a new picture to a contact

1. Click to open Windows Contacts.
2. Double-click the contact with the picture you want to change. (Windows adds a default

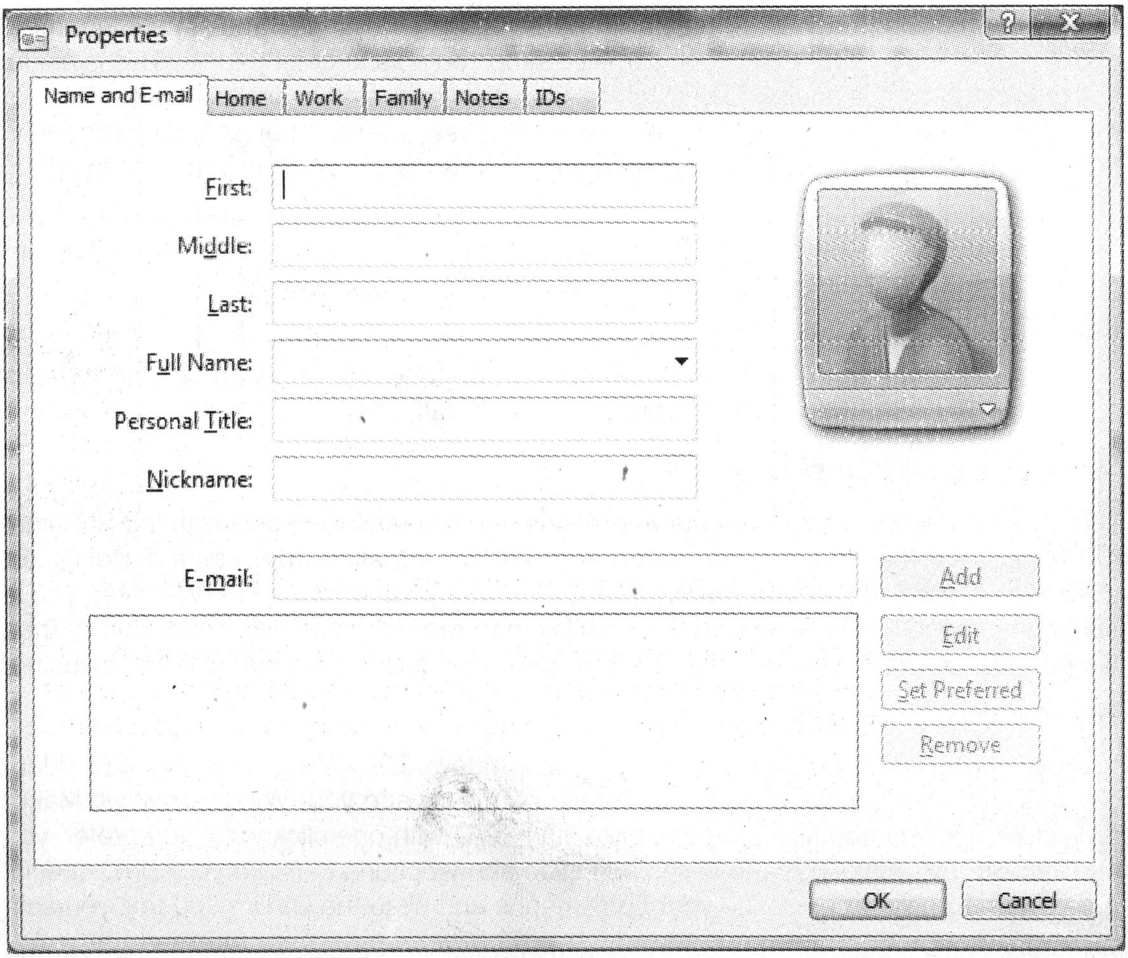

image for each contact which you can change to any picture or graphic you want.)

3. On the Name and e mail tab, click the contact picture, and then do one of the following:
   - To add a new picture, click Change picture, locate the picture you want to use for the contact, click it, and then click Open.
   - To remove an existing picture, click Remove picture. The picture will revert to the default contact image used by Windows. (You cannot remove this default image.)

Creating contact groups (mailing lists)

You can also create contact groups, which combine multiple individual contacts into a single group. Creating a contact group enables you to send e mail to many people at once. If you send an e mail message to a contact group, it will be sent to everyone you added to the group. Sending e mail to a contact group can be a lot easier than adding names one at a time to an e mail message, especially if you often send messages to the same group of people.

Sending contacts to other people

In addition to using Windows Contacts to address e mail messages and store information about people and organizations, you can also send contacts to other people. This is useful if you want to send someone contact information about yourself or someone else. There's no need to type a bunch of phone numbers, addresses, and other contact information into an e mail message—just send them a contact with the information you want to share.

To send a contact to someone who is not using this version of Windows, you may first need to export the contact to another format. For more information, see Import, export, or change the format for contacts.

Note

- If you upgrade to this version of Windows from Windows XP, each of your contacts in the Windows Address Book will be automatically stored in Windows Contacts.

Windows DVD Maker

DVD Maker, a new program, debuts with Windows Vista, and then only iwth the Premium or Ultimate editions. You can export your finished Movie Maker project as a digital file, or save it to a good old VHS cassette. But preserving your work on a DVD gives you a boatload of benefits, including better durability than tape, dramatically better quality than a movie file, no need for rewinding, duplication without quality loss, and cheaper shipping.

Burn a DVD-Video disc

You can create DVDs quickly and easily using Windows DVD Maker. You can add video, pictures, and audio, make slide shows for your DVD, or add your Windows Movie Maker projects. Once you add files, you can burn your DVD with one click, or, if you prefer, you can choose from several menu styles and slide show options to make your DVD special before you burn it, or customize your DVD menus and write the DVD menu text yourself.

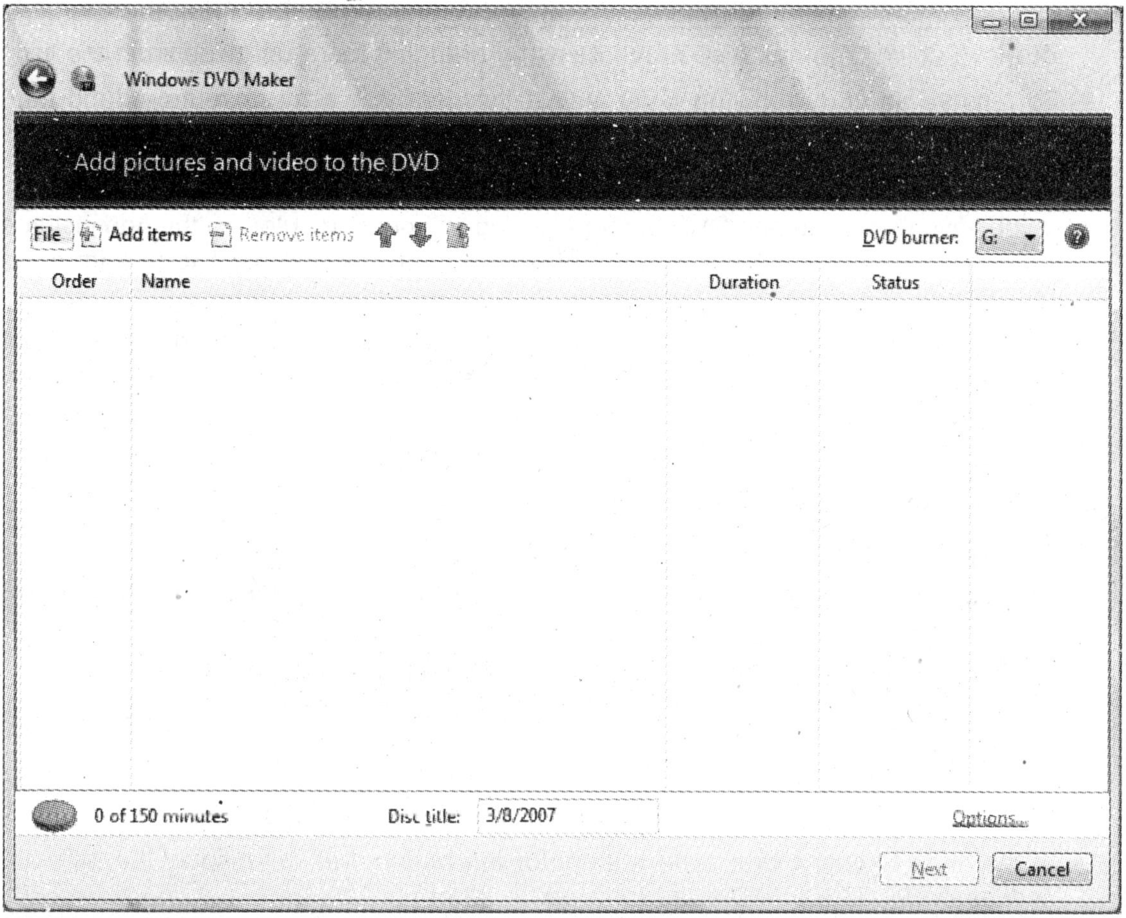

After you create a DVD, you can play the DVD in a DVD player and watch your movies and slide shows on TV. The following steps explain how to use Windows DVD Maker to burn a DVD.

To open Windows DVD Maker

- Click Start, click All Programs, and then click Windows DVD Maker.

Note

- You can also open Windows DVD Maker by inserting a blank recordable or rewriteable DVD into your DVD burner. When the AutoPlay dialog appears automatically, click Burn a DVD video disc using Windows DVD Maker.

To add and arrange items on a DVD

1. On the Add pictures and video to the DVD page, click Add items.
2. Locate and select the video files, pictures, and Windows Movie Maker project files that you want to include on your DVD, and then click Add.
3. To arrange items and specify the order that the different items will play from the DVD,

click the video, picture, or slide show that you want to move, and then click Move up or Move down. You can also move items by dragging them up or down in the list.

4. To remove an item from the DVD, select the item you want to remove, and then click Remove items.

To choose a DVD burner and enter a DVD title

1. If you have more than one DVD burner installed on your computer, on the Add pictures and video to the DVD page, select the DVD burner that you want to use from the DVD burner list.
2. If you want to set different options for your DVD, click Options. For information about the different options you can specify when burning a DVD, see Change DVD-Video settings.
3. Click the Disc title box, and then type a title for the DVD.

To change the menu text for your DVD

1. Once you've added all of your files and chosen the burner and title, click Next.
2. To customize the text for the DVD menu, click Menu text, and then do one or more of the following:

- Click the Font box, and then select the font for the menu text.
- Click the Font Color, Bold, or Italics buttons to select the font color and formatting.
- In the Disc title box, type the title you want to use for your DVD.
- In the Play button box, type a label for the button that plays your DVD.
- In the Scenes button box, type a label for the button that will display the different scenes on the DVD.
- In the Notes button box, type a label for the button that will display any notes you enter for the DVD.
- In the Notes box, type any notes that you want to appear on your DVD.

  The Notes button and Notes page only appear on the DVD if you include information in these fields.
- Click Change Text.
- You can see a static preview of your settings in the preview pane at the right side of the screen. Or, to see how the menu text will look when you burn your DVD, click Preview.

To customize the menu style for your DVD

1. To customize the menu style for your DVD, click one of the DVD menu styles along the right side of the screen, or click Customize menu and then do one or more of the following:

- Click the Font box, and then select a font.
- Click the Font Color, Bold, or Italic buttons to select the font color and formatting.

- If you've chosen a menu style with both foreground and background video options, near Foreground video, click Browse, locate the video that you want to appear in the foreground, and then click Open.
- To have a picture or video appear as the background for the main DVD menu, near Background video, click Browse, locate the video that you want to appear in the background, and then click Open.
- To add a digital media audio file to play as background music while the menu is displayed for your DVD, near Menu audio, click Browse, locate the audio file that you want to use, and then click Open.
- Click the Scenes button styles box, and then select the shape for the scenes buttons on your DVD.
- If you want to see the menu as it will appear when you play your DVD, click Preview.

2. If you want to save the customized DVD menu settings as a new DVD menu style, click Save as new style. In the Style name name box, type a name for the customized menu style, and then click OK. You can then choose to use this customized DVD menu style for the current DVD and for other DVDs you create using Windows DVD Maker.
3. If you did not save the style as a new style, click Change Style to save the changes you made for this DVD and to return to the previous page.

To choose the settings for a slide show on the DVD

1. To set the photo settings for the slide show on your DVD, click Slide show.
2. On the Change your slide show settings page, do one or more of the following:
   - Click Add Music, navigate to the music files you want to add, and then click Open.
   - Depending on the length and settings for the slide show, you might want to add additional audio files. To do so, repeat the previous step.
   - If you added more than one audio file and you want to change the order in which the music files play in the slide show, click an audio file that you want to move, and then click Move Up or Move Down.
   - To remove an audio file from the list, in the Music for slide show list, select the audio file, and then click Remove.
   - To automatically change the slide show length so it matches the duration of the music you have added, select the Change slide show length to match music length check box.
   - To specify the duration for each picture to display in the slide show, select the duration (in seconds) from the Picture length box.
   - To choose the kind of transitions you want to use between pictures, select a transition type from the Transition box.
   - To add pan-and-zoom effects to the pictures you include in your slide show, click Use pan-and-zoom effects for pictures.

3. Click Change Slide Show to save the changes you made and to go to the previous page.

To burn your DVD

1. When you've finished adding files and customizing your DVD menus, click Burn..
2. After the DVD disc has been successfully burned, you can do one or more of the following on the Your disc is ready page:
   - To make another copy of the current DVD, remove the completed DVD, insert a new recordable DVD, and then click Make another copy of this disc.
   - To close Windows DVD Maker, click Close.

Windows Photo Gallery

Photo Gallery approaches digital photo management as a four-step process; importing the photos to your Picture folder; organizing, tagging, and rating them; editing them; and sharing them (via prints, onscreen slideshows, design DVD slideshows, email, screen saver, and so on).

Find a picture on your computer

The easiest way to locate and view pictures on your computer is by using Windows Photo Gallery. By default, Photo Gallery shows all the pictures and videos that are located in the Pictures folder, but you can add other folders to Photo Gallery. You can search for pictures and videos by typing in the Search box or by clicking tags, ratings, or dates in the Navigation pane.

Click to open Windows Photo Gallery.

To browse and view pictures

To	*Do this*
See all your pictures and videos in Photo Gallery	In the Navigation pane, click All Pictures and Videos. All Pictures and Videos in the Navigation pane
See all pictures or all videos, but not both	In the Navigation pane, under All Pictures and Videos, click either Pictures or Videos.
See a larger preview of a picture thumbnail	Rest the mouse pointer over a picture thumbnail.
See the picture in a larger view	Double-click the picture.
Return to the thumbnail view	Click Back to Gallery.

To find pictures

To	*Do this*
Find a picture by tag	In the Navigation pane, under Tags, click a tag to see all of the pictures and videos using that tag.Tags in the Navigation pane

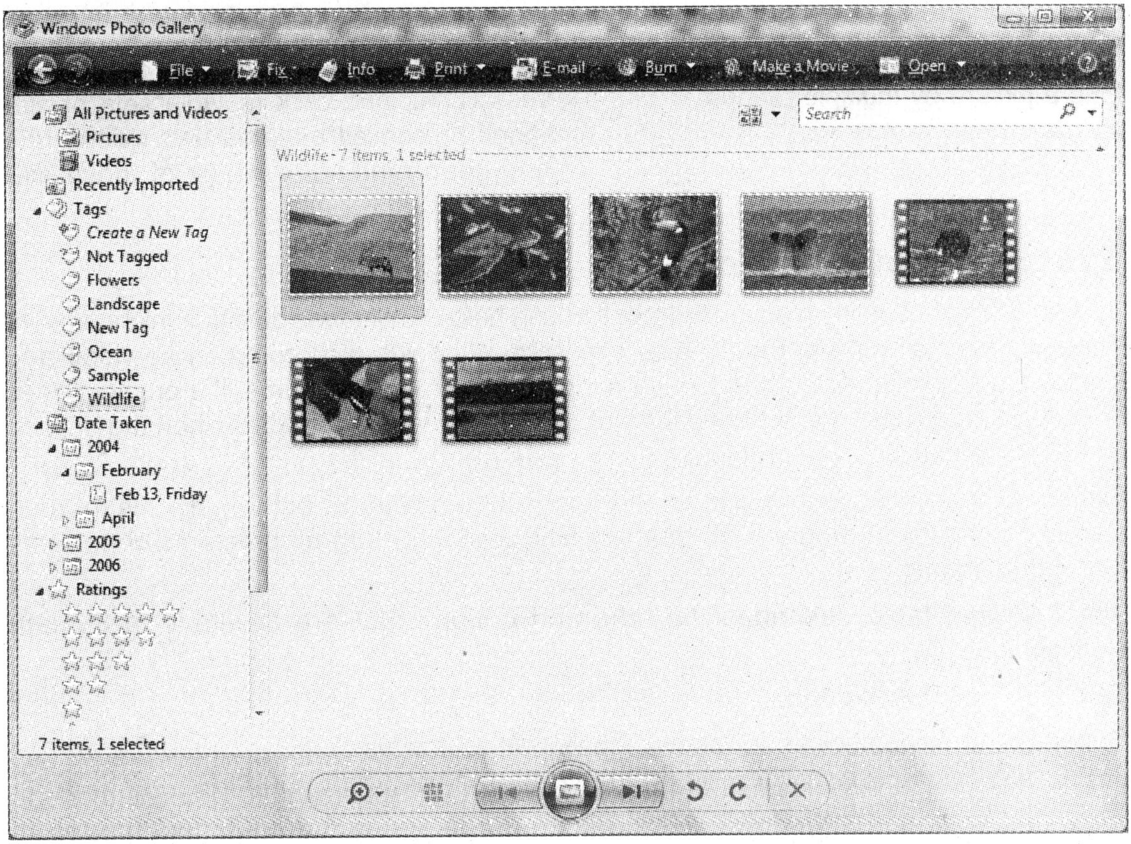

Find a picture by multiple tags	Press the CTRL key and click multiple tags to see all of the pictures and videos that include any of those tags.
Find a picture by file name or tag	Type the name of the file or tag in the Search box. You can type the entire name, or just the first few letters.The Search box
Find a picture by file extension	Type the file extension in the Search box to quickly limit the results to certain file formats, such as .jpg, .tif, or .wmv.
Find a picture by year, month, or date taken	In the Navigation pane, under Date Taken, click a year to see all of the pictures and videos taken during that year, or expand the year to select a month or date.
Find a picture by multiple dates	Press CTRL and click multiple dates to see all of the pictures and videos taken on any of those dates.
Find a picture by rating	In the Navigation pane, under Ratings, click a set of stars (from Not Rated to five stars)

	to see all of the pictures and videos that have been marked with that star rating.
Find a picture by multiple ratings	Press CTRL and click multiple sets of star ratings to see all pictures and videos that have been marked with any of those star ratings.

System Configuration

System Configuration is an advanced tool that can help identify problems that might prevent Windows from starting correctly. You can start Windows with common services and startup programs turned off and then turn them back on, one at a time. If a problem does not occur when a service is turned off, but does occur when turned on, then the service could be the cause of the problem.

System Configuration is intended to find and isolate problems, but it is not meant as a startup management program. To permanently remove or turn off programs or services that run at startup.

The following table describes the tabs and options that are available in System Configuration:

Tab	*Description*
General	Lists choices for startup configuration modes: • Normal startup. Starts Windows in the usual manner. Use this mode to start Windows after you are done using the other two modes to troubleshoot the problem. • Diagnostic startup. Starts Windows with basic services and drivers only. This mode can help rule out basic Windows files as the problem. • Selective startup. Starts Windows with basic services and drivers and the other services and startup programs that you select.
Boot	Shows configuration options for the operating system and advanced debugging settings, including: • Safe boot: Minimal. Boots to the Windows graphical user interface (Windows Explorer) in safe mode running only critical system services. Networking is disabled. • Safe boot: Alternate shell. Boots to the Windows Command Prompt in safe mode running only critical system services. Networking and the graphical user interface are disabled. • Safe boot: Active Directory repair. Boots to the Windows graphical user interface in safe mode running critical system services and Active Directory. • Safe boot: Network. Boots to the Windows graphical user interface in safe mode running only critical system services. Networking is enabled.

- No GUI boot. Does not display the Windows splash screen when booting.
- Boot log. Stores all information from the boot process in the file %SystemRoot%Ntbtlog.txt.
- Base video. Boots to the Windows graphical user interface in minimal VGA mode. This loads standard VGA drivers instead of display drivers specific to the video hardware on the computer.
- OS boot information. Shows driver names as drivers are being loaded during the boot process.
- Make all settings permanent. Does not track changes made in System Configuration. Options can be changed later using System Configuration, but must be changed manually. When this option is selected, you cannot roll back your changes by selecting Normal startup on the General tab.

Services

Lists all of the services that start when the computer boots, along with their current status (Running or Stopped). Use the Services tab to enable or disable individual services at boot time to troubleshoot which services might be contributing to boot problems.

Select Hide all Microsoft services to show only third-party applications in the services list. Clear the check box for a service to disable it on your next boot. If you have chosen Selective startup on the General tab, you must either choose Normal startup on the General tab or select the service's check box to start it again at boot time.

Warning

- Disabling services that normally run at boot time might cause some programs to malfunction or result in system instability. Do not disable services in this list unless you know they are not essential to your computer's operation. Selecting Disable all will not disable some secure Microsoft services required for the operating system to start.

Startup

Lists applications that run when the computer boots, along with the name of their publisher, the path to the executable file, and the location of the registry key or shortcut that causes the application to run.

Clear the check box for a startup item to disable it on your next boot. If you have chosen Selective startup on the General tab, you must either choose Normal startup on the General tab or select the startup item's check box to start it again at boot time.

If you suspect an application has been compromised, examine the Command column to review the path to the executable file.

- Disabling applications that normally run at boot time might result in related applications starting more slowly or not running as expected.

Tools

Provides a convenient list of diagnostic tools and other advanced tools that you can run.

To start Windows in Diagnostic startup mode

1. Click to open System Configuration. If you are prompted for an administrator password or confirmation, type the password or provide confirmation.
2. Click the General tab, click Diagnostic startup, click OK, and then click Restart.
3. If the problem occurs, then basic Windows files or drivers might be corrupted. For more information, search Windows Help and Support for "Startup Repair."
4. If the problem does not occur, then use Selective startup mode to try to find the problem by turning individual services and startup programs on or off.

To start Windows in Selective startup mode

1. Click to open System Configuration. If you are prompted for an administrator password or confirmation, type the password or provide confirmation.
2. Click the General tab, click Selective startup, and then clear the Load system services and Load startup items check boxes.
3. Select the Load system services check box, click OK, and then click Restart.
4. If the problem occurs after restarting, do one or both (if necessary) of the following tasks:

Identify the system service that is causing the problem

1. Click the Services tab, click Disable all, select the check box for the first service that is listed, and then restart the computer. If the problem does not occur, then you can eliminate the first service as the cause of the problem.
2. With the first service selected, select the second service check box, and then restart the computer.
3. Repeat this process until you reproduce the problem. If you cannot reproduce the problem, then you can eliminate system services as the cause of the problem. Perform the following task:

Identify the startup item that is causing the problem

1. Click the General tab, and then select the Load startup items check box.
2. Click the Startup tab, click Disable all, select the check box for the first startup item that is listed, and then restart the computer. If the problem does not occur, then you can eliminate the first startup item as the cause of the problem.
3. With the first startup item selected, select the second startup item check box, and then restart the computer. Repeat this process until you reproduce the problem.

Windows Calender

In addition to using Windows Calendar as your primary calendar, you can use it to subscribe to web calendars from any partic'pating organization's website or to share your schedule with others. It has the following features:

- It can automate the process of entering repeating events, such as weekly staff meeting or gym workout dates.
- Calender can give you a gentle nudge, with a dialog box and a sound, if you like; when an important appointment is approaching.
- You can "publish" your calendar on the Internet, so all your family members/ classmates/baseball team members/downtrodden employees know the schedule. For example, you can susbscribe to your spouse's calender, thereby finding out when you have been committed to after-dinner drinks on the night the big game's on TV.

To open Windows Calendar

1. Click to open Windows Calendar.

To change the calendar view

You can view your calendar by day, work week, week, or month.

- Click the View menu, and then click the view you want. A check mark appears next to the view you select.

To view the details pane

- If you can't see the details of a task, date, or calendar, click the View menu, and then click Details Pane so that a check mark appears. To close the Details pane, click Details Pane again, so that the check mark disappears.

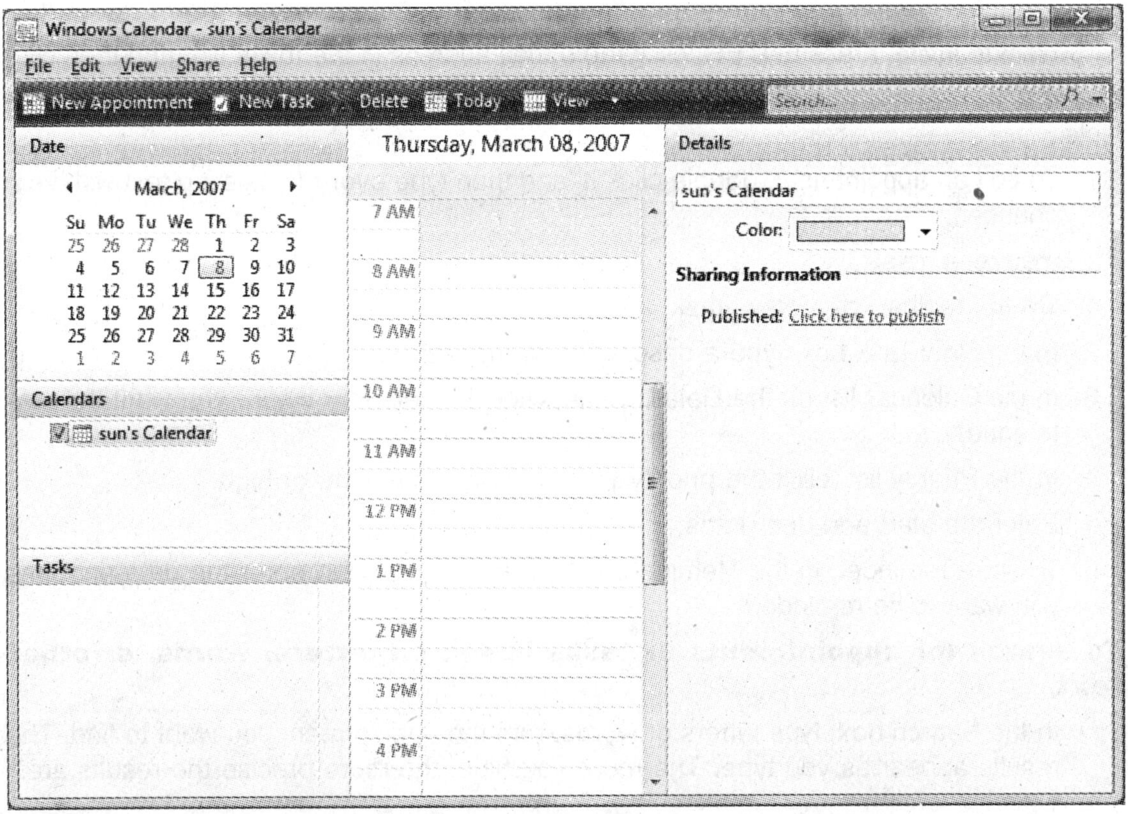

To create a calendar

1. Click the File menu, and then click New Calendar.
2. In the New Calendar box, type the name you want for the calendar, and then press ENTER.
3. To choose the color of your appointments, in the Details pane, click Color, and then click the color you want.

To create an appointment

1. On the toolbar, click New Appointment.
2. In the New Appointment box, type a description of the appointment.
3. In the Location box on the Details pane, type the location of the appointment.
4. In the Calendar list, click the calendar where you want the appointment to appear.
5. To make an all-day appointment, select the All-day Appointment check box.
6. Enter start and end times.
7. To make the appointment recur, in the Recurrence list, click the type of recurrence you want.
8. To set a reminder, in the Reminder list, click how long before the appointment you want to be reminded.
9. To invite someone, in the Attendees list, type the e mail address of the person you want to invite, press ENTER, click the e mail address in the Invite list, and then click Invite.

Note

- To edit an appointment, double-click it, and then type over the existing text with your changes.

To create a task

1. On the toolbar, click New Task.
2. In the New Task box, type a description of the task.
3. In the Calendar list on the Details pane, click the calendar where you want the task to appear.
4. In the Priority list, click the priority you want: low, medium, or high.
5. Enter the start and due dates.
6. To set a reminder, in the Reminder list, click On date, and enter the date and time you want to be reminded.

To search for appointments or tasks based on letters, words, or other text

- In the Search box, type letters or words from the appointment you want to find. The results appear as you type. The more you type, the more precise the results are.

To subscribe to a calendar

Many major sports teams, television and radio shows, and academic institutions offer calendars on the Internet. When you subscribe to one of these calendars, you can set how often your personal calendar is updated with the subscription calendar's event dates. Windows Calendar works with calendars in the iCalendar format (.ics).

- On the toolbar, click Subscribe, and then follow the instructions.

Note

- To see a list of calendars that you can subscribe to online, click Windows Calendar website.

To publish a calendar

You can publish your own calendar on the Internet through a web host so that others can see and share it. If you want, you can publish your personal schedule with password protection, so that you can choose who can access and view it.

1. Click the Share menu, and then click Publish.
2. In the Calendar name box, type the calendar name that you want to share.
3. In the Location to publish calendar box, enter the location (such as a website) where you want to publish the calendar.
4. Select any other options you want, and then click Publish.

Note

- To see locations where you can publish your calendar online, click Where can I publish this calendar?

To print a calendar

You can print your calendar by day, work week, week, or month.

1. On the toolbar, click Print.
2. Under Print Style, click one of the following: Day, Work Week, Week, or Month, and then click OK.

Windows Meeting Space

Windows Meeting Space gives you the ability to share documents, programs, or your desktop with other people. Some advantages are:

- You can share your desktop or any program with other meeting participants.
- You and other meeting participants can distribute and co-edit documents.
- You can pass notes to other participants.
- You can connect to a network projector to give a presentation.

Windows Meeting Space uses peer-to-peer technology and automatically sets up an ad hoc network if it can't find an existing network. So you can use it in a conference room, a favorite hotspot, or a place where no network exists. You can join a meeting that someone else sets up, or you can start a new meeting and invite other people to join it.

Join a meeting using Windows Meeting Space

With Windows Meeting Space, you can collaborate and share documents, programs, or your desktop with other people on the Internet, a local network, or a wireless ad hoc network.

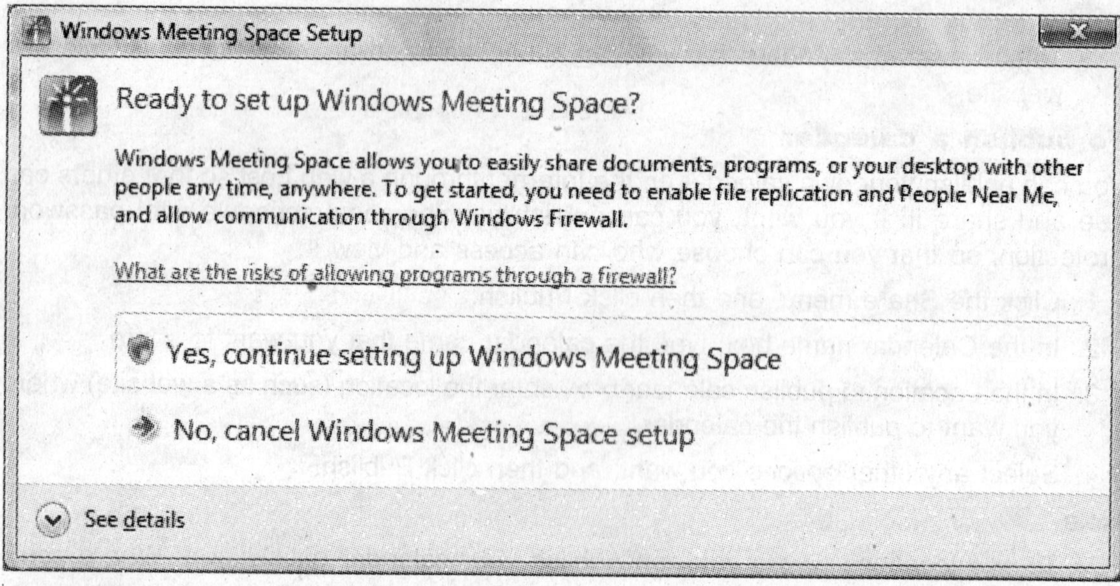

You can join a meeting by double-clicking the invitation file that you receive from someone in the meeting. You can also join a meeting by following these steps:

1. Click to open Windows Meeting Space.

   If this is the first time you open Windows Meeting Space, you will be prompted to turn on some services and sign in to People Near Me. If you are prompted for an administrator password or confirmation, type the password or provide confirmation.
2. Click Join a meeting near me, type the password for the meeting, and then click the arrow.

Mobility Center

It is there if you are using Vista on the laptop. It is a handy, centralized hub for everything that makes a laptop battery; wireless networking; external projector connection, and so on. Following are the options which you can use for the Mobility.

What's new for using your mobile PC while traveling?

If you've ever traveled with your mobile PC, you've probably experienced that moment of dread when you realize that you don't have the most recent version of your files or that your battery charge will last only several more minutes. This article discusses four ways that you can use Windows Vista to travel more efficiently with your mobile PC.

Before You Leave—Sync Center

If you use more than one computer, such as a desktop computer in addition to your mobile PC, it can be difficult to keep track of all your files. How can you make sure that you have the most recent versions of your files on your mobile PC before you travel? The easiest and most efficient way is to automatically sync information on your mobile PC, desktop computer, and other devices by using Sync Center. Just create a set of rules that tells Sync Center what files you want to sync, where to sync them, and when. You can schedule Sync Center to run as frequently as you want, such as daily or weekly, or you can sync files manually before you travel.

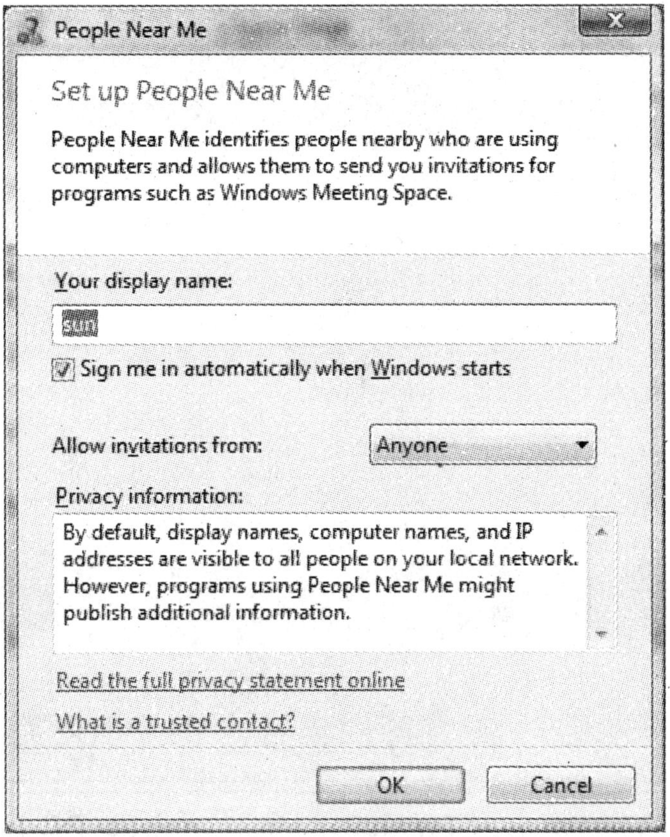

While you're traveling—Power plans

If most of your travel time will be spent on a bus or a commuter train, you'll need to rely on battery power. Even with recent advancements in battery cell technology and software that makes more efficient use of power, a single charge lasts only several hours on most mobile PCs. In Windows Vista, you can use a power plan called Power saver, which reduces your power consumption by lowering system performance. This plan is best suited for activities such as reading e-mail messages and listening to music.

Windows Meeting Space

If you're traveling with coworkers, you may need to share information with them. For example, you may need to work together on a presentation. With Windows Meeting Space, you can work with up to 10 other people on the Internet, a local network, or an ad hoc network. If no network exists, Windows Meeting Space will set one up automatically. You can share your desktop or any program with other session participants, distribute and edit documents on each other's computers, and pass notes to other participants.

Windows Mobility Center

If you're traveling to different locations with your mobile PC, you may have to check your network connectivity, adjust your power plan, or change your display brightness. Changing settings in Windows Mobility Center is faster than changing them in Control Panel because it provides a single location where you can adjust all of the most frequently used mobile PC settings.

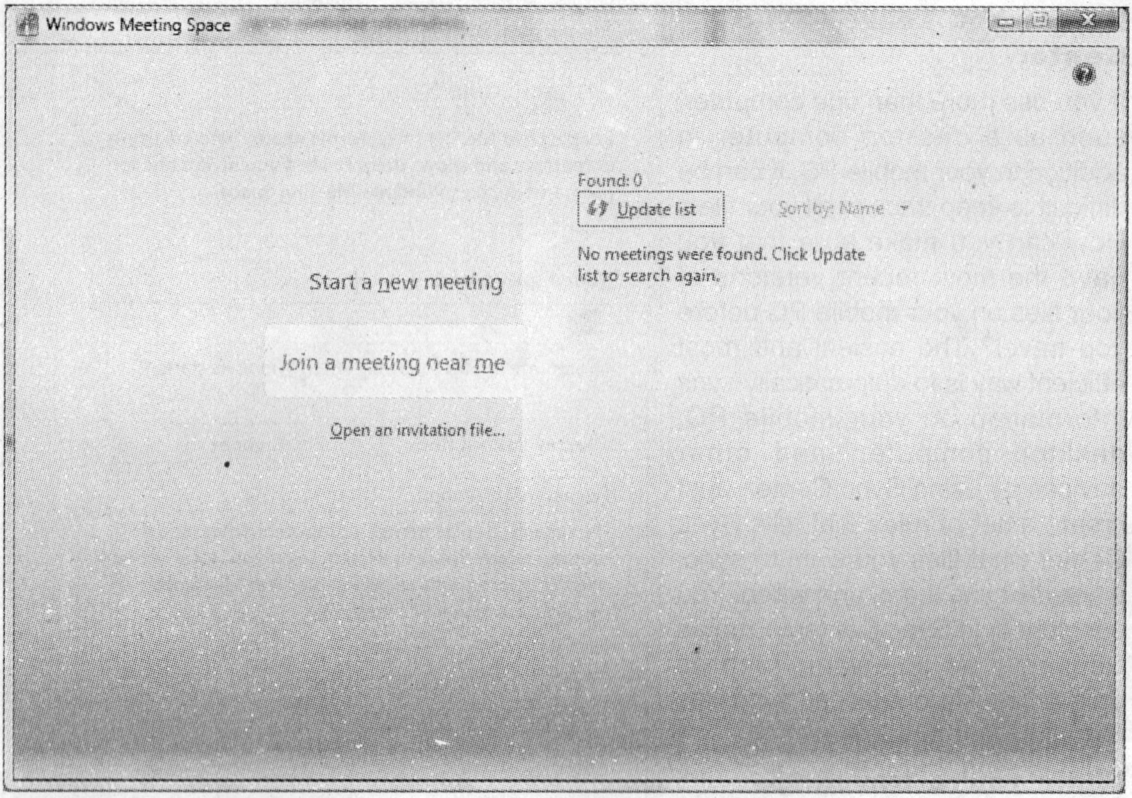

What's new for using your mobile PC in meetings?

Mobile PCs are becoming essential when you're away from your desk, especially when attending meetings. This article discusses three ways that you can use a mobile PC running Windows Vista to be more productive in meetings.

Windows Mobility Center

Now there is a single location where you can adjust mobile PC settings. You can adjust the volume on your mobile PC, check your network connectivity, adjust the brightness of your display, and more. Mobility Center provides the quickest way to adjust settings before you give a presentation or when you're in a meeting.

Presentation Settings

Have you ever had your display turn black in the middle of a presentation? Or has the desktop background image made your children the center of attention when you were presenting a proposal to a group of clients? With Presentation Settings, you can automatically turn off the screen saver, prevent system notifications from appearing, change your desktop background image, and adjust the volume level on your mobile PC when you connect to a projector to broadcast a presentation. Or, you can manually adjust Presentation Settings in Mobility Center.

Network projection

With Windows , you can easily use a network projector to give a presentation from a mobile PC. A network projector is a shared resource that you can access from your mobile PC, similar to finding a printer on a network. By using the Connect to a Network Projector wizard, you can connect to any available network projector over a wireless or a wired network.

Windows Meeting Space

When you use your mobile PC in a collaborative environment away from your office, you may want to share data with others. With Windows Meeting Space, you can collaborate with up to 10 people on the Internet, a local network, or an ad hoc network. If no network exists, Windows Meeting Space sets up one for you. You can share your desktop or any program with other session participants, distribute and coedit documents on each other's computers, and pass notes to other participants.

Power plans

If you've given a presentation or taken notes on your mobile PC when it was using the battery, you've probably worried about running out of power before completing the task. Even with recent advancements in battery cell technology and software that make more efficient use of power, a single charge lasts only several hours on most mobile PCs. In Windows Vista, you can use a power plan called Power saver, which reduces your power consumption by lowering system performance. This plan is best suited for activities such as reading e-mail messages and listening to music.

Windows Search

Every computer offers a way to find files. And every system offers several differnt ways to open them. But Search, a star feature of Vista combines these two functions in a way that's so fast, so efficient, and so spectular, it reduces much of time. Its important to note, though, that you can search for files on your Pc using the superfast Search box in two different places:

- The Start Menu The Start Search box at the bottom of the Start menu searches everywhere on your computer.
- Explorer windows The Search box at the top of every desktop window searches only that window, including folders within it. You can expand it, too, into something called the Search pane—a way to limit the scope of your search to certain file types or date ranges, for example.

Search boxes also appear in the Control Panel window, Internet Explorer, Windows Mail, Windows Media Player, and other spots where it is useful to perform small-time, limited searches.

Snipping Tool

Snipping tool takes pictures of your PC's screen.

You can use Snipping Tool to capture a screen shot, or snip, of any object on your screen and then annotate, save, or share the image. Simply use a mouse or tablet pen to capture any of the following types of snips:

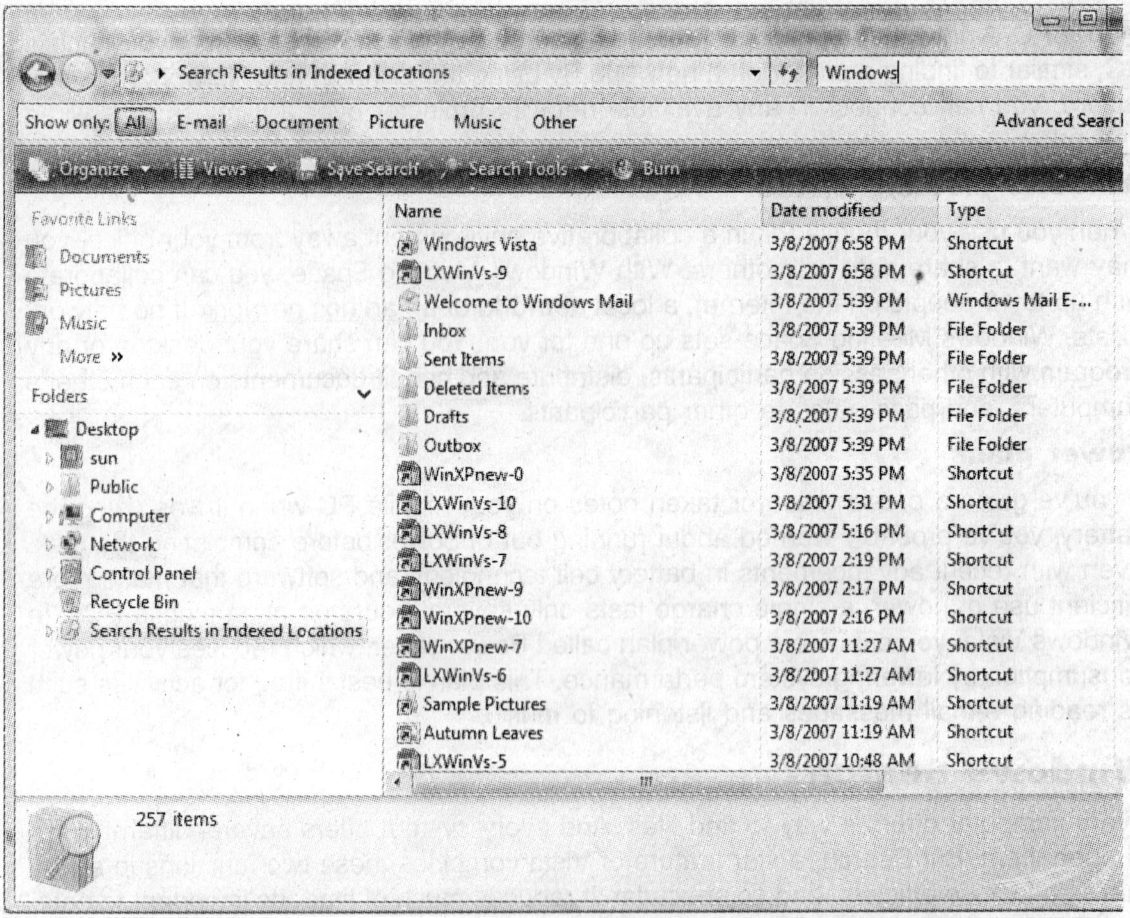

- Free-form Snip. Draw an irregular line, such as a circle or a triangle, around an object.
- Rectangular Snip. Draw a precise line by dragging the cursor around an object to form a rectangle.
- Window Snip. Select a window, such as a browser window or dialog box, that you want to capture.
- Full-screen Snip. Capture the entire screen when you select this type of snip.

After you capture a snip, it's automatically copied to the mark-up window, where you can annotate, save, or share the snip.

Let's see how it is done.

1. Open Snipping Tool

   The first thing you open it, Vista offers you the chance to add its micor-icon to your Quick Launch toolbar, so you can get to it faster the next time.

2. From the New Shortcut menu, specify what area of the screen you want to capture.

   Your choces are as mentioned above.

What you do with your finished graphic is up to you. For example,

- Paste it. The edited image may be in the window in front of you, but the original, unedited image is also on your invisible Windows Clipboard. Close the editing window without saving changes, pop into your graphics, word processing, or email program, and paste what you have copied. Often, that is exactly what you will want to do.
- Send it. The little envelope button on the eidting-window toolbar automatically prepares an outgoing email message with your graphic alrady pasted in for, if your email program is set to send plain, unformatted text message only, as an attachment.
- Save it. If your intention is to save the capture as a file, click the Save icon, or choose File, Save, or press Ctrl+S. When the Save As dialog box appears type a name for your graphic, choose a file format for it pop-up men, specify a folder location, and then click Save.

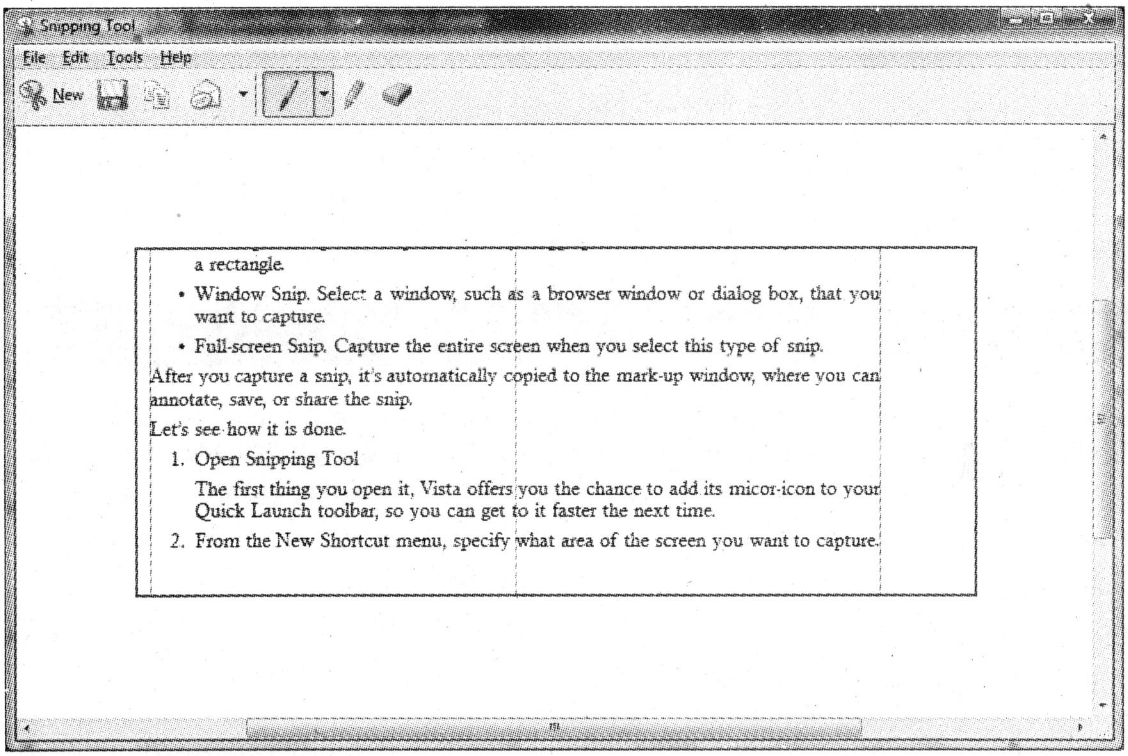

Windows Media Player

The new Windows Media Player is not only meant for listing to songs, copying them, burning them, etc., it can also be used for seeing the various types of videos and DVDs. Once you start using Media Player, you would like to use the various keybcard commands too for easy and fast actions.

Windows Media Player keyboard shortcuts

All features and buttons in Windows Media Player are accessible to you by using the keyboard only. The Player provides a variety of keyboard shortcuts for the more commonly

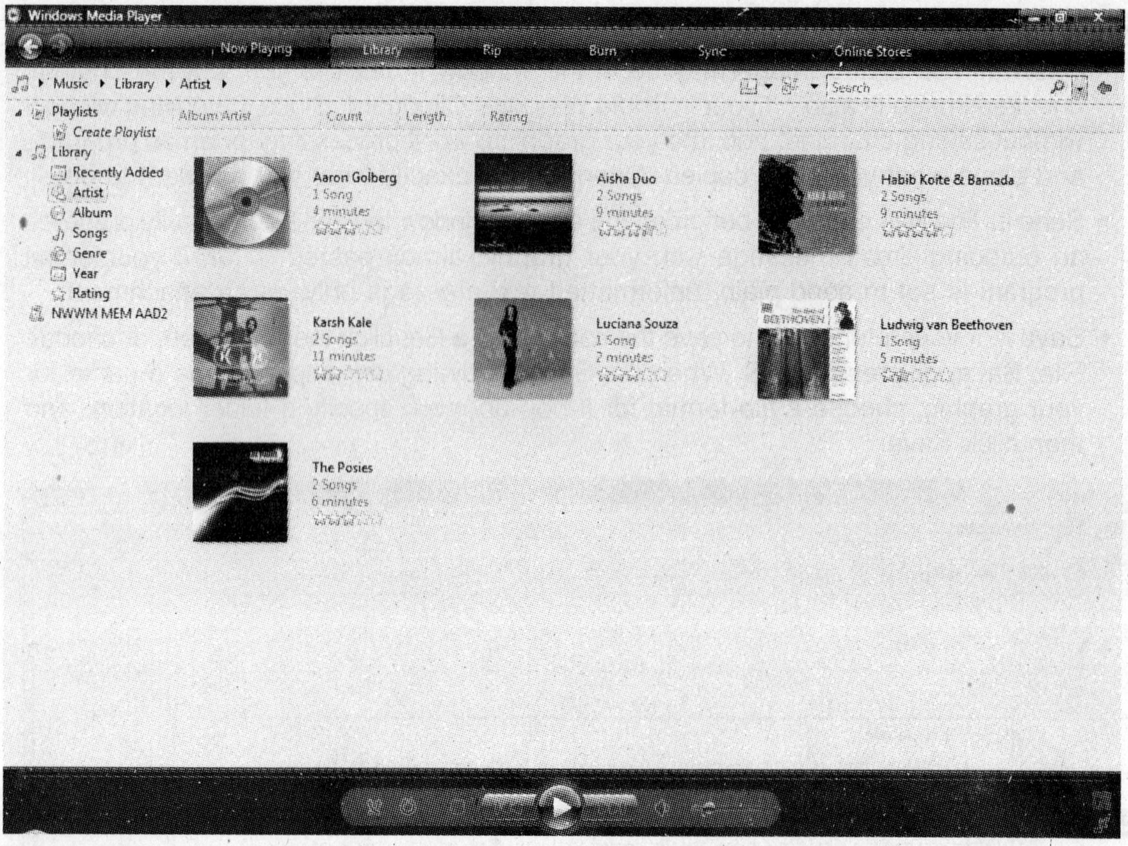

used commands and buttons that you can use to control the Player from your keyboard or with macros. The following table shows the various keyboard shortcuts for the Player.

To do this	Use this keyboard shortcut
Zoom to 50%	ALT+1
Zoom at 100%	ALT+2
Zoom to 200%	ALT+3
Toggle display for full-screen video	ALT+ENTER
Retrace your steps back through your most recent views in the Player	ALT+LEFT ARROW
Retrace your steps forward through your most recent views in the Player	ALT+RIGHT ARROW
Switch to full-screen mode	CTRL+1
Switch to skin mode	CTRL+2
Switch to the first view in a media category after Recently Added (such as Artist in Music)	CTRL+7

Switch to the second view in a media category after Recently Added (such as Album in Music)	CTRL+8
Switch to the third view in a media category after Recently Added (such as Songs in Music)	CTRL+9
Previous (item or chapter)	CTRL+B
Put the focus on the search box in the library	CTRL+E
Next (item or chapter)	CTRL+F
Turn shuffle on or off	CTRL+H
Eject CD or DVD (note that this does not work on computers equipped with two or more CD or DVD disc drives)	CTRL+J
In full mode, show or hide the Classic Menus (menu bar)	CTRL+M
Create a new playlist	CTRL+N
Open a file	CTRL+O
Play or pause playing	CTRL+P
Stop playing	CTRL+S
In audio playback, turn repeat on or off	CTRL+T
Specify a URL or path to a file	CTRL+U
Close or stop playing a file	CTRL+W
Rewind video	CTRL+SHIFT+B
Turn captions and subtitles on or off	CTRL+SHIFT+C
Fast forward through video or music	CTRL+SHIFT+F
Use a fast play speed	CTRL+SHIFT+G
Play at normal speed	CTRL+SHIFT+N
Use a slow play speed	CTRL+SHIFT+S
Rate an item that is playing as zero stars	CTRL+Windows logo key+0
Rate an item that is playing as one star	CTRL+Windows logo key+1
Rate an item that is playing as two stars	CTRL+Windows logo key+2
Rate an item that is playing as three stars	CTRL+Windows logo key+3
Rate an item that is playing as four stars	CTRL+Windows logo key+4
Rate an item that is playing as five stars	CTRL+Windows logo key+5
Return to full mode from full screen	ESC
Display Windows Media Player Help	F1
Edit media information on a selected item in the library	F2

Add media files to the library	F3
Switches the view of items in the Details pane using the options available with the View Options button	F4
Refresh information in the panes	F5
Increase size of album art	F6
Decrease size of album art	SHIFT+F6
Mute volume	F7
Decrease volume	F8
Increase volume	F9
Show the Classic Menus (menu bar)	F10
Switch to full screen mode	F11

7 Keyboard Shortcuts of Windows Vista

Introduction

Keyboard shortcuts can make it easier to interact with your computer because you don't need to use the mouse as often.

Ease of Access keyboard shortcuts

The following table contains keyboard shortcuts that can help make your computer easier to use.

Press this key	To do this
Right Shift for eight seconds	Turn Filter Keys on and off
Left Alt+left Shift+Print Screen (or PRTSCRN)	Turn High Contrast on or off
Left Alt+left Shift+Num Lock	Turn Mouse Keys on or off
Shift five times	Turn Sticky Keys on or off
Num Lock for five seconds	Turn Toggle Keys on or off
Windows logo key +U	Open the Ease of Access Center

General keyboard shortcuts

The following table contains general keyboard shortcuts.

Press this key	To do this
Ctrl+C	Copy the selected item
Ctrl+X	Cut the selected item
Ctrl+V	Paste the selected item
Ctrl+Z	Undo an action
Delete	Delete the selected item and move it to the Recycle Bin
Shift+Delete	Delete the selected item without moving it to the Recycle Bin first
F2	Rename the selected item
Ctrl+Right Arrow	Move the cursor to the beginning of the next word
Ctrl+Left Arrow	Move the cursor to the beginning of the previous word

Ctrl+Down Arrow	Move the cursor to the beginning of the next paragraph
Ctrl+Up Arrow	Move the cursor to the beginning of the previous paragraph
Ctrl+Shift with an arrow key	Select a block of text
Shift with any arrow key	Select more than one item in a window or on the desktop, or select text within a document
Ctrl+A	Select all items in a document or window
F3	Search for a file or folder
Alt+Enter	Display properties for the selected item
Alt+F4	Close the active item, or exit the active program
Alt+Spacebar	Open the shortcut menu for the active window
Ctrl+F4	Close the active document (in programs that allow you to have multiple documents open simultaneously)
Alt+Tab	Switch between open items
Ctrl+Alt+Tab	Use the arrow keys to switch between open items
Windows logo key +Tab	Cycle through programs on the taskbar by using Windows Flip 3-D
Ctrl+Windows logo key +Tab	Use the arrow keys to cycle through programs on the taskbar by using Windows Flip 3-D
Alt+Esc	Cycle through items in the order in which they were opened
F6	Cycle through screen elements in a window or on the desktop
F4	Display the Address bar list in Windows Explorer
Shift+F10	Display the shortcut menu for the selected item
Ctrl+Esc	Open the Start menu
Alt+underlined letter	Display the corresponding menu
Alt+underlined letter	Perform the menu command (or other underlined command)
F10	Activate the menu bar in the active program

Right Arrow	Open the next menu to the right, or open a submenu
Left Arrow	Open the next menu to the left, or close a submenu
F5	Refresh the active window
Alt+Up Arrow	View the folder one level up in Windows Explorer
Esc	Cancel the current task
Ctrl+Shift+Esc	Open Task Manager
Shift when you insert a CD	Prevent the CD from automatically playing

Dialog box keyboard shortcuts

The following table contains keyboard shortcuts for use in dialog boxes.

Press this key	To do this
Ctrl+Tab	Move forward through tabs
Ctrl+Shift+Tab	Move back through tabs
Tab	Move forward through options
Shift+Tab	Move back through options
Alt+underlined letter	Perform the command (or select the option) that goes with that letter
Enter	Replaces clicking the mouse for many selected commands
Spacebar	Select or clear the check box if the active option is a check box
Arrow keys	Select a button if the active option is a group of option buttons
F1	Display Help
F4	Display the items in the active list
Backspace	Open a folder one level up if a folder is selected in the Save As or Open dialog box

Microsoft keyboard shortcuts

The following table contains keyboard shortcuts for use with Microsoft keyboards.

Press this key	To do this
Windows logo key	Open or close the Start menu
Windows logo key +Break	Display the System Properties dialog box
Windows logo key +D	Display the desktop
Windows logo key +M	Minimize all windows
Windows logo key +Shift+M	Restore minimized windows to the desktop

Windows logo key +E	Open Computer
Windows logo key +F	Search for a file or folder
Ctrl+Windows logo key +F	Search for computers (if you are on a network)
Windows logo key +L	Lock your computer (if you are connected to a network domain), or switch users (if you're not connected to a network domain)
Windows logo key +R	Open the Run dialog box
Windows logo key +T	Cycle through programs on the taskbar
Windows logo key +Tab	Cycle through programs on the taskbar by using Windows Flip 3-D
Ctrl+Windows logo key +Tab	Use the arrow keys to cycle through programs on the taskbar by using Windows Flip 3-D
Windows logo key +Spacebar	Bring all gadgets to the front and select Windows Sidebar
Windows logo key +G	Cycle through Sidebar gadgets
Windows logo key +U	Open Ease of Access Center
Windows logo key +X	Open Windows Mobility Center

Windows Explorer keyboard shortcuts

The following table contains keyboard shortcuts for working with Windows Explorer windows or folders.

Press this key	To do this
End	Display the bottom of the active window
Home	Display the top of the active window
Num Lock+Asterisk (*) on numeric keypad	Display all subfolders under the selected folder
Num Lock+Plus Sign (+) on numeric keypad	Display the contents of the selected folder
Num Lock+Minus Sign (-) on numeric keypad	Collapse the selected folder
Left Arrow	Collapse the current selection (if it is expanded), or select the parent folder
Alt+Left Arrow	View the previous folder
Right Arrow	Display the current selection (if it is collapsed), or select the first subfolder
Alt+Right Arrow	Vie.⁄ the next folder
Alt+D	Select the Address bar

Windows Sidebar keyboard shortcuts

The following table contains keyboard shortcuts for working with Windows Sidebar.

Press this key	To do this
Windows logo key +Spacebar	Bring all gadgets to the front and select Sidebar
Windows logo key +G	Cycle through Sidebar gadgets
Tab	Cycle through Sidebar controls

Windows Photo Gallery keyboard shortcuts

The following table contains keyboard shortcuts for working with Windows Photo Gallery.

Press this key	To do this
Ctrl+F	Open the Fix pane
Ctrl+P	Print the selected picture
Enter	View the selected picture at a larger size
Ctrl+I	Open or close the Details pane
Ctrl+Period (.)	Rotate the picture clockwise
Ctrl+Comma (,)	Rotate the picture counter-clockwise
F2	Rename the selected item
Ctrl+E	Search for an item
Alt+Left Arrow	Go back
Alt+Right Arrow	Go forward
Plus Sign (+)	Zoom in or resize the picture thumbnail
Minus Sign (-)	Zoom out or resize the picture thumbnail
Ctrl+B	Best fit
Left Arrow	Select the previous item
Down Arrow	Select the next item or row
Up Arrow	Previous item (Easel) or previous row (Thumbnail)
Page Up	Previous screen
Page Dn	Next screen
Home	Select the first item
End	Select the last item
Delete	Move the selected item to the Recycle Bin
Shift+Delete	Permanently delete the selected item
Left Arrow	Collapse node
Right Arrow	Expand node

Keyboard shortcuts for working with videos

J	Move back one frame
K	Pause the playback
L	Move forward one frame
I	Set the start trim point
O	Set the end trim point
M	Split a clip
Home	Stop and rewind all the way back to the start trim point
Alt+Right Arrow	Advance to the next frame
Alt+Left Arrow	Go back to the previous frame
Ctrl+K	Stop and rewind playback
Ctrl+P	Play from the current location
Home	Move the start trim point
End	Move to the end trim point
Page Up	Seek to nearest split point before the current location
Page Dn	Seek to nearest split point after the current location

Windows Help viewer keyboard shortcuts

The following table contains keyboard shortcuts for working with the Help viewer.

Press this key	To do this
Alt+C	Display the Table of Contents
Alt+N	Display the Connection Settings menu
F10	Display the Options menu
Alt+Left Arrow	Move back to the previously viewed topic
Alt+Right Arrow	Move forward to the next (previously viewed) topic
Alt+A	Display the customer support page
Alt+Home	Display the Help and Support home page
Home	Move the to beginning of a topic
End	Move to the end of a topic
Ctrl+F	Search the current topic
Ctrl+P	Print a topic
F3	Move to the Search box

8 Questions

Answer the Following Questions

Chapter 1 — Introduction to Windows Vista

1. Describe the various items of the Taskbar.
2. What is Computer used for? Describe its constituents.
3. Describe the process of copying of files.
4. How is Recycle Bin used in Windows Vista?
5. Describe the process of creating a shortcut.
6. Describe what's new in Windows Vista.

Chapter 2 — Accessories of Windows Vista

1. Describe the various options available under the following Accessories heads.

Calculator	Command Prompt
Connect to a Network Projector	Notepad
Paint	Remote Desktop Connection
Run	Snipping Tool
Sound Recorder	Sync Center
Welcome Center	Windows Explorer
Windows Sidebar	WordPad
Ease of Access	System Tools
Internet Explorer	System Information
System Restore	Task Scheduler
Windows Easy Transfer	Tablet PC

Chapter 3 — Control Panel of Windows Vista

1. Describe the various tasks and icons available under:

Add Hardware	Adminstrative Tools

AutoPlay
BitLocker Drive Encryption
Date and Time
Device Manager
Folder Options
Game Controllers
Internet Options
Keyboard
Mouse
Offline Files
Pen and Input Devices
Performance Information
Phone and Modem Options
Printers
Programs and Features
Scanners and Cameras
Sound
Speech Recognition
System
Taskbar and Start Menu
User Accounts
Windows CardSpace
Windows Firewall
Windows SlideShow
Backup and Restore Centre
Color Management
Default Programs
Ease of Access
Fonts
Indexing Options
iSCSI Initiator
Mail
Network and Sharing Centre
Parental Controls 40
People Near Me
Personalize
Power Options
Problem Reports and Solutions
Regional and Language Options
Security Center
SoundMAX
Sync Center
Table PC Settings
Text to Speech
Welcom Center
Windows Defender
Windows Sidebar Properties
Windows Update

Chapter 4 — Configuring Your System with Windows Vista

1. Describe the process of setting up of Date, Time and Regional Settings in Windows Vista.
2. Describe the various options of Keyboard under Keyboard Settings.
3. How would you manage fonts on your computer? Describe.
4. How would you change passwords in your system?
5. How would you change Taskbar properties?
6. How would you change the various properties of Monitor Display?
7. What role does the Screen Saver plays?

8. Describe the process of setting up Home Networking.
9. Describe the process of setting up of Internet on your computer.

Chapter 5 — Maintaining and Protect Your System with Windows Vista

1. What does Disk Fragmentation do? Explain.
2. What does Disk Cleanup do? Explain.
3. How would you tune up your system using Task Scheduler? Describe.
4. Describe the various security and privacy options in Windows Vista.
5. Describe the following options:

   User Account Control

   BitLocker Drive Encryption

   Trusted Platform Module Services

Chapter 6 — Additional Commands of Windows Vista

1. Describe the working of Windows Mail?
2. How would you install a USB Drive?
3. What does Windows Contacts do?
4. How would you create a DVD using Windows DVD Maker?
5. What are the functions of Windows Photo Gallery?
6. What sort of calender in there in Windows Calender?
7. How would you search using Windows Search?
8. What is Snipping Tool used for?
9. What is new in Windows Media Player of Windows Vista?
10. How would you use Windows Vista for Mobile PC?

Titles in the Learning Series

1. Windows 98
2. Word 2000
3. PageMaker 6.5
4. Excel 2000
5. Access 2000
6. CorelDRAW 9
7. PowerPoint 2000
8. Outlook 2000
9. FrontPage 2000
10. MS Office 2000
11. Photoshop 5.5
12. Internet and e-mail
13. Flash 4
14. HTML 4
15. C++
16. DOS 6.0/6.22
17. Visual FoxPro
18. e-commerce
19. JAVA
20. JAVA Servlets
21. Windows ME
22. UNIX
23. JavaScript
24. Visual Basic 6.0
25. Tally 5.4
26. AutoCAD 2000
27. XML/XHTML
28. Flash 5.0
29. Photoshop 6.0
30. Oracle 8i
31. CorelDRAW 10
32. Word 2002
33. Excel 2002
34. Access 2002
35. PowerPoint 2002
36. FrontPage 2002
37. Microsoft Office XP
38. C#
39. Computer Fundamentals
40. C
41. Dreamweaver 4.0
42. Red Hat Linux 7.1
43. Windows XP
44. Tally 6.3
45. Simple Networking
46. HTML (Rev.)
47. Photoshop 6 (Rev.)
48. PageMaker 7.0
49. Illustrator 9.0
50. Flash 5 (Rev.)
51. SQL Programming
52. JavaScript (Rev.)
53. Multimedia
54. PC Hardware
55. Internet & e-mail (Rev.)
56. Unix (Rev.)
57. C++ (Rev.)
58. Microsoft Office 2000 (Rev.)
59. Visual Basic (Rev.)
60. Java 2 (Rev.)
61. Visual FoxPro (Rev.)
62. Photoshop 7
63. Illustrator 10
64. Visual C++
65. AutoCAD 2002
66. Microsoft Office XP (Rev.)
67. Flash MX
68. Oracle 9i
69. CorelDRAW 11
70. Linux 8
71. 3d Max 5.0
72. MCQ in Unix
73. MCQ in C++
74. MCQ in C
75. Microsoft Office 2003
76. Microsoft Office Word 2003
77. Microsoft Office Excel 2003
78. AutoCAD 2004
79. DreamWeaver MX 2004
80. Flash MX 2004
81. Microsoft Office Access 2003
82. Microsoft Office FrontPage 2003
83. Microsoft Office PowerPoint 2003
84. CorelDRAW 12
85. Photoshop 2004 CS
86. AutoCAD 2005
87. Tally 7.2
88. Computer Fundamentals (New Format)
89. HTML 4 (New Format)
90. Microsoft Office 2003 (New Format)
91. CorelDRAW 12 (New Format)
92. Photoshop CS 2004 (New Format)
93. Internet and e-mail (New Format)
94. JavaScript (New Format)
95. e-commerce (Revised and New Format)
96. Windows XP (New Format)
97. AutoCAD 2006
98. Flash 8
99. Dreamweaver 8
100. PC Hardware (Revised and New Pattern)
101. CorelDRAW X.3 (CorelDRAW 13)
102. Adobe Photoshop CS 2 (version 9)
103. UNIX (Revised and New Pattern)
104. MySQL 5.0
105. Illustrator CS 2
106. Tally 8.1
107. PHP
108. Visual Basic 2005
109. ASP 2.0
110. CSharp.Net
111. AutoCAD 2007
112. Tally 9.0
113. DTP
114. Windows Vista